D0163395

"*From Belief to Knowledge* is a timely contribution to a key debate within the organizational studies literature: what is the role of knowledge in change processes within modern and complex organizations? While leaders proceed in their leadership of organizations in the belief that they have a body of knowledge that they draw upon as they lead, it is often the case that their knowledge is essentially a series of assumptions or beliefs and these determine the decisions they make and the actions they pursue. This book puts forward the proposition that how we form the beliefs we hold significantly influences what we believe and is the key process in shaping our personal anchors in knowledge that informs our actions. This well-written, thoughtful, and thought provoking book will challenge leaders to consider the fundamental differences between belief and knowledge. It provides a novel contribution in its integrative analysis of the issue of learning and change in organizations. It offers leaders and scholars of change a considered opportunity to explore the transitions along the continuum from belief to knowledge that can lead to sustainable change."

Sue Dopson, PhD
Rhodes Trust Professor of Organisational Behaviour
Director of Research Degrees
Said Business School
University of Oxford

"Organizational learning has been defined in various ways. Some of these definitions and designs for implementation have been elegant; some have been simplistic, yet none seem to have had a lasting impact. Douglas and Wykowski in *From Belief to Knowledge* address organizational learning as an integrated system where knowledge provides the linkage to adapt to changing environments all the while delivering improved performance. They answer the question that lingers in the minds of many managers: what does organizational learning mean and how does it influence ongoing organizational success? I expect this book to be highly influential."

Lee Newick
General Manager, Contracting and Procurement
Global Manufacturing
Shell Downstream

"*From Belief to Knowledge* represents a paradigm shift in understanding knowledge and has added significantly to critical thinking. This book has the potential to shift thinking from firmly held assumptions and beliefs to real knowledge when readers have the courage and motivation to confront their beliefs in the search for truth. Douglas and Wykowski challenge us to become conscious of our own beliefs and how we form them, which affect all our actions. Although this book is geared to organizational change, it has the potential to change all areas of human endeavor. My understanding of culture and culture change has been greatly enhanced by this thorough scholarship and practical application to knowledge."

David Julian Hodges, PhD
Professor of Anthropology
Hunter College of the City University of New York

"If you accept, as I do, that in a knowledge economy, the successful organizations are those that continuously invest in their knowledge producing capability, then this book provides valuable insights for thought and action. Uniquely, they make the case for the growth of knowledge as a defining characteristic of culture in contrast to the treatment of knowledge as one asset among many. Douglas and Wykowski drill down into theories of knowledge and, importantly, of knowing, to argue that multiple approaches to knowledge capability-building are required. They seek to translate these arguments into practice and then address what sort of leadership and human interaction are required."

Michael Earl
Emeritus Professor of Information Management
University of Oxford

From Belief to Knowledge

Achieving and Sustaining
an Adaptive Culture
in Organizations

From Belief to Knowledge

Achieving and Sustaining an Adaptive Culture in Organizations

Neil Douglas
Terry Wykowski

CRC Press
Taylor & Francis Group
Boca Raton   London   New York

CRC Press is an imprint of the
Taylor & Francis Group, an **informa** business

CRC Press
Taylor & Francis Group
6000 Broken Sound Parkway NW, Suite 300
Boca Raton, FL 33487-2742

© 2011 by Taylor and Francis Group, LLC
CRC Press is an imprint of Taylor & Francis Group, an Informa business

No claim to original U.S. Government works

Printed in the United States of America on acid-free paper
10 9 8 7 6 5 4 3 2 1

International Standard Book Number: 978-1-4398-3734-4 (Hardback)

Library of Congress Cataloging-in-Publication Data

Douglas, Neil, 1962-
    From belief to knowledge : achieving and sustaining an adaptive culture in organizations / Neil Douglas, Terry Wykowski.
        p. cm.
    Includes bibliographical references and index.
    ISBN 978-1-4398-3734-4 (hardcover : alk. paper)
    1. Organizational learning. 2. Organizational change. I. Wykowski, Terry. II. Title.

HD58.82.D683 2011
658.4'038--dc22   2010026472

Visit the Taylor & Francis Web site at
http://www.taylorandfrancis.com

and the CRC Press Web site at
http://www.crcpress.com

To our families, friends, and colleagues

who believed in and supported us

Contents

Preface

How do organizations create and sustain the ability to adapt to changing environments and improve performance? How can a knowledge producing, adaptive, and performance enhancing culture be created and sustained? Why do we encounter both unwillingness and apparent inability to change when there is a clear and compelling need to change? Are there reliable and effectual practices for producing knowledge in contrast to mere belief? Working to formulate potential answers to these questions framed the development of this book and led us to face an additional set of questions—How are beliefs and knowledge different, how does this difference affect organizational behavior, and how do the roots of our beliefs influence our ability to change and adapt?

Belief is *not* knowledge, but we tend to hold our beliefs as if they represented knowledge, assuming them to be true and supported by the existence of evidence that justifies them. The essential ideas in this book are 1) the widely acknowledged premise that our beliefs or assumptions largely determine the decisions we make and the actions we take, and 2) the relatively novel conception that *how* we form the beliefs we hold significantly influences *what* we believe and whether our beliefs are likely to be true and, therefore, representative of knowledge. These essential ideas are straightforward and closely connected. Their development, however, requires exploration of the meaning and implications of such abstract-seeming concepts as knowledge, belief, truth, and reality.

This book is about the growth of knowledge in organizations as a positive attribute of culture and a result of able and purposeful human interaction. The action we take or fail to take based on what we *know* rather than what we merely believe aligns what we *do* with reality and tends to produce desirable effects. Depending on the organization, these beneficial effects may be expressed in terms of operations or research productivity, earnings, safety, product relevance, customer service, market share, educational outcomes, or quality of patient care. In contrast, the action we take grounded in ignorance or false belief is likely to produce undesirable consequences and to account for under achievement and failure.

The beliefs we hold reflect our diversity as individuals and our character as groups and organizations. More fundamentally, *how* we form our

xiii

beliefs is an aspect of individual diversity and pertains to the process or processes we use to establish and sustain such beliefs. Perhaps we rely on the opinions of other people. Perhaps we ground our beliefs in our own ability to reason, or in our own experience and that of others. Perhaps we believe in the truth of an argument or proposition based on the results or utility of the argument or on whether or not the elements of the argument fit together logically. Perhaps we believe based on some absolute notion of truth or perhaps we shape our beliefs based on how circumstances vary over time and place. Reality is also diverse. When we speak about belief or knowledge, questions pertaining to relevant reality or the character of the object of such belief or knowledge must arise. Do we seek to know about mechanics or chemistry or physics or business or economics or society or politics or ethics?

We have been working in organizations as consultants on problems of learning, change and development for twenty years. Our client organizations are large and small, global companies and academic institutions, hospitals and biotechnology companies. Our work has been with management, operations, research, and clinical teams. Prior to working together, we had separate careers as managers and consultants. Through our work and study, we have observed a number of circumstances including these: Individual, group, and organizational change is difficult to bring about (seemingly impossible at times); the beliefs and assumptions of individuals and those shared by groups are the primary barriers to learning and change; cultures have a tendency to endure in spite of the presence of urgent need for change; irrespective of the best efforts of leaders and others, organizations often fail to achieve their potential.

The set of perceived factors giving rise to the writing of this book are 1) the need for a deeper and more integrative analysis and treatment of the problem of learning in organizations, including the need to look beneath beliefs and assumptions to find their roots and their sources of persistent influence; 2) the need for a broader thesis regarding knowledge than that associated with information technology and the idea of knowledge as an asset; and 3) an alternative view of culture and culture change defined by the ability to continually align collective beliefs with reality. The title of the book, *From Belief to Knowledge*, suggests movement or growth as the active theme. Knowledge, therefore, is not seen as absolute or static. Rather, the emphasis is on a continuum of transitions along the continuum *from belief to knowledge.*

Our clients are unnamed in this book, but our gratitude is enormous for the opportunity to work with them, for their insights, and for their confidence in us. We also appreciate the time and candor of the individuals we interviewed and who participated in our research. In looking beyond the literature of organizational studies for insights and inspiration, we are indebted to the work of many scholars in the fields of epistemology, ontology, social psychology, sociology of knowledge, and cognitive science. We especially wish to acknowledge Michael Williams, Alvin Goldman, Peter Berger, Thomas Luckman, Rom Harre and Donald Campbell. We also express our appreciation for the work of A. J. Ayer, Laurence BonJour, Lorraine Code, Fred Dretske, Catherine Elgin, Robert Kegan, Jaegwon Kim, Thomas Kuhn, Susann M. Laverty, Richard Palmer, W. V. O. Quine, Richard Rorty, John Searle, and Ernest Sosa. Dare we also presume to pay respects to the work of William James, Jean Piaget, Immanuel Kant, and David Hume? The memory of Dan Gowler, Terry's mentor at the University of Oxford and Neil's by proxy, continues to influence and inspire our work. We appreciate the work and support of the editors at Taylor & Francis: Amy Blalock, Lara Zoble, and Michael Sinocchi. We are grateful to Sandy Birtwistle for carefully reading the entire manuscript. Finally, we thank our families, friends, and colleagues who both encouraged and challenged us.

The Authors

Neil Douglas and Terry Wykowski have been working together in organizations in North America and Europe as consultants on problems of learning, change, and development for twenty years. Their client organizations are large and small, global companies and academic institutions, hospitals and technology-based companies. Their work has been with management, operations, research, and clinical teams. Prior to working together, they had separate careers as managers and consultants. Neil Douglas, although trained as a systems engineer, held a number of technical and management posts including chief executive officer of two high technology firms and a biotechnology startup company, and senior manager and chief information officer of a large health services organization. Terry Wykowski's training in psychology and management studies and organizational behavior at the University of Oxford led her to internal consulting assignments for a global energy company and work as an external consultant for an organizational development firm.

1

Introduction

We live in the midst of rapidly expanding knowledge, which often seems to be very close to complete if not actually so. As a result of the Human Genome Project, we know that 46 human chromosomes house almost 3 billion chemical base pairs of DNA and that human DNA contains about 30,000 protein-encoding genes that govern virtually all aspects of human biology. We know how to organize and store this information to learn how to more effectively diagnose and treat diseases.

In the world of digital electronics, our knowledge of how to achieve exponential growth of capacity and reduction of cost over time accounts for the dramatic year-to-year increase of function in an ever widening set of applications. This driving force of technological change in the last half century has occurred through a doubling every two years of such factors as processing speed of computing, memory capacity, and even the number of pixels in digital cameras. In terms of the movement of people and goods, we know how to build and operate a machine that will safely transport more than 500 people almost 10,000 miles from Paris to Tokyo in 16 hours. We are proud of what we know and, in many instances, keenly aware of the consequences of knowledge versus ignorance.

There are also consequences to failing to know or believing falsely and, in all too many instances, our lack of knowledge relates to those things that most profoundly matter to us. We don't know how to avoid war and settle our differences peacefully. We don't know how to reconcile our political, religious, and cultural differences to improve the lives of all people. We don't know how to equitably distribute the world's resources to eliminate poverty, hunger, and suffering and create an expanding base of potential and wealth at the same time. At the time of this writing, it has become clear that the highly educated and excessively compensated Wall Street executives, those assumed to be among the best and the brightest

1

members of our society did not know about the frailty of finance capitalism and about the consequences of unrestrained market forces. Or perhaps they did know and relied on everyone else's ignorance to enable them to shape a system that would reward them so lavishly.

We don't always know how to see things whole and bring about successful interdisciplinary collaboration in science and medicine. Frequently, we don't know how to produce optimal solutions to problems and how to achieve the potential of our organizations. As individuals and collections of individuals, what we *think* we know about our common reality and *how* we come to believe and seek to know about that reality seem to keep us from producing real knowledge about our persistent dilemmas. It will be obvious that knowledge about multi-layered and unremitting sets of circumstances is not the same as knowing about a commonly observed experience or a simple physical object. Further, it will be obvious that the truth about vexing and paradox-laden circumstances is not knowable in the sense that we usually think we know about "things." This should not, however, in any way suggest that we are not compelled to seek to rise above ignorance and to know about complex and layered sets of factors and situations, even if what we come to know is probabilistic and less than absolute.

In terms of what we don't know, it could be argued that it's not a matter of knowing but rather a matter of will. Perhaps we don't want to avoid war or equitably distribute the world's resources or reconcile our differences. There are vested and parochial interests that are pleased with the status quo, not enthusiastic about comprehending wholes, achieving the potential of the greater community or organization, and enhancing the common good. Granting the valid if cynical substance of such an argument, we contend that lack of knowledge does in fact lie somewhere in the chain of perceptions and beliefs that result in our failure to answer our deepest questions and solve our most unyielding problems. Our lack of knowledge may pertain to the implications and consequences of the actions we clearly know how to take. Our lack of knowledge may relate to the character of reality associated with the circumstances of our collective life. In her book, *This Republic of Suffering,* Drew Faust, the historian and president of Harvard University, asks why we accept war. Not so much why do governments wage war, but why do populations accept it? We are all members of the same species, we share a common biology and psychology. We fight for reasons our states invent.[1] We need to know why, in an age of universal education, ubiquitous technology, communication, and political democracy in the developed world, do we act inconsistently in our own self interests; why do economic systems designed to promote the well-being and economic power of the few as opposed to the many persist? Our beliefs may serve our narrow purposes for a time, but when the common good suffers because of our failure to grasp the character of our common reality, all of us ultimately lose. When we act within the framework of flawed conceptions of reality we act in ignorance or false belief.

Knowledge is highly prized in human society. The person who *knows*, as opposed to one who desires or hopes or believes, is the one to whom we turn when danger or threat is present. Shakespeare expressed our deep and enduring regard for knowledge in his exhortation, "Go to your bosom: knock there and ask your heart what it doth know." Socrates is reported to have said, "There is only one good, knowledge and one evil, ignorance." Knowledge is set against ignorance and accounts for our progress in natural and social science, medicine, technology, economics, public health, and public policy. On the other hand, lack of knowledge or, more profoundly, the illusion of knowledge, given substance and influence as mere belief, is responsible for our lack of progress. "The greatest obstacle to discovering the shape of the earth, the continents and the oceans was not simple ignorance, but the illusion of knowledge (or the belief that we know)."[2] Knowledge seeking is likewise highly prized and considered by most of us to be virtuous and a liberating and elevating aspect of human nature. Of the forces and motivations that frame the human condition, the pursuit of knowledge is among our noblest and most useful. Will Durant, the historian and author of *The Story of Civilization*, expressed the belief that "there are not many things finer in our murderous species than this noble curiosity, this restless and reckless passion to understand."[3] Knowledge that results in action is responsible for the progress we achieve. The action we take, or fail to take, based on what we know, will align what we do with reality and will be likely to produce desirable and beneficial effects. In an imperfect world, however, actions are often pursued in the absence of knowledge. Except through some accident of circumstance, the actions we take founded on fallacy or false belief or flawed conceptions of reality are doomed to ultimate failure.

BELIEF, KNOWLEDGE AND THE CONSEQUENCES OF HUMAN ENDEAVOR

Medicine and public health provide many positive examples of action aligned with knowledge that result in important benefits for human beings. These examples range from disease prevention and treatment stemming from knowledge expressed in the germ theory of infectious disease in the nineteenth century to changes in clinical practice based on the knowledge that life-threatening dehydration in children is a consequence of gastroenteritis. Fifty years ago, physicians believed that atherosclerosis was inevitable in aging people and that blood pressure should increase with age to enable the heart to pump blood through narrowed arteries. We did not know that, in addition to age, there is a set of risk factors for cardiovascular disease and these can be identified and measured. In 1948, the National Heart, Lung, and Blood Institute embarked upon and directed an ambitious project in health research, which came to be known as the Framingham Heart Study. The researchers recruited men and women in the town of Framingham, Massachusetts with the objective of identifying the common factors or characteristics that contribute to cardiovascular disease. Through regular and periodic physical examinations including measurement of blood chemistry and other variables and lifestyle interviews, a large group of participants who had not yet developed symptoms of cardiovascular disease were followed over long periods of time.

Two generations of study participants and researchers from the United States and around the world have produced findings regarded as among the most significant in the history of medicine. Before Framingham, the role of serum cholesterol in the evolution of cardiovascular disease was neither widely understood nor accepted by physicians as a major contributing factor. The study established a relationship between cholesterol levels and risk of disease and, further, that high levels of LDL cholesterol are positively linked to disease while high levels of HDL cholesterol have a protective effect. Investigations of blood pressure exposed a number of misconceptions regarding blood pressure and led to perceptions of hypertension as an important factor in the risk of disease. Researchers also learned that certain lifestyle factors such as diet, sedentary living, and unrestrained weight gain contributed to high rates of disease and disability. Before Framingham, cigarette smoking was not accepted as a hazard in the development of heart disease. The study demonstrated that smokers were at increased risk of having a heart attack and experiencing sudden death.

As late as the mid-twentieth century, children diagnosed with leukemia rarely lived longer than three months. Today, according to the National Academy of Sciences, 80 percent of childhood leukemias are cured and more than 30,000 lives have been saved.[4] This remarkable achievement of medicine was not fueled by a single breakthrough, but rather by a chain of knowledge events, cumulatively leading to treatments that restore children to health. The initial insight in non-surgical intervention to treat cancer, based on knowledge about cells from a series of basic science discoveries in the late nineteenth and early twentieth centuries, was that interfering with reproduction in cancer cells can inflict disproportionate damage from which they sometimes don't recover. The next step in the knowledge chain was the discovery of the role of enzymes as the crucial proteins that drive chemical reactions in cells and affect function, including cellular reproduction. Scientists learned that the interaction of enzymes and chemicals within a cell resemble a lock-and-key mechanism, progressively unlocking sequences and enabling completion of chemical reactions and activating functions. Researchers also came to know that the introduction of certain chemical compounds that looked like or mimicked a key could jam or stop chemical reactions and interfere with vital cellular functions in cancer cells.

Knowledge about specific chemicals that interfered with the functions of cancer cells converged with knowledge about how to demonstrate and prove the effectiveness of these chemicals in the laboratory. Targeting specific diseases through intentional and rational drug design led to early application of chemotherapy in children with leukemia with little success; with no other treatment options, however, the children had nothing to lose. With the discovery of the DNA molecule, scientists came to understand how cell division actually occurs and to understand more fully how blocking cells from making new DNA bases could cause cancer cells to be unable to reproduce. Possessing new knowledge about cellular processes, signaling pathways and chemical reactions, new chemicals were synthesized that showed promise in the laboratory and in animal models. New compounds were given to children suffering from leukemia and some rare and brief remissions were achieved. Further synthesis of promising compounds produced two drugs that consistently brought about remission, although lives were only extended from three months to one year in most cases.

Additional knowledge was needed about combinations of drugs, dosages, and frequency. In the mid 1950s, the state of the art of conducting clinical, chemotherapy trials, including the concept of the double blind study, was greatly advanced. New trials enabled answering questions pertaining to combination, dose, and frequency as well as measuring the effects of transfusions of blood platelets and other treatment options. Remission became routine, but the cancer returned in most cases. Ongoing laboratory research led to the knowledge that only a single leukemic cell was required to restart the fatal process. The final step in the knowledge chain was the identification of the brain and spinal cord as hideouts for the dangerous cancer cells. Direct injection of drugs and target radiation proved to be successful in killing even the smallest number of residual cancer cells. The combination of treatments, the two drugs discovered and developed early in the process, and new drugs have produced a very high cure rate and the promise of normal, healthy lives for thousands of children.

Another example from medicine, albeit one where knowledge has yet to be fully developed is the role, function, and clinical application associated with human stem cells. There can be little doubt that political, cultural, and moral considerations, at least in the United States, have restrained the growth of knowledge related to stem cells and potentially beneficial applications for human health. There are significant gaps in knowledge about stem cells that impose constraints on the development of new therapies from either adult- or embryo-derived stem cells, according to an Institute of Medicine report entitled Stem Cells and the Future of Regenerative Medicine. "As knowledge of stem cells grows, investigators will be able to ask meaningful questions about therapeutic approaches, including whether to implant cells in an undifferentiated state or a differentiated state, and which of the various sources of stem cells are best suited to address a specific clinical need. For now, all of these questions must wait for the establishment of a more firm scientific foundation."[5]

A major obstacle to the growth of knowledge related to stem cells and the development of new therapies is opposition to embryonic stem cell research on ethical and religious grounds. While the Institute of Medicine report does not comment on the validity of the ethical or moral arguments for or against embryonic stem cell research, it does identify key points in the scientific position, including that adult stem cells alone will not provide the basis for the work that must be done and that the small number of available cell lines has seriously limited the cellular diversity necessary for fruitful research. Although current legal constraints on funding embryonic stem cell research is limited to public funding, it must be borne in mind that basic research is needed, and public funding through the National Institutes of Health supports most basic research in the United States. Publicly funded research is published in peer-reviewed journals, thereby making results of research available to other scientists anywhere in the world. Regardless of how one feels about the arguments for and against embryonic stem cell research, the consequence of lack of knowledge related to stem cells is lack of action in the development of promising treatments for a variety of life threatening and debilitating illnesses. The essential question is whether there are negative consequences pertaining to human life in general and the pursuit of this kind of research, the knowledge of which would trump the benefits of relatively unburdened research in regenerative medicine.

There are times when knowledge, or something very close to knowledge, exists among a subset of a community, but the masking or corruption of that knowledge, for economic or political reasons, inhibits comprehension of that knowledge by the larger community resulting in inappropriate action or no action at all. There is a scientific consensus on the reality of climate change induced by human activity. The journal *Science* reported on this scientific consensus as expressed in the report of the Intergovernmental Panel on Climate Change, on behalf of the World Meteorological Organization and the United Nations Environmental Programme.[6] The report concluded that human activities are modifying the concentrations of greenhouse gases, which are likely to be responsible for the observed climatic warming over the past fifty years. In the United States, the National Academy of Sciences, the American Meteorological Society, and the American Association for the Advancement of Science have all issued statements concluding that the evidence for human modification of climate is compelling.

In the face of this evidence, policy makers in the United States through most of the first decade of the twenty-first century, as well as some large corporations and segments of the media, have asserted that the conclusions of the climate science community are inconclusive. These claims have been used as an argument against adopting measures to reduce greenhouse emissions. This failure of the United States to respond responsibly to what we know about climate change is especially harmful because, among the community of nations, the United States produces the largest proportion of greenhouse gases. As the report in *Science* concludes: "The scientific consensus might, of course, be wrong. If the history of science teaches anything, it is humility, and no one can be faulted for failing to act on what is not known. But our grandchildren will surely blame us if they find that we understood the reality of anthropogenic climate change and failed to do anything about it." There is an analogy with the tobacco industry and its campaign to confuse and obfuscate what was known about the dangers of smoking. That tobacco was addictive and harmful to the health of smokers had been known for years and, since the 1950s, the scientific evidence had been overwhelming. The industry, however, with the help of public relations experts, created doubt about the health warnings and advocated for the public's right to smoke. The strategy worked by misleading the public and delaying action on a variety of initiatives designed to reduce tobacco consumption.

There are times when knowledge is constrained by sheer denial. The historian Barbara Tuchman describes wooden-headedness in geopolitics as a source of self-deception. It consists of assessing a situation in terms of preconceived beliefs while ignoring facts to the contrary. "A classic case in action was Plan 17, the French war plan of 1914, conceived in a mood of total dedication to the offensive. It concentrated everything on a French advance to the Rhine, allowing the French left (flank) to remain virtually unguarded, a strategy that could only be justified by the fixed belief that the Germans could not deploy enough manpower to extend their invasion around western Belgium and the French coastal provinces. This assumption was based on the equally fixed belief that the Germans would never use reserves in the front line. Evidence to the contrary, which began seeping through to the French General Staff in 1913, had to be, and was, resolutely ignored in order that no concern about a possible German invasion on the west be allowed to divert strength from a direct French offensive eastward to the Rhine. When war came, the Germans could and did use reserves in the front line and did come the long way around on the west with results that determined a protracted war and its fearful consequences for our century."[7]

Sometimes what we believe with justification and what we think we know changes. What we knew about biology changed with Darwin and what we thought we knew about physics based on Newton's clockwork metaphors changed with quantum mechanics. Sometimes what we know at one level doesn't translate to knowledge at another yet connected level, although there is often an assumption that it does. As we've seen above, narrow interests, politics, religion, and conceptions of morality can be constraints on the growth of knowledge. The process of inferring the probable truth of one proposition from the apparent truth of another is fundamental to the human faculty of reason, but this process itself is subject to the same constraints as well as to the additional constraint of our innate propensity for flawed reasoning. The evidence to date is compelling and we can humbly (and provisionally) say that we *know* that capitalism within some framework of law and regulation produces an economic system that provides material well-being to an extent greater and for more members of a society than others. The distance is short from this assertion to an inference proclaiming that if capitalism is good, the purest or the most extreme capitalism is best. But do we *know* this or is it an unjustified belief, incongruent with reality? The answer may depend on what we hold to be true about a deeper, existential question. If we believe that the creation of wealth is the greatest economic good, it may be assumed to follow that the purest capitalism, in the form of "market fundamentalism," maximizes this good. While believing that the creation of wealth is the greatest good, market fundamentalists imagine that the market magically transforms market participants into moral agents who mitigate self-interest through the "invisible hand" as described by Adam Smith.[8] In addition to charges of misreading Adam Smith and seeing completely free markets where few if any exist, market fundamentalists are accused of misinterpreting the "greatest good." As the first decade of the twenty-first century draws to a close, the collapse of deregulated financial markets, losses of trillions of dollars of wealth, and a global recession of greater depth than any since the Great Depression seem to have answered the market fundamentalism question, at least for the present. To be specific, not only have questions about the morality of markets been answered, we have to be far less certain about unbridled capitalism as the unchallenged engine of wealth creation.

Advocates for an alternative view argue that, "Envisioning a moral economy does not require any heroic assumptions about human nature; it does not assume that people are always cooperative and kind. On the contrary, it starts from the idea that the individual pursuit of self-interest has to be controlled or it will turn destructive. The moral economy narrative recognizes that there is no 'royal road,' no magic formula that will produce the desired combinations of prosperity, order, and justice. Rather, it is through the continuous exercise of democratic self-governance that we can reform our institutions to make both the economy and the government work better to achieve our shared objectives."[9] Of course, if we don't *know* the answer to the deeper, existential question, namely, what is the greatest good underlying the organizing principles of a modern economy, we will be inevitably led to other questions pertaining to how we can come to form justified and (arguably) true beliefs about such a thing.

ORGANIZATIONS

Peter Drucker argued that knowledge underlies the imperative to manage organizations for and through a state of persistent change. "Society, community, family are all conserving institutions. They try to maintain stability, and to prevent, or at least to slow down, change. But the organization of the post-capitalist society of organizations is a destabilizer. Because its function is to put knowledge to work—on tools, processes, and products; on knowledge itself—it must be organized for constant change."[10] Although the subject matter of this book pertains to the growth of knowledge in any setting, the focus is on the growth of knowledge in organizations. The argument is made that action based on knowledge versus action driven by mere belief is the crucial difference between successful adaptation and the long-term health of organizations and the underachievement and failure of such organizations. The process of aligning belief with relevant reality results in a transition from belief to knowledge. *Knowing* about these *realities*, rather than only having beliefs about them, represents a passage out of ignorance and inertia and an opportunity to act based upon what is justified and closer to the truth rather than farther from it. "Ignorance is not bliss, it's our worst enemy," according to one of our clients. Although the consequences of knowing may be greater at higher levels in an organization's belief generating chain, for example, at the level associated with organizational strategy or the allocation of limited and constrained resources, consequences exist at the level of every operating unit and contributing individual. The challenges to knowing are also greater in settings where emotion, vested interest, and hardened perspectives are factors in learning and the creation or growth of knowledge.

While families and some other collections of individuals may exist to *be*, organizations exist to *do*. This assertion holds whether we speak about hospitals, universities, small businesses, global corporations, foundations, or governments. While there may be few common traits across this wide range of organizations, the imperative to act is one trait common to all of them. Even though purpose can become obscured in some organizations at some times, taking action within some concept of purpose is assumed to be the rationale for existence in all organizations. Action results from beliefs shaped by information and the belief-forming processes of people concerning widely understood and sometimes explicit answers to questions such as: What must we do to achieve our goals? What is the right thing to do in these circumstances? What is the most effective action to take in this situation? What is the most efficient use of our resources given the relevant variables? How can we produce more of what we exist to produce? How we answer these as well as other important questions and the nature and quality of the answers we produce determine whether our actions will be driven by knowledge or something else. The something else is belief, laden with emotion and conviction, but lacking the distinction of reflecting reality. For our purposes, knowledge is characterized simply as that which is closer to the truth than alternative conceptions. If we assume that organizations at least *seek* to act rationally, the information that informs and sets action in motion must either *be* knowledge or the members of the organization must *believe* the information to be knowledge. The difference between acting based on knowledge and acting based on belief is the difference between acting within an accurate perception of reality and acting within what we hope is reality. Action shaped and informed by reality will produce desired results; action driven by information, which is inconsistent with reality, will not. Successful action always reflects a lively and operative convergence of knowledge about the organization itself and its operating environment.

The convergence of two, incompatible systems of belief provides an example of knowledge at the intersection of an organization's internal and external realities. A manufacturing company based in the United States acquired a single-site manufacturing company in Canada. The rationale for the acquisition was to enhance the global reach of the U.S. company in what was perceived to be an increasingly global market for the company's products. At the strategic level, the logic of the acquisition appealed to both parties, but at the operational level, integration brought significant difficulties. Operational members of the previously independent Canadian company *believed* they knew what was best for their organization, that how they had done things had worked for them for years. and that the changes introduced by the U.S. company were incompatible with their reality. These *beliefs* were embedded in a highly evolved local culture shaped by local perceptions and circumstances.

The U.S. company was in the process of focusing on global markets and operations based on its *belief* that the nature of markets and successful operating models had changed. By default and design, its culture was evolving in the direction of a global orientation. Early steps to integrate U.S. and Canadian operations were not successful. The lack of success was attributed to the effects of what was observed to be a clash of cultures, or the interplay of incompatible beliefs. The essential question was which, if either, belief about the relevant reality was closest to the truth and represented knowledge instead of mere belief. One of the managers in the new organization observed that "the beliefs and assumptions people internalize affects everything they do; I think my world is real, they think their world is real. ...It simply turned out that one perception of reality was more real than the other." Through a rigorous and joint process of analysis and an even more rigorous and intentional process of cultural reconciliation, the reality of a global industry and market became the assumed reality facing the merged operation. The new organization succeeded and sustained its success, providing evidence that the belief about the global nature of the market was accurate and consistent with the relevant and then current reality.

Another example of the operation of incompatible beliefs has a less than happy ending. A 15-year-old technology-based products and services company had grown slowly but steadily to occupy a near dominant position in a small but highly visible and prestigious niche market. Two entrepreneurs, who had led the company from its inception and were deeply and personally committed to its underlying technology and business model, had founded the company. At a certain time in the life of the company, a professional manager was hired as CEO, enabling the founders to remove themselves from active management and reap the rewards of their past efforts. Linear projections were provided for the new CEO, which suggested that the proper course for the future was to continue on the same path with higher levels of revenue to be driven by improved sales and operating performance. After a brief period of settling in to the job, the CEO began to discover a number of troubling facts including rumblings among the customer base about the company's old and unchanging technology. New competitors with updated technologies were entering the company's market. Potential new clients, who would have chosen the company's products and services in the past, were choosing a competitor's products. Gross margins on the company's products and services were declining. The cost to maintain and extend the company's products was increasing. The new CEO and a small number of senior managers and engineers came to believe that the company was on a path of decline and that significant investment would be required to reinvigorate and refresh the company's product and service offerings and to provide an economically viable framework for moving forward.

The founders and some senior employees continued to believe that the company's technology and products were superior to its competitors. Although the new leadership was successful in raising additional capital to fund development and to launch updated products, the new direction for the company was short-lived. The underlying dynamics of the business and the market eventually led to losses and a decision of the board to terminate efforts to redesign the company and its products in favor of cutting costs and returning to business as usual. Two incompatible beliefs were facing each other. One belief was aligned with reality and represented knowledge; the other belief was false. Two years after the board's decision, the company filed for bankruptcy; it was acquired by a competitor for its customer base and disappeared from the scene with the loss of jobs and ongoing support for its customers. The belief that the company's existing products were competitive and viable was false. The belief that the company's underlying economics and product attributes would not sustain success was a true belief. Actions based on false beliefs and lack of knowledge led to the demise of the company.

Linking accurate perceptions of internal and external realities is the primary responsibility of business managers and will lay solid foundations for market success. In other words, *knowing*, rather than *believing* about the strengths, weaknesses, and internal characteristics of the organization and the forces and dynamics in relevant markets will provide the basis for effective performance. As a result of a planning process projecting a 15-year horizon, a decision was made by the managers of a commodity manufacturer to close an old plant. Given the cyclical nature of the company's business, some members of the organization wondered about the validity of such a long planning horizon with current market conditions as the baseline. Irrespective of these questions, plans to close the plant because of projected costs to modernize moved forward.

The strategy manager for the company began to see indicators of a shift from a "down market" to one of an "up" disposition. At the same time, a new manager at the site designated for closure produced a plan for modernizing the plant at a vastly lower cost, which would enable several years of continued operation. As it became clearer that the market was indeed turning back to one of high demand, the decision to close the plant was reversed. The modernization occurred, the market turned up, the plant continued to operate through the up cycle, and it generated significant economic returns for the company. If the plant had closed, the company would not have had the capacity to meet the demand for its products. One of the managers observed, "As we become more driven by the results of our planning processes, we reduce our ability to respond to changing realities." Another manager noted that in situations shaped by something less than absolute knowledge such as forecasting and planning processes, "we should become more hypothesis oriented and less belief oriented."

A manufacturing manager recounted an example of how two sets of beliefs, both flawed in her opinion, and each almost the opposite of the other, came together to produce a near tragic event in her plant. The subsequent analysis of this event set the stage for what may result in a culture more aligned with reality. According to the manager, the company had developed an orientation described as the mindset of a financial analyst. The company was seen as a "black box" and attention was centered on numerical inputs and outputs. What happened inside the box, i.e., how the numbers were achieved, was of limited interest. The result, again in the opinion of the manager, was a companywide loss of knowledge about important processes including safety and risk assessment processes. At the same time, the plant in question, located in a densely populated region of the United States, had been moving over the years in the direction of a socio-technical orientation. Briefly, socio-technical design is associated with a set of beliefs and a clear principle to increase the ability of individuals to participate in decision making and to exercise significant control over their immediate work environment. A consequence of this potentially positive orientation in the plant was a strong focus on subjective factors, arguably, to the detriment of objective factors such as uncluttered patterns of accountability for performance and results.

Because of what was determined to be a breakdown in process and accountability, a dangerous situation developed and a significant accident occurred. The manager believed that only a set of fortuitous circumstances made the difference between a serious accident and a disastrous one. The incident triggered a deep and comprehensive causal analysis, which pointed to a lack of understanding of certain basic manufacturing processes. The answer to the question why such a lack of understanding could exist turned out to be the most basic of "root cause" questions. The answer to this question identified two causes. The progressive loss of process knowledge, coupled with ambiguous accountability represented the conflation of the two strong cultural influences described above. Knowing about the existing culture and seeking to evolve a different culture more closely consistent with the operative reality of the plant were among the necessary ingredients in mapping the way forward.

Seeking to answer questions pertaining to "the right thing to do" from a social or an environmental perspective is an example of seeking knowledge about an ethical reality. We had occasion to work with the leadership team of one of the business units of a global petrochemical company. The business unit had adopted an operating model developed by the larger corporation as its own framework for planning and allocation of resources. The model referenced a range of activities connected with key business and developmental initiatives. Sustainable development occupied the center of the model. According to the Earth Institute at Columbia University, sustainable development is defined as "meeting the needs of the present without compromising the ability of future generations to meet their own needs." Sustainable development is controversial. Some people, even some working within this company, question whether sustainable development is even possible. The company sought, however, to integrate sustainable development into its day-to-day activities in substantive ways.

Over the course of a multi-day planning session in a retreat setting, the leadership team addressed each business and development activity category. Strategic and near term outcomes were identified, action steps were devised, and resources were allocated. Nothing connected with sustainable development had been discussed and we wondered if the *alleged* commitment to sustainable development would be anything other than a public relations strategy. Happily, a sustainable development project was defined and adopted by the team. The project would recycle the used output of one of its manufacturing processes to produce low cost and durable building materials to be used in the third world. Not only would the new materials meet a social need, the removal and use of discarded waste would mitigate environmental concerns. This project was an example of doing the right thing. Although the company would acknowledge that they believe doing the right thing is good for business, there is a strong element of seeking to *know* how to be socially responsible and how to minimize its own footprint on the planet.

RATIONALE AND STRUCTURE OF THIS BOOK

The central argument in this book is that *how* we form the beliefs we hold influences *what* we believe and whether or not our beliefs are likely to be true. Since what we do is largely determined by what we believe, our actions tend to be valid and beneficial depending on the knowledge content or degree of truth represented by our beliefs. Section I of the book, Foundations, addresses the foundational aspects of *how* and *what* we know within the framework of the general topics of knowledge (meaning and theory), truth, belief, justification, and the nature of reality. The central argument is deconstructed and presented as a set of arguments and hypotheses and developed through the chapters of Section II, Applications, arrayed around the human organizational dimensions of *individuals* as knowing subjects, *groups* as they relate to collective knowing, *leaders* as stewards of knowledge, and *culture* as knowing context.

The subject matter of the book is the growth of knowledge in organizations as the essential outcome of learning. Since the key active idea is growth, knowledge is seen neither as absolute nor static and the emphasis is on transitions along a continuum from belief to knowledge. The focus in this book is on the growth of knowledge as a cultural attribute, as a *way of working and being* in contrast to the narrower conception of knowledge, as in technology or process expertise, as one asset among many. Knowledge as an asset is the idea underpinning the field of knowledge management, which the authors see as useful and worthy of pursuit but distinctly not the subject matter of this book. More to the point, the growth of knowledge as a defining aspect of culture is seen as complementary to knowledge management, providing a necessary precondition for the successful pursuit of knowledge as a strategic asset.

This book is both analysis and synthesis regarding the factors influencing an organization's ability to create or improve the knowledge required for adaptation, growth, and success. As indicated above, there are theoretical or foundational and practical aspects to this book. The arguments embodied in the application-oriented portion of the book are the context for exploring reality, belief, truth, knowledge, and justification as foundational conceptions or arguments. Regarding Section I, there is an assumption that useful insights exist within the philosophical disciplines associated with reality or ontology and knowledge or epistemology pertaining to the growth of knowledge in organizations. Further, the assumption is that these insights and perspectives, generally undeveloped in the fields of organizational behavior and learning, lay the foundations for practical applications. The foundational arguments, summarized below, are developed in Section I.

- Whenever we seek to know, we seek to know about something, about some reality. There are multiple realities that affect and are affected by life in organizations. These realities pertain to natural or physical objects, to the human constructed yet material world of money and property, to the constructed and non-material world of culture, politics, etc., and to concepts such as ethics. Questions having to do with the nature and dimensions of reality are the subject matter of ontology.
- How we form the beliefs we hold is determined by our conceptions of reality and the application of one or more approaches to knowing. Various theories of knowledge and approaches to knowing exist. All of these have something to say about belief, truth, and justification. These theories range from a complete reliance on experience as the basis of all knowledge to a complete reliance on individual reflection and the application of reason. Theories of knowledge and approaches to knowing are the subject matter of epistemology.
- No single theory and approach to knowing applies to all realities. For example, while theories based on experience may apply to the physical world of objects and phenomena but not to the non-material and conceptual worlds, theories based on some form of idealism or human mediation may apply to the conceptual world but not to the physical or material worlds. Multiple approaches to knowing may apply to the same reality.

A chain of linked arguments provides the basis for the practical focus in Section II, Applications. These arguments are listed below:

- Human action is set in motion by belief. Belief connotes trust and confidence in an idea or proposition and is generally held both collectively and by individuals. Beliefs tend to be embodied in organizational culture. It is self-evident that while beliefs may lead to beneficial action, they are not necessarily truth-bearing and may not be held in an organization's best interests.
- Action is valid and has value when the belief that drives it is aligned with reality. Reality refers to manifestations of culture, operating and

environmental circumstances, as well as to conceptions of relevant technological and market factors.

- Individuals and their collectives tend to be predisposed to one or a closely related set of approaches to forming beliefs and knowing and to seek to apply these *epistemic* approaches to *any* reality. Epistemic style or approach to knowing is a fundamental element of diversity among individuals. Individual diversity is brought about and seasoned by cognitive style or way of thinking, training, socialization, and other background factors.

- Diverse approaches to knowing can facilitate or constrain creativity, problem solving, and the growth of knowledge. There are approaches to knowing that can beneficially bridge and reconcile divergent approaches to knowing (or epistemic styles).

- Learning and the growth of knowledge is a collective matter resulting from the interaction of individuals in group settings. As previously established, four organizational dimensions influence the effective interaction of individuals for the purpose of learning and creating knowledge. These dimensions are *individuals, groups, leaders,* and *culture.*

Most of the arguments defining the rationale for this book, taken individually, are self-evident and are offered as "givens." Four of these arguments, however, are presented as hypotheses. These hypotheses are addressed throughout the book and supported by experience, related consequences and inference, by reflection, and by research associated with sources in epistemology and ontology. While seeking to make a positive case for application based on these hypotheses, the reader is encouraged to view them as conjectural and to validate or invalidate them within the framework of their own experience. These four hypotheses are further elaborated as follows:

- *The growth of knowledge is a function of the relevance and efficacy of the approach to knowing employed, subject to the nature of the reality about which we hope to know.* We live in a world of multiple and diverse realities. It is clearly different to speak about the reality of an object in front of us with physical dimensions than to speak about the reality associated with culture or with perceptions of success or with a moral or ethical question. There are also multiple and diverse ways of knowing and no single approach to knowing applies to everything about which we hope to know. For example, empiricism asserts that we can only know through experience and observation by way of our senses; rationalism argues that our ability to reason is the only reliable path to knowledge; pragmatism posits that knowledge is associated with the beneficial consequences of action; theories embracing idealism focus on human subjectivity as the mediator of all knowledge. Growth of knowledge can be achieved when the approach to knowing matches the nature of the reality in question. More than one approach to knowing may apply to a single reality and the acknowledgement and understanding of that fact can result in improved knowledge of the reality in question.

- *The growth of knowledge is influenced by the personal and subjective attributes of the individuals engaged in the process of coming to know, specifically including approach to knowing or epistemic style.* Individuals bring the complete bundle of their characteristics and traits to their encounters with each other. These attributes include assumptions about meaning and how the world works, biases, ways of thinking and solving problems, personality traits, motivations and, not least, ways of knowing or approaches to knowing. The personal characteristics of the individuals involved in any group setting will help shape the character and knowledge creating quality of the group.

- *Within the work of groups, specific approaches to knowing can transcend and help reconcile the diverse approaches to knowing of individuals.* Collections of individuals, whether existing at the same time and place or separated from each other by time and place, are responsible for most of what we learn and come to know. Within the context of individuals working in groups, diverse approaches to knowing can facilitate or constrain creativity, problem solving, and the growth of knowledge. Groups can provide the framework to clarify, sharpen, and reconcile the perspectives of individuals and, through dialogue and bridging divergent approaches to knowing, produce learning and knowledge.

- *The essential task of leadership is to bring about and sustain an environment conducive to the growth of knowledge.* The growth of knowledge is a clear and effective basis for leading organizations to achieve higher levels of relevance and performance. The first requirement for leaders is to create and sustain a set of conditions hospitable to the truth. Such an environment is underpinned and expressed by organizational culture. Culture is defined as that which is both objective, as existing independently and apart from individuals, and subjective, as having become internalized and made a part of the beliefs of individuals. A culture characterized as one where there is a collective belief that the growth of knowledge is objectively valuable and where that collective belief is subjective and real for the members of the culture provides the foundation for an environment conducive to the growth of knowledge.

REFERENCES

1. Faust, Drew. 2008. *The Republic of Suffering: Death and the American Civil War*. New York: Knopf, a Division of Random House.
2. Boorstein, Daniel. 1983. *The Discoverers: A History of Man's Search to Know His World and Himself*. New York: Vintage Books, a Division of Random House.
3. Durant, Will. 1935. *The Story of Civilization, Vol. 1*. New York: MJF Books.
4. Wells, William, Gertrude Elion and John Laszlo. 2003. *Beyond Discovery: The Path from Research to Human Benefit*. Washington: The National Academy of Sciences.
5. Committee on the Biological and Biomedical Applications of Stem Cell Research. 2002. Stem Cells and the Future of Regenerative Medicine. Washington.
6. Report on Intergovernmental Panel on Climate Change, on behalf of the World Meteorological Organization and the United Nations Environmental Programme. 2004. *Science*, Vol. 304, No. 5670.
7. Tuchman, Barbara. 1984. *The March of Folly: From Troy to Vietnam*. New York: Alfred A. Knopf, Inc.
8. Smith, Adam. 1999/1776. *The Wealth of Nations*. London: Penguin Group.
9. Block, Fred. 2006. A Moral Economy. *The Nation* March 20.
10. Drucker, Peter. 1993. *Post Capitalist Society*. New York: Harper Business.

Section I

Foundations

Knowledge, belief, truth, and reality are the foundational concepts that underpin this book. Revisiting the essential ideas proposed, they are: 1) the premise that individual and collective beliefs or assumptions largely determine decisions that are made and actions that are taken, and 2) the conception that *how* beliefs are formed influences the *content* of such beliefs and whether they are likely to be true and, therefore, representative of knowledge. Given that *what* we believe plays a dominant role in defining what we *do*, the basis of our beliefs and the degree of truth associated with them are important factors in influencing whether or not we succeed as individuals and organizations. If *how* we form our beliefs and seek to know influences the content and veracity of our beliefs, the mode or manner of belief formation is an even more fundamental factor in shaping our ability to make good decisions and take appropriate actions. The development of these ideas requires exploration of the meaning and implications of the foundational concepts. Theories of knowledge and reality are surveyed and analyzed and relevant theories of knowledge, expressed as approaches to belief formation, are integrated with conceptions of reality. The subject matter of Section I comes into focus around the following arguments:

- There are multiple realities that affect and are affected by life in organizations.
- Various theories of knowledge or approaches to knowing (belief formation) exist.
- No single theory or approach to knowing applies to all realities. Multiple approaches to knowing may apply to the same reality.

2

What Does It Mean to Know?

ANTICIPATORY SUMMARY

We say we *know* when what we mean is we *believe*. We say we have knowledge when what we have is an opinion. We say our beliefs are justified when our evidence is subjective and often fanciful. Knowledge—as easily as we speak of it, as important as it is and as desirable as we take it to be—is not well understood. In this chapter, the conception of knowledge is deconstructed and defined in a practical and operative way.

The "Standard Analysis" of Knowledge

The conventional definition or the "standard analysis" of knowledge refers to three individually *necessary* and jointly *sufficient* conditions for knowledge—justification, truth, and belief. Necessary and sufficient are the terms used to identify the validating factors of knowledge. Necessary refers to that which is *required*; sufficient refers to the condition of *enough*. Knowledge, in other words, is justified true belief. The individual conditions of belief, truth, and justification and their interaction are explored in this chapter.

Challenges to the Standard Analysis

Although the standard analysis seems to embody the comfortable claim of common sense, it gives the dubious impression that the quality of knowing is binary and absolute, which is contrary to our conception. There are important challenges to the standard analysis. These are accounted for in this chapter within the practical perspective that there *are* realities about

23

which we can know and our knowing about them has meaning in our lives as individuals and members of groups and organizations.

WHAT DOES IT MEAN TO KNOW?

It seems self-evident that it is good to live in a state of knowing, rather than in ignorance; to act based on accurate perceptions rather than error or false belief. We are taught from an early age that achieving knowledge is a worthy aim. We boast about being members of the "knowledge society" and count ourselves fortunate to live in an age of widely available information, even if we often wonder if such information is knowledge or something else. We take *knowing* and the reasons why we want to know for granted, however, as we glibly speak about knowledge and the value of it. The stories from the previous chapter illuminate how knowledge is profoundly beneficial in a practical and real sense and how the lack of knowledge leaves us vulnerable and disadvantaged; yet most of us give little thought to these questions: What does it mean to know? What is knowledge? How do we know what we know?

If knowledge could be defined as a distinct and fully objective "something," such as a material or physical thing or sunlight or oxygen or temperature, it wouldn't matter a great deal in practical terms whether or not we fully understood it; we could easily come to apprehend whether or not it was present and in what quantity and what its effects would likely be. Knowledge, however, is not well defined in an explicit and universal sense, and the term *knowledge* is often used ordinarily and in general speech to refer to circumstances that have little or nothing to do with knowledge. We say we *know* when what we mean is we *believe*; we say we have knowledge when what we mean is we have an opinion. We say we have *justification* for what we believe when our evidence is highly subjective and sometimes fanciful. Knowledge, to the extent that we actually think about it, can mean different things according to the nature of that about which we hope to know. It can also mean different things to different people according to disposition, training, and assumptions about the world. Knowledge, therefore, as important as it is and as desirable as we take it to be, turns out to be not well understood. Conceptions of knowledge are varied, confusing, elusive, often mysterious, and generally far more complex than we have come to suppose.

The growth of knowledge is the central matter of interest in this book. The growth of knowledge as a collective and intentional effort is affected in a positive way by a common understanding of what knowledge means within any given context and pertaining to any relevant reality. Further, framed by a common perception of the reality we seek to know about, the diversity of approaches to knowing or how we seek to know, closely related to the varied conceptions of knowledge, acknowledges and provides the basis for uniquely and beneficially exploiting individual diversity. Conversely, the failure to achieve a common and operative understanding of the meaning of knowledge and the reality about which knowledge is sought will tend to result in a fragmented and incoherent framework for pursuing the growth of knowledge. An understanding, therefore, of the various conceptions, forces, challenges, and dynamics surrounding knowledge itself is necessary to the analysis and arguments presented in the book. This is the rationale for the chapters in Section I: Foundations.

THE "STANDARD ANALYSIS" OF KNOWLEDGE

As human beings, we have struggled with knowledge, what it means and how we come to know, throughout our recorded history. Socrates is said to have claimed that he knew either nothing or very little. Plato's views of knowledge initially followed Socrates' in expressing a skeptical stance, but later evolved to a more positive doctrine. Aristotle was influenced by the questions raised in Plato's dialogues pertaining to the definitions of knowledge and the conditions for justification. Conceptions of knowledge have emerged, become combined and differentiated, and evolved from the time of Socrates to the present. Also, disputes about what it means to know have been an ever-present feature of the knowledge landscape from the earliest times. As we undertook this project, we decided to begin the development of our understanding of knowledge with what has become known as the standard definition or "the standard analysis" of knowledge. Michael Williams, the philosopher, identified the analytic problem as the first "problem of knowledge" and the standard analysis as a "precise explication or analysis of the concept of knowledge."[1] The standard analysis refers to *propositional knowledge*. Propositional knowledge is expressed in a declarative statement or phrase expressing the validity or truth of some proposition in the form—to *know that* such and such. Examples of propositional knowledge are to *know that* the color green is a mixture of yellow and blue; to *know that* water freezes at thirty-two degrees Fahrenheit; to *know that*, given a set of conditions, it will rain tomorrow; to *know that* the consistency and coherence of the evidence points to the guilt or innocence of an accused offender; to *know that* the desirable outcome of an action suggests its truth. There seem to be other kinds of knowledge. To know how to get around Paris or to know the face of an old friend or to know how to ride a bicycle feels like non-propositional knowledge, but some set of propositions, however subtle, tends to underpin such knowledge. Other conceptions and views of differences in kinds or types of knowledge exist, but our analysis will center on the sort of knowledge that can be reduced to propositions.

Within the language of epistemology or the theory of knowledge, the terms "necessary" and "sufficient" are used to name the validating factors of knowledge. Necessary refers to that which is absolutely needed or required; sufficient refers to the condition of "enough." The conventional definition of knowledge, according to the "standard analysis" also known as the "tripartite definition of knowledge," refers to three individually necessary and jointly sufficient conditions or constituents: justification, truth, and belief.[2] Knowledge, in other words, as in the case of a three-legged stool, rests on the three conditions expressed as justified, true belief. The belief condition requires that anyone who *knows* something, believes or accepts it, trusts and has confidence in it. The truth and justification conditions assert that anything that can be *known*, rather than just believed, must be *true* and must be adequately *justified* or supported by evidence. We can believe something and have credible justification for believing it, but if it turns out not to be true, we can't be said to have knowledge; in other words, we can't be said to *know*. We can believe something, which is in fact true but if our basis for believing it is not warranted as in the case of astrology or superstition, for example, we can't be said to have knowledge. Accident, serendipity or discredited systems of thought can't bestow the state or validate the claim of having knowledge according to the standard analysis.

Something like the standard analysis appears to have been in the mind of Plato in the Dialogues through his description of a ladder. The bottom rung of the ladder represents unjustified belief or ignorance and rises rung by rung through justified belief, unjustified true belief, and so on arriving at the state of justified true belief or knowledge. The standard analysis has been revisited and augmented by philosophers throughout the centuries and articulated in the twentieth century, for example, by the American philosopher Roderick Chisholm[3] and the British philosopher A. J. Ayer. Ayer argued, "I conclude then that the necessary and sufficient conditions for knowing that something is the case are first that what one is said to know be true, secondly that one be sure of it, and thirdly that one should have the right to be sure."[4] While some theorists disavow the standard analysis, their arguments tend to be developed using the language of the standard analysis and such arguments are usually placed along side it as a frame of reference

We acknowledge that within the standard definition there is controversy about the meaning of the constituents of this definition and these will be addressed below. We also acknowledge that there are important challenges to the "standard analysis" and these will be addressed in this chapter as well. Further still, we acknowledge, perhaps most importantly, that when we think about knowledge, knowledge about *what* becomes the crucial question. This question will be taken up in Chapter 3 and will play a central role throughout the book.

Belief

Our actions are driven by what we believe, by what we assume to be true about the world and our place in it. Beliefs have been described as maps, but not merely maps. Beliefs not only supply information about the terrain through which we move, they help determine the direction in which we steer.[5] If what we believe is, in fact, true and justified, our actions will be driven by knowledge or something approaching it, with favorable consequences. Unless we happen to be beneficiaries of blind luck, our actions based on beliefs induced by ignorance or fallacy will leave us disadvantaged and less well off. In the language of cultural anthropology, it is common to refer to the *operative* beliefs embedded in culture as knowledge. Following that practice and without an appropriate degree of sensitivity to the dynamics and implications associated with the differences between belief and knowledge, we referred to the effectual cultural beliefs of an organization as institutional knowledge in our 1999 book *Beyond Reductionism*. It is important to amend our earlier perspective and reiterate, therefore, that belief is *not* knowledge.

Belief that is both true and justified accounts for the conception of knowledge in the standard analysis. We will begin our exploration of the constituents of the standard analysis with, arguably, its core component—belief. The generally accepted definition of belief centers on the idea of belief as a state of mind that embodies trust and confidence in something. Belief refers to a commitment to the perceived truth of some proposition. The Scottish philosopher David Hume embellished the meaning of belief. He wrote, "It is evident that belief consists not in the peculiar nature or order of ideas, but in the manner of their conception, and in their *feeling* to the mind. I confess that it is impossible perfectly to explain this feeling or manner of conception. We may make use of words which express something near it. But its true and proper name is belief, which is a term which everyone sufficiently understands in common life. And in philosophy, we can go no farther than assert that belief is something felt by the mind, which distinguishes the ideas of the judgment from the fictions of the imagination. It gives them more weight and influence; makes them appear of greater importance; enforces them in the mind; and renders them the governing principle of our actions."[6]

Belief is the relatively unrestricted acceptance of an argument or proposition with the added dimension of feeling about the "something" believed. Other "feeling" states of mind such as desiring, hoping, fearing, and intending do not, to recall Hume, have the "weight and influence" of belief to underpin knowing as a special state of mind, which also possesses a normative or conforming to the truth status. The treatment of knowledge as a special kind of belief is not without controversy. Timothy Williamson in *Knowledge and Its Limits* argues against the standard analysis by claiming that "knowing (unaffected by belief) is a state of mind. ... In contrast (to the standard view), the claim that *knowing* is a state of mind is to be understood as the claim that there is a mental state, being in which, is necessary and sufficient for knowing."[7] (Parenthetical comments are those of the authors.) It is also not always immediately obvious to non-specialists in the normal course of their lives that belief is necessary for knowledge. Advocates of the standard analysis, however, argue that it makes no sense to say that one *knows* something but doesn't *believe* it. Without becoming an advocate for the standard view, there is something reassuring to common understanding to the notion of a ladder regarding knowledge, to borrow the metaphor from Plato, beginning with belief and progressing through the rungs of truth and justification. At this stage in the development of this book, we *believe* that exploring the foundations of knowledge will have something useful to say about the growth of knowledge in organizations and organizational effectiveness but the *truth* of that belief is yet to be shown.

There is a connection between belief and knowledge that is not expressed in the standard analysis. This connection has to do with the active role of belief in creating its own reality. One of our industrial clients who was strongly motivated to improve safety in his company spoke about his hopes for *belief* to create a self-fulfilling prophecy. Rather than defining safety goals based on classical assessments of acceptable risk, his aim is to inculcate the *belief* that "all accidents can be prevented." He reckons that if this belief becomes strong enough, it will, in fact, become true and there-fore knowledge. This phenomenon has been called the "Tinker Bell effect," suggesting that something can be true as long as we all believe it.

Truth

Truth is a relation that may exist between an idea (belief, opinion, state-ment) and its object. Truth is a property of certain of our ideas, connot-ing agreement with reality as falsity connotes disagreement with reality. The standard analysis asserts that knowledge of "something" requires that the condition of truth exist for the "something." There is an obvious assumption in the standard analysis that the condition of "being true" is a state that exists and can be grasped. There are well-formed objections to this assumption, which will be described below under Challenges, and there are alternative, nontraditional conceptions of truth, which will be explored subsequently in this and other chapters. The standard analysis of knowledge, however, is traditional with practical implications and a strong appeal to common sense. The discussion of truth in this chapter, therefore, within the framework of the standard analysis, will be confined to traditional conceptions of truth, given the qualification that a meaning-ful conception of truth may be less than absolute.

The table in Figure 2.1 introduces the three traditional conceptions of truth. An observation, made repeatedly throughout this book is that

Traditional Conceptions of Truth	Knowledge Implications
Correspondence: Truth is that which corresponds to simple reality.	Reality is objective. We can know about any such reality.
Coherence: The truth of any reality is that which exists within a rational and coherent whole.	Knowledge is found in the search for mutual coherence among beliefs.
Pragmatism: The truth associated with any reality is that which attaches to good (useful) consequences.	Knowledge is found in the "what and how" of producing desirable results.

FIGURE 2.1
Truth and knowledge.

scholars and champions of a specific conception of truth, theory of knowledge, or approach to knowing tend to see its exclusive application irrespective of the *what* about which one hopes to know. Ideas pertaining to the existence of relevant conceptions of truth and knowledge according to the reality in question as well as to their non-mutual exclusivity will be fully developed in Chapter 4 and subsequent chapters. For our purposes in this chapter, these ideas of reality-specific conceptions of truth and the related limited set of approaches to knowing apply, as well as the view that even these traditional conceptions of truth are not mutually exclusive.

Correspondence

That truth corresponds to facts is an intuitive, commonly accepted idea. When propositional knowledge refers to statements or sentences corresponding to facts, the correspondence conception of truth is expressed in the language of logic as: *a statement is true if and only if it corresponds to the facts.* That the month of April has thirty days, or that the Battle of Hastings occurred in the year 1066, or that the computer screen is thirty inches in front of my eyes are statements that are true or not depending on the accuracy of what they assert. The scientific method relies on the correspondence conception of truth. The essential role of observation and experimentation in natural science is based on the assumption that there is an objective reality, independent of the observer, about which it is possible to have knowledge. For example, in the childhood leukemia story in Chapter 1, laboratory studies proved the truth of the hypotheses that enzymes are the triggers of chemical reactions in cells and that certain chemicals interfere with cellular functions; double blind clinical trials demonstrated that certain chemotherapeutic agents caused remission.

Realists defend the idea that there is a reality totally independent of us and the idea that truth is a matter of correspondence to facts. "'True' comes from the same etymological root as 'trust' and 'trustworthy,' and all these from the Indo-European root 'deru' for 'tree,' suggesting uprightness and reliability. There are not only true statements, but also true friends (real or genuine), true emotions (sincerely felt, not fake), true heirs (rightful or legitimate), as well as true north, knives that cut true, and true believers. These various senses of true show family resemblances. If truth has some general connection to trustworthiness and reliability, we need to ask: Under what conditions would we find a statement trustworthy or reliable?

Obviously, when it does what it purports to do; that is, when it accurately states how things are (when the statement comports with facts)."[8] Regarding facts, the term "fact" connotes something that has an actual existence in space and time. The term fact has come to mean the existence of that which makes true statements true. It's important to note that true statements and facts are not the same. Facts refer to the quality of being "actual" while true statements are expressions of the relation of being in accordance with an actual state of affairs. Factual circumstances may be causal in a way that true statements cannot be. The true statement that "it is raining" is a linguistic construct. The fact that it is raining will produce the consequences of rain. Also, the same fact may be expressed in different true statements. The fact that April has thirty days is always the same, but could be stated truly by "April has thirty days" or "April has one less day than July" or "April has the same number of days as September."

In a practical sense, the validity of the correspondence conception of truth seems obvious. This is the common sense way of assessing the truth or falsity of the physical world. Yet, this ancient idea is alleged by some theorists to have never been adequately articulated. Regarding the world of objects we can perceive through the senses and know about, Kant, who sought to reconcile divergent perspectives on truth and knowledge, called *correspondence* into question and argued that we can only *know* about "appearances" and not "things-in-themselves."[9] Kant used the expression "things-in-themselves" to differentiate the substance and essence of objects from how they appear to observers. Further, the meanings of correspondence and reality have been criticized for being obscure. In this connection, we will explore challenges to the definitions of truth and the other definitions that make up the standard analysis later in this chapter and in subsequent chapters.

Further still, there are radical and idiosyncratic notions of truth pertaining to what, how, and if we can know about the physical world. Given our focus on practical knowledge in this book, we will not substantively pursue those conceptions of truth. Since not everything about which we hope to know will neatly fit into what can be known through the senses as physical objects, we will also explore diverse realities in Chapter 3.

Coherence

In our experience, especially from the interviews we conducted for this book, some individuals find truth in internal consistency in "how the pieces fit together." Among those who expressed this idea regarding truth, it occurred to them only upon reflection as the second or third answer to our question about how they would define truth. Having formulated this conception and expressed it, however, it seemed to be comfortable and satisfying; it seemed to "feel" right to them. At its simplest level, *coherence* would call into question the truth of a network of beliefs if, according to the logical principal of noncontradiction, one or more constituent beliefs expressed truth and falsity at the same time. In other words, within a set of beliefs, affirmation and nonaffirmation of a perceived reality could not simultaneously exist. The attraction to the notion of *coherence* as an indicator of truth seemed to feel as natural to these people as *correspondence* did to others, although, to restate a point made earlier, the two conceptions regarding truth are not necessarily mutually exclusive, even within a single truth-seeking individual. In a practical sense, coherence perspectives on truth may point the way to relevant and powerful conceptions of functional truth when self-interested, proprietary, and influential forces use anomalous and inconsistent findings to cast doubt on the validity of a large and coherent body of scientific findings. The reference to the controversy over human-induced global warming described in Chapter 1 is an example.

Although the *idea* of coherence can be present for those who haven't given much thought to the meaning of knowledge and truth, there are formal coherence theories of belief, justification, and truth that combine in various ways to yield theories of knowledge. Since coherence seeks to find truth in the consistency and mutual support or entailment of beliefs, coherence theories of belief are strongly related to coherence notions of truth. Coherence is a matter of how well a body of beliefs "hangs together": "how well its component beliefs fit together, agree, or dovetail with each other so as to produce an organized, tightly structured system of beliefs rather than either a helter-skelter collection or a set of conflicting subsystems. It is reasonably clear that this "hanging together" depends on the various sorts of inferential, evidential, and explanatory relations among the various members of a system of beliefs and especially on the more holistic and systematic of these.[10] As described in Chapter 1, a manufacturing organization facing two conceptions of reality was forced to choose and alter its own operating circumstances based on the conception determined to be closest to the truth. The lack of coherence associated with one set of beliefs in relation to the other is an example of an analysis supported by a coherence conception of truth.

Pragmatist

In ordinary usage, "pragmatic" is an adjective describing a person. A pragmatist, in general, is seen as a person who exhibits a practical approach to problems and the affairs of living. A person who is seen as practical is disposed to action as opposed to speculation or abstract thinking; a practical person is "down to earth" and has "both feet on the ground." Consistent with more formal usage, the word "pragmatist" has a more specific meaning in this chapter and designates a conception of truth. According to the pragmatist's view, truth is found in utility or the consequences of action. While truth adheres to good consequences, falsity is associated with results which exhibit little or no utility. Leaders in organizations with an orientation to outcomes or results closely connected with fundamental purpose and direction are essentially pragmatic. For them, truth resides in the idea or concept and related action that produces desired consequences. For pragmatists, both the correspondence and coherence conceptions of truth and knowledge are not seen as invalid, but only incomplete or inadequate.

Pragmatist refers to a concept pertaining to truth emanating from the philosophy of pragmatism. Pragmatism, as a school of philosophical thought, is considered to be primarily American in origin, but with the influence of Kant, Hegel, and Francis Bacon, who in rejecting traditional Scholastic philosophy, held that the practical success of a theory was the hallmark of its truth. (Scholastic philosophy is the result of a highly influential medieval intellectual movement designed to bring articles of faith and reason into a single system.) Charles S. Pierce and William James are usually credited with first articulating pragmatism as a philosophy. According to James, the pragmatic method means, "The attitude of looking away from first things, principles, "categories," supposed necessities; and of looking toward last things, fruits, consequences, facts.... True assumptions (beliefs) are said to be, by definition, those which provoke actions with desirable results.... Pragmatism is willing to take anything, to follow either logic or the senses, and to count the humblest and most personal experiences.... Her only test of probable truth is what works best in the way of leading us, what fits every part of life best and combines with the collectivity of experience's demands, nothing being omitted."[11] While there are common themes within the various interpretations of pragmatism, it has been observed by Schiller, an important pragmatist, that there are as "many pragmatisms as there are pragmatists."

Returning again to the climate change story, the following is a quotation from Chapter 1. "The scientific consensus might, of course, be wrong. If the history of science teaches anything, it is humility, and no one can be faulted for failing to act on what is *not* known. But our grandchildren will surely blame us if they find that we understood the reality of anthropogenic climate change and failed to do anything about it." Given the complexity of climate science and the difficulty of achieving a consensus regarding action based on either a correspondence or a coherence conception of truth, a pragmatist's approach to truth could offer a path through the dilemma to acceptable and consensual knowledge. This example also points to the nonmutually exclusive and potentially complementary nature of the three traditional conceptions of truth.

Justification

Within the framework of the standard analysis of knowledge and its assertion that knowledge is justified true belief, justification is the third leg. The intent of the standard analysis is to define the conditions, which if present, would confer the status of *knowing* on the potential knower. It could be argued that true belief is adequate for knowledge, but that interpretation has been found wanting by most theorists who contend that something more is required. We could guess at the rightness of some proposition or concept, which could turn out to be right by mere accident or chance event. A belief, based on the wrong reasons or on no fully understood reasons at all, could be true. Under such circumstances, since knowledge is assumed to be a conscious mental state, one could have true belief, but not knowledge. Justification, then, as an evaluative concept related to grounds or warrant, has come to be required for conferring the status of having knowledge. Writing in the journal *Philosophical Perspectives*, Jaegwon Kim argues that "there is a simple reason for our preoccupation with justification: It is the only specifically epistemic (pertaining to knowledge) component in the classic (or standard) tripartite conception of knowledge." (Parenthetical comments are those of the authors.) "Neither belief nor truth is a specifically epistemic notion: Belief is a psychological concept and truth is a semantical-metaphysical one. These concepts may have an implicit epistemological dimension, but if they do, it is likely to be through their involvement with essentially normative epistemic notions like justification, evidence, and rationality. Moreover, justification is what makes knowledge itself a normative concept."[12] "There is a close connection between justification and the social practice of providing reasons to back up our claims. The practice of giving grounds in defense of our assertions provides the background against which the concept of justification has been developed."[13]

"Justified," like "true," within the context of the standard analysis, is an adjective of belief. Justification has attracted a large body of scholarly literature and, as a topic of scholarship, has generated numbingly subtle differentiations among types or modes of justification. Justification in principle is simple; it refers to the grounds one has for believing that a proposition or circumstance is true. Evidence, or the presence of a set of known facts that provide grounds for inferring further facts, could confer justification. For example, the belief that Peterson owns a Ford could be justified by the facts that he owns a car, that he works for Ford, that Ford gives discounts to employees, and that his father owned a Ford. As another example, the existence of a strong and increasing pattern of demand for a product and the relatively low cost of entry for new firms could provide the justification for the belief that new competitors will enter a particular market. The reliance on a process that has reliably predicted the truth of arguments or circumstances in the past could provide justification for one's related beliefs. A detective could justifiably depend on her tried and tested processes of observation and attribution to support her beliefs pertaining to the guilt of a crime suspect. Seeking justification in a dutiful and responsible manner could bestow the state of "justified" on beliefs. For example, establishing and adhering to stringent requirements for documentation and analysis associated with clinical trials in medicine could provide justification for believing in the results describing the potential efficacy of a new drug.

Should the process of justification lead us to focus on justification of the belief itself, whether or not the believer is fully aware of the evidence or justification? Or is it more relevant and consequential to pay attention to the believer and the believer's justification in holding the belief? Questions pertaining to whether our justification concerns are more legitimately connected to the belief or to the believer lead to the consideration of the two broad categories of theories pertaining to justification. The first requires that all factors necessary for a belief to be justified be cognitively and *internally* accessible to the potential believer; existing somehow, in other words, *within* the believing subject. The second allows that at least some of the justifying factors not be internally accessible and, therefore, *external* to the believer's cognitive perspective. The first of these categories is identified as *internalist*; the second as *externalist*. The core idea behind internalist conceptions of justification is that for any justified belief, one can become aware of the justifier(s) *solely* through reflection. The essential contentions of the externalist argument are that the propensity of a process or method to reliably produce and sustain true beliefs is all that is required for justification and that the awareness of this propensity need not be internally accessible to the believer.

The reasons for the internalist/externalist distinction seem to reduce to two. First, theories under the internalist category depend upon sophisticated and complex internal (to the believer) resources and therefore may inappropriately deny justification of beliefs to unsophisticated adults and young children. Externalist conceptions do not impose such limits and support the view that such limits should not be imposed. Second, internalist conceptions require that justification and acceptance of beliefs be rational, responsible, and complete and that the believer be aware of the reasons for believing in the truth of the proposition. Internalists argue that externalist theories do not meet all requirements for justification; externalists counter that to impose such requirements is to fail to understand the meaning and implications of justification. In a practical sense, irrespective of scholarly differences over the standards for justification, the idea of justification is simple and refers to the grounds one has for believing a proposition or circumstance to be true.

CHALLENGES TO THE STANDARD ANALYSIS

The standard analysis of knowledge appears to embody the comfortable claim of common sense. It feels intuitively correct. The standard analysis of knowledge, however, gives the dubious impression that the quality of knowing is binary and absolute. A proposition is either believed, justified, and true or it is not; one either knows or one does not know. We are strongly led to the conviction that knowledge and truth are usually not absolute, especially when we consider that the character of the reality about which we seek to know can vary from the mathematical to the physical to the material to the nonmaterial to the conceptual. While there will be little controversy over treating mathematical and physical realities as independent of human agency, material, nonmaterial and conceptual realities exist only within the context of human mediation. The topic of multiple realities will be explored in the next chapter. For now, embracing the questions pertaining to the absoluteness of knowledge and going beyond, there are challenges to the standard analysis regarding such questions as: Can we ever be certain that we know anything? Whose truth and whose justification relates to our knowing? Are there circumstances where we are justified in holding our true beliefs, yet still cannot be said to know? In describing the challenges to the standard analysis below, incompletely but representatively, it is worth noting again that, while some disavow the standard analysis, challenges are usually set against the standard analysis as a frame of reference and the terms of disavowal are usually expressed in standard analysis terms.

Skepticism

In ordinary usage, skepticism is a term which describes the attitude of one who questions and seeks confirming evidence when confronted with a proposition. The skeptic is one who doubts, suspends judgment, and often withholds it. The skeptic is not usually part of the crowd rushing to embrace some new idea or some article of faith. Ordinary or common skepticism, however, represents only one strand of formal or philosophical skepticism, which refers to a general outlook regarding human knowledge. Skepticism in its various forms, in one degree or another, questions our ability to ever really know anything. Some forms of skepticism express the view that we can never know because we can never meet the truth condition; others hold that we can't know because the justification condition can never be satisfied.

Epistemology, the branch of philosophy concerned with knowledge, has been in a state of tension with skepticism since ancient times. Socrates and Plato wondered about their ability to truly know anything. The roots of classical skepticism are traced through Sextus Empiricus, a second century follower of Pyrrho, to the fourth century BCE Greek, Pyrrho himself and his school of extreme skeptics who suspended judgment on everything. Throughout history, skeptical arguments have emerged to counter virtually every theory of knowledge ever articulated, and philosophers have sought to answer critical skepticism as a way to provide grounding for their theories of knowledge. Many philosophers go to the extent of identifying the problem of knowledge with that of skepticism. Paradoxically, skeptics and dogmatists (the formal and narrow term applied to those who are not skeptics) agree on the *definition* of knowledge; the disagreement pertains to the *possibility* of knowledge.

Radical or absolute, global skepticism is closely related to nihilism, a doctrine that denies the existence of objective truth in any form. Radical skepticism rejects both reason and experience as justification for knowing anything. More precisely, since objective truth does not exist, seeking to know is an empty enterprise. This breed of skeptic has been described as "atheistic" regarding knowledge. It is doubtful if many serious philosophers embrace radical skepticism, but the arguments of moderate skeptics are often difficult to separate from a radical view. Critics of radical skepticism argue that the assertion that knowledge is not possible is itself a knowledge claim. The skeptical "agnostic" doesn't deny the existence of objective truth, but questions our ability to know about it. She or he may reject reason or experience as justification for knowing but usually not both. The less "dogmatic" skeptic seeks to show that there is no better reason for believing a proposition than denying it and advocates for continual searching to avoid error.

Relativism

The quest of those engaged in traditional and philosophical epistemology has been to develop and articulate a single, unified, neutral, and universal theory of knowledge. Such a theory would integrate all relevant perspectives and apply to all realities in all times and all places. Although the champions of certain theories of knowledge seem to make claims of neutrality, singularity, and universality, there are in fact multiple, competitive theories. Controversy over the validity and relevance of the various theories is a constant feature of life among those who develop and defend theories. Unlike skepticism, which questions the existence of *any* valid theory of knowledge, relativism is defined as the general conception that knowledge (and/or truth and justification) is relative to (contingent upon the nature and character of) time, place, culture, historical era, personal disposition, or some other conceptual framework. Relativism is seen as a challenge to the standard analysis of knowledge because it asserts that knowledge and, therefore, truth is relative.

We tend to think that relativism is a product of the modern age or, more precisely, the postmodern age. Relativism is linked with epistemic postmodernism in its criticism of absolutism in the quest for knowledge and truth. The fourth century BCE Greek philosopher, Protagoras, however, was a relativist through and through. Protagoras, who was more interested in thought than things, introduced the notion of subjectivity in philosophy.

"No absolute truth can be found," said Protagoras, "but only such truths as hold for given men under given conditions; contradictory assertions can be equally true for different persons or at different times. All truth, goodness, and beauty are relative and subjective; man is the measure of all things."[14] Protagoras further said, "Relativism takes two main forms, subjective and cultural. The subjectivist says that nothing is justified (simply and naturally): things are only justified for me. The cultural relativist is less individualistic; he thinks that beliefs are justified for particular cultures. Cultural relativism sometimes leads to the embrace of a 'standpoint epistemology,' according to which ethnic, class, gender, or other 'cultural' differences are associated with distinct 'ways of knowing.'"

Beyond relativism as a thesis about justification, relativism pertains to conceptions of truth, asserting that " something" is only true for me or within the context of some culture. "Relativists reject the idea of objective truth because they have grave doubts about the existence of neutral methods or criteria for establishing the truth."[15]

The Gettier Problem

In 1963, Edmund Gettier, arguing for a fourth criterion of knowledge, produced a number of counterexamples to the traditional account of knowledge in the paper, "Is Justified True Belief Knowledge?" in the journal *Analysis*. There are variations and embellishments to Gettier's counterexamples, but the following captures their essence. "Smith and Jones have applied for the same job. Smith is justified in believing that (a) Jones will get the job, and that (b) Jones has ten coins in his pocket. On the basis of (a) and (b), Smith infers, and thus is justified in believing (c) that the person who will get the job has ten coins in his pocket. As it turns out, Smith himself will get the job, and he also happens to have ten coins in his pocket. So, although Smith is *justified* in *believing* the *true* proposition (c), Smith does not *know* (c)."[16] What Gettier noted is that a well-justified belief can be as fortuitously true as the most blatant guess. Gettier's counterexamples are thus cases where one has justified true belief regarding a proposition, but lacks knowledge pertaining to that proposition. There have been numerous attempts to solve Gettier-like problems, but no consensus regarding a fourth condition to knowledge has emerged. Within the framework of the tripartite definition of knowledge, one strategy for dealing with Gettier problems is to supplement the justification condition, specifying a narrower kind of justification. Another strategy is to drop the justification requirement entirely.

Naturalized Epistemology

The term "naturalized epistemology" brings to mind the idea of Walden Pond and theories of knowledge produced by members of a community who had given up academia for living and working in the forests and mountains. Or, the term could elicit the thought of becoming a citizen of a community of knowledge theorists into which one is not born. The actual meaning is less obvious, but possibly more interesting. The term refers to a set of theories about knowledge based on continuity with natural science, especially with cognitive psychology, neurophysiology, artificial intelligence, linguistics, evolutionary biology, and the social sciences of sociology, social psychology, and anthropology. According to Phyllis Rooney in *Putting Naturalized Epistemology to Work,* there is an assumption that scientific knowledge is the paradigm example of knowledge. "This is partly—and I think not unreasonably—based on the view that scientific knowledge is more systematic, regulated, and documented, and thus it more readily lends itself to naturalistic scientific study.... Yet, the privileging of scientific knowledge also regularly presumes that scientific knowledge is like knowledge generally, only better; in fact, the best we have, and thus it merits the status of paradigmatic knowledge."[17]

Rene Descartes, correctly or not, has been called the Father of Modern Philosophy because he placed questions about knowledge as primary and central to philosophy. It was what he called First Philosophy. On the Cartesian or classical view, an epistemological theory must be developed independently of and prior to any scientific theorizing; proper scientific theorizing could only occur after such a theory was developed and deployed.[18] Proponents of a "naturalistic" conception of knowledge pay respect to W. V. O. Quine as the contemporary source of their inspiration as a consequence of his influential paper *Epistemology Naturalized.*[19] Quine challenged Cartesian or classical theorizing about knowledge based on his view that sensory stimulation was the only basis for knowing and that the natural sciences were the only valid route to acceptable belief and knowledge.

It would be misleading to say that the standard analysis of knowledge is essentially Cartesian, but challenges to the standard analysis and classical or Cartesian epistemology seem to fall into the same basket. This linking is valid only to the extent that an extreme form of naturalized epistemology is advanced. Under such an extreme view, traditional views of epistemology would be abandoned and the entire enterprise of theorizing about knowledge turned over to the natural sciences. A moderate view of naturalized epistemology finds a degree of comfort and compatibility with traditional conceptions, especially those related to the idea that epistemology is normative or related to some principle of right action. "Just as it is the business of normative ethics to delineate the conditions under which acts and decisions are justified from the moral point of view, so it is the business of epistemology to identify and analyze the conditions under which beliefs, and perhaps other propositional attitudes, are justified from the epistemological point of view. Epistemology is a normative discipline as much as, in the same sense as, normative ethics."[20] For example, Goldman's conception of "reliabilism" as a theory of knowledge takes a naturalistic turn in its orientation to psychological processes associated with justification of belief.[21] However, the ability of certain cognitive processes to reliably produce justified belief is as fully oriented to "rightness" and, therefore, as fully normative as any traditional approach to justification based on evidence, or the presence of a set of known facts that provide grounds for inferring further facts.

The challenges to the standard analysis and to conventional perspectives concerning knowledge in general stimulate thought and inquiry, and contribute to our own perspectives regarding knowledge, and to the conclusions reached in this book. These perspectives include the ideas that knowledge is not absolute and that it varies in character by the reality about which we hope to know. As previously stated, our interest in knowledge is practical and centers on questions of how knowledge can be produced and become available and useful in practice. To the extent, therefore, that challenges to the enterprise of seeking to know represent attempts to "throw the baby out with the bath water," we take issue with them. Regarding skepticism, David Hume, a renowned skeptic himself, argued that action in the form of the occupations of common life is the great defeater of the excessive principles of skepticism. Further, while skeptical principles may flourish in the academy, when they leave the "shade" of the academy and are put in opposition to the presence of real objects and the principles of our nature, they "vanish like smoke" and leave the avowed skeptic in the same condition as the rest of us.[22] As challengers to the standard conception of knowledge, both skepticism and relativism are self-defeating in that the defense of either requires that they be given up. A radical skeptical argument calls everything into question including itself, thereby eliminating it as a positive alternative; an extreme relativist argument has no objective defense because it denies all notions of objective reality. Critics of naturalized epistemology assert that without a normative dimension such approaches to knowing are empty. Critics also assert that naturalized and traditional epistemologies are like apples and oranges, with different objects and investigating different relations. Gettier-style examples seem to suggest the need for a fourth condition for knowledge beyond belief, truth, and justification, but no consensus on a fourth condition exists.

The challenging, postmodern and quasi-naturalist views of the well-known American academic Richard Rorty regarding knowledge are both constructive and destructive. We agree with his arguments against Cartesian mind/body dualism and against the notion that there could be such a thing as "foundations of knowledge" (all knowledge—in every field, past, present, and future) or a "theory of representation" (all representation, in familiar vocabularies and those not yet dreamed of). In his book *Philosophy and the Mirror of Nature*, however, Rorty aims to undermine all theorizing about the process of knowing and the "reader's confidence in knowledge as something about which there ought to be a theory and which has foundations."[23] Rorty equates those who seek to understand how knowledge develops with politicians who seek to govern as "cultural overseers" and places them both in a context of culture, which tends to disable or dampen any assumed authority to oversee.

Peter Munz, in his stinging critique of Rorty's book, asserts that he (Rorty) "calls the philosophers who claim to know something about knowledge and who are therefore critical of those cultures in which knowledge is mishandled or perverted ' cultural overseers.' The question whether, under certain circumstances, some cultures need reform is never asked by Rorty. He takes it for granted that none of them ever do.... There is indeed something to be known about knowledge, just as there is something to be known about equality and wealth. There are many different opinions held by different people, and all people interested in knowledge or in politics must pay attention to these opinions and weigh them and evaluate them. Then there are some people who do not engage much in politics or in science themselves, but who prefer to specialize in the questions of what we can know or how we can promote or, for that matter, prevent social justice. Whether we call these specialists philosophers and politicians or not does not really matter. The only thing that matters is the acceptance of the fact that there is something to be known about all these things; that it is better to know something about them than not to know anything about them."[24]

For our purposes, at the level of the practical, it is clear that there are realities about which we can know and our knowing about them has meaning in our lives as individuals and members of groups and organizations. Our knowing about the attributes of these realities rather than having beliefs about them represents a movement out of the darkness and an opportunity to align our organizations and ourselves more closely with reality. Reality itself is the subject matter of the next chapter.

REFERENCES

1. Williams, Michael. 2001. *Problems of Knowledge: A Critical Introduction to Epistemology*. Oxford: Oxford University Press.
2. Moser, Paul K. 1992. Tripartite Definition of Knowledge. In *A Companion to Epistemology*, ed. Jonathan Dancy, Ernest Sosa, 509. Oxford: Blackwell Publishers.
3. Chisholm, Roderick. 1996. *Theory of Knowledge*. 2nd ed. Englewood Cliffs, NJ: Prentice Hall Foundations of Philosophy Series.
4. Ayer, A.J. 1956. The Right to be Sure. In *The Problem of Knowledge*, 25–44. London: Penguin Books Ltd.
5. Dretske, Fred. 1988. *Explaining Behavior: Reasons in a World of Causes*. Boston: The MIT Press.
6. Hume, David. 1952. *An Enquiry Concerning Human Understanding*. Ed. L.A. Selby-Bigge. Oxford: Oxford University Press.
7. Williamson, Timothy. 2000. *Knowledge and Its Limits*. Oxford: Oxford University Press.
8. Searle, John R. 1995. *The Construction of Social Reality*. New York: The Free Press.
9. Kant, Immanuel. 1963. *The Critique of Pure Reason,* Trans. Norman Kemp Smith. London: Macmillan and Co Ltd.
10. BonJour, Laurence. 1985. The Elements of Coherentism. In *Structure of Empirical Knowledge*, 87–110. Cambridge: Harvard University Press.
11. James, William. 1975. *Pragmatism*. Cambridge: Harvard University Press.
12. Kim, Jaegwon.1988. What is Naturalized Epistemology? In Philosophical Perspectives, 2, *Epistemology*, ed. James E. Tomberlin, 381–405. Atascadero, CA: Ridgeview Publishing Co.
13. Tanesini, Alessandra. 1998. The Practices of Justification. In *Epistemology: The Big Questions,* ed. Linda Martin Alcoff, 152–164. Oxford: Blackwell Publishers Ltd.
14. Durant, Will. 1939. *The Life of Greece*. New York: MJF Books.
15. Williams, Michael. 2001. *Problems of Knowledge: A Critical Introduction to Epistemology*. Oxford: Oxford University Press.
16. Moser, Paul K. 1992. Gettier Problem. In *A Companion to Epistemology*, ed. Jonathan Dancy, Ernest Sosa, pp. 157–159. Oxford: Blackwell Publishers, Ltd.

17. Rooney, Phyllis. 1998. Putting Naturalized Epistemology to Work. In *Epistemology: The Big Questions,* ed. Linda Martin Alcoff, pp. 285–305. Oxford: Blackwell Publishers Ltd.

18. Kornblith, Hilary. 1992. Naturalized Epistemology. In *A Companion to Epistemology,* ed. Jonathan Dancy, Ernest Sosa, 297–300. Oxford: Blackwell Publishers, Ltd.

19. Quine, W. V. O. 1969. Epistemology Naturalized. In *Ontological Relativity and Other Essays,* pp. 69–90. New York: Columbia University Press.

20. Kim, Jaegwon, 1988. What is Naturalized Epistemology? In Philosophical Perspectives, *Vol. 2, Epistemology,* ed. James E. Tomberlin, 381–405. Atascadero, CA: Ridgeview Publishing Company.

21. Goldman, Alvin I. 1986. *Epistemology and Cognition.* Cambridge: Harvard University Press.

22. Hume, David, 1952. *An Enquiry Concerning Human Understanding.* Ed. L.A. Selby-Bigge. Oxford: Oxford University Press.

23. Rorty, Richard. 1979. *Philosophy and the Mirror of Nature.* Princeton: Princeton University Press.

24. Munz, Peter. 1987. Philosophy and the Mirror of Rorty. In *Evolutionary Epistemology, Rationality, and the Sociology of Knowledge,* ed. G. Radnitzky, W.W. Bartley, III, 345–398. Chicago: Open Court.

3

Reality and Knowing

ANTICIPATORY SUMMARY

Thinking about knowledge leads inevitably to the question: Knowledge about what? When we seek to know, we seek to know about some demonstrable or objective set of facts, some *real* circumstance where *real* means that which is actual and true. Chapter 3 aims to address the "knowledge about what" question, expressed as the nature of relevant reality and to lay the groundwork for integrating the following assertions:

- The identification and treatment of the multiple realities of organizational life have practical implications.
- Specific approaches to knowing are relevant to specific realities.
- Knowledge is not absolute and the quality of knowing varies according to the nature of the reality in question.

Multiple Realities

For the sake of simplicity and clarity, the traits and related implications of diverse and varied aspects of reality are referred to as multiple realities. Learning and the growth of knowledge occur within the context of relevant yet variable reality. In addition to exploring the realities of everyday life, mathematical reality and the objective and subjective dimensions of reality, a classification of realities bearing specifically on organizational life, is defined and explored. The line of direction embodied in this definition is the distinction between natural or physical reality and reality constructed by human beings. The key points are that multiple realties have a bearing on life in organizations and how these realities are conceived and how knowledge about them is sought have practical consequences for organizations and individuals.

Knowledge Implications

How we conceive the character of reality determines how we understand knowing in general and how we seek to know in particular. The argument is made that while knowledge is never absolute, relevant and actionable knowledge is achievable given that we speak in terms of 1) the reality about which we hope to know, 2) degrees of belief, 3) the quality of justification, and 4) the probability of truth.

REALITY AND KNOWING

We say that Helen was "in touch" with reality to suggest that Helen *knew* about some objective set of facts and this knowledge informed the actions she took. We say that an illusion or Howard's false conception of reality was responsible for the failure of his actions to produce desired results. The term "facts on the ground" has come to refer to the practical and operative reality about which one must know in order to make good decisions and take effective action. "Living in a dream" is taken to mean living and working within a distorted and fallacious understanding of *real* circumstances where *real* means that which is authentic and true, not artificial, not fraudulent, and not illusory. Reality sometimes refers to practical or everyday concerns as when we say Jane left academia for life in the *real* world, suggesting that life among scholars and theorists is not real. Reality is often taken to mean that which is subjectively real to a person or a group. We say, the event "shattered his world," "we live in different worlds," "for them, the spirits were as real as the rocks and trees." Sometimes we wonder, "What planet is he from?" thereby suggesting that his reality is vastly different from our own.

Thinking about knowledge leads inevitably to the question: Knowledge about what? When we seek to know, we seek to know about some reality. The character of reality has long been a subject of interest for ordinary people as well as for philosophers, natural scientists, social scientists, and theologians as well as for sages and gurus of any number of common and bizarre orientations. In *The Social Construction of Reality*, Berger and

Luckman define *reality* as "a quality appertaining to phenomena that we recognize as having a being independent of our own volition (we cannot wish them away) and *knowledge* as the certainty that phenomena are real and that they possess specific characteristics. ... It is in this (admittedly simplistic) sense that the terms have relevance both to the man in the street and to the philosopher."[1] For Kant, "Reality is that which corresponds to a sensation in general; it is that, therefore, the concept of which, in itself, points to being (in time)—the real is that which accords with the material conditions of experience."[2]

Metaphysics is the division of philosophy concerned with the fundamental nature of reality and being; ontology is the branch of metaphysics that seeks to describe the categories and relationships of reality. Ontology seeks to answer such questions as: What is existence? What features are the essential attributes and characteristics of a specific object? What constitutes the identity of an object or circumstance? Regarding the nature of reality, the longest running dispute in philosophy pertains to whether only individual entities such as specific chairs, trees, stars, molecules, circumstances, and events are real or whether general attributes or characteristics of such entities such as red, tall, bright, good, just, and useful are real as well. General characteristics are referred to as "universals" and specific characteristics associated with individual items or occurrences are "particulars"; the conflict is framed as the "universals versus particulars dispute." Although it seems counterintuitive given that the term *realist* is usually associated with those who are practical and oriented to concrete facts, adherents of the independent existence of universals are described as realists. In this context, following Plato who postulated the independent existence of "forms" as universals, the specific use of the term *realist* connotes belief in the external reality of these abstract conceptions of general characteristics. Adherents of the *particularist* school are defined as nominalists or conceptualists. There are various expressions of realism and nominalism and the dispute continues to this day. A full treatment of this dispute is beyond the scope of this book. The essential nature of the dispute, however, is relevant for the perspectives developed in this chapter.

The term ontology has been borrowed from philosophy by computer science, particularly by artificial intelligence. The indefinite article "an" is used in artificial intelligence to denote "an ontology" (one among possibly several) that denotes an explicit specification of concepts, a reality in other words, within which queries and assertions may be exchanged. We will adapt the license taken by artificial intelligence to develop "an ontology" in this chapter, one (among possibly several) that relates to the multiple realities of life in organizations. Our aim in this chapter is to address and begin to integrate the set of foundational arguments from Chapter 1, summarized as follows.

- There are multiple realities that have a bearing on life in organizations.
- The identification and treatment of these realities have practical implications for organizations.
- Specific approaches to knowing (epistemic styles/approaches) are relevant to specific realities. In other words, optimal ways of knowing are reality-specific.
- Based on various factors, individuals tend to see all realities as uniform in character and seek to apply favored and narrow approaches to knowing about any reality.
- Knowledge is not absolute and the quality of knowing varies by the reality in question. In spite of this assertion, actionable knowledge about any reality is achievable.

MULTIPLE REALITIES

In a practical and functional sense, what do we mean by reality? What can we know about reality? Although the meaning of reality is often taken to refer to the totality of real things and events, when we think about these questions, we come to realize that we live in a world of multiple realities. We could frame our reflections in this chapter as pertaining to multiple *aspects* of a singular and overarching reality rather than to multiple realities. However, given that our intent is to bring attention to bear on the *diverse natures* and *related implications* of the diverse and varied aspects of reality, we will refer to *multiple realities* for the sake of simplicity and semantical clarity. Berger and Luckman speak of our guarded ability to relate to multiple realities. "My consciousness is capable of moving through different spheres of reality. Put differently, I am conscious of the world as consisting of multiple realities. As I move from one reality to another, I experience the transition as a kind of shock. This shock is to be understood as caused by the shift in attentiveness that the transition entails."[3] The boundaries of the realities we will explore in this chapter are not always clearly marked. In other words, while we will assume a degree of operative uniqueness in the natures of these realities, the constitution, quality, and character of them may not be mutually exclusive in all respects.

The Realities of Everyday Life

The reality that most readily comes to mind is the reality of everyday life or the set of common sense realities we encounter day in and day out. We know a great deal about these realities as we go about the routine of our lives. We know about our status and circumstances in life in relation to others and about our limits and possibilities. We know how to use telephones and computers. We know how to drive a car and how to get to work and back home again. We know how to relate to our boss, our spouse, the traffic police, our doctor, our accountant. Knowledge about the realities of everyday life is embodied in what Berger and Luckman define as the "social stock of knowledge." The validity of the knowledge about these realities is taken for granted, as long as the knowledge produces satisfactory outcomes. Although we don't usually deconstruct what we think we know about the everyday world, there are natural or physical dimensions to this reality, pertaining, for example to the physics of driving a car. There are dimensions of reality pertaining to money and success and other material yet non-natural constructs, for example, in how we come to know about our social and economic situations in life. There are dimensions pertaining to culture and politics, in how we come to know about marriage and paying our taxes, and to ethics and morality pertaining to how we treat the planet and our fellow human beings.

Conceptions of everyday reality and knowledge about various specific realities are transmitted from generation to generation and pragmatism is the driving force in the creation and preservation of such knowledge. That which produces useful and beneficial results is the standard for knowledge about everyday life. We learn how to operate an automobile to get us from one place to another safely and dependably. We know how to use our computers to access the Internet and read our email. We know how to relate to our family members to give rise to peace and stability in our homes and to relate to traffic police to avoid being arrested and taken to jail. But knowing about the reality of everyday life leaves the totality of the world obscure. In other words, what we know about the realities we encounter in the normal course of our daily activities appears as a "zone of lucidity behind which there is a background of darkness."[4] We can understand the operational reality of cars and trucks and know how to use them to get from here to there without understanding the realities of internal combustion. We can understand the reality of how our behavior affects the behavior of others and know how to elicit the behavior we want without comprehending the reality of the needs, motivations, emotions, and perceptions of others.

The darkness that defines the fullness of reality, that surrounds and frames everyday reality, must be penetrated if we wish to know more than what it takes to get through the day. If we hope to move out of the life situation into which we are born, we need to know more than how to survive in that static environment; we need to know about the realities of alternative ways of living and success. In order to challenge something that works to produce something that works better, we may need to know about the realities of mechanics or physics or software or chemistry or biology. We may need to know something about the operating reality of our car to keep it running reliably. If we hope to have a richer and more satisfying relationship with another person, we may need to comprehend the subjective reality of that person. In order to understand the meaning and relevance of an ethical position, we may need to know about the roots and underpinnings of dogmatic morality and its consequences.

An Ontology for Organizational Life

Writing in his book the *Problems of Knowledge*, Michael Williams asserts, "One of the founding distinctions of Western philosophy is that between what the Greeks called *physis*, nature and *nomos*, custom or convention." This distinction refers to conceptions of reality. One reality seems to exist "in virtue of facts that hold independently of human wish and will.... Stones fall to earth always and everywhere, whether we like it or not.... Such facts belong to nature." But there are other realities, for example, having to do with social conventions, values, and right conduct, and these realities seem to vary from time to time and place to place, reflecting the customs or traditions of particular groups of people. Williams argues, in what will be obvious to many, that customs and conventions, as human creations, do not belong to nature.[5]

That reality is partitioned into two domains, the first physical or natural and the second constructed by human beings, is widely accepted in philosophy and science. To the extent that ordinary people in everyday life contemplate the character of reality, this segmentation will be self-evident and acknowledged by many of them. There is controversy, however, among specialists as well as ordinary people concerning where the *natural* ends and the *constructed* begins and to what extent both realities share characteristics. Also, in the course of daily living, individuals with limited exposure to cultures and societies different from their own and those strongly influenced by dogma from whatever source tend to see independent, even natural reality in what others see as a reality created and maintained by human society. Among the readings connected with work on this book, we have seen that some philosophers and social scientists with an orientation to realism in the extreme see the independent and natural existence of universals. Concepts such as ethical, beautiful, just, and fair, which are universals to realists, are seen by others as constructed by society within a context of time and place.

Acknowledging the independent existence of natural or physical reality, social or constructed reality has been reduced to a finer set of categories for purposes of clarity and utility. For example, Morgan and Smircich in their paper, *The Case for Qualitative Research,* developed a typology in their Table 1 defining the range of potential conceptions of social reality that could be held by certain individuals at certain times.[6] The table in Figure 3.1 below adapts the portion of their typology that further categorizes such core ontological assumptions or, in other words, *how* constructed or social reality may be conceived.

"Reality as a concrete structure," on the right of the table, is a conception of social reality closely aligned with how physical or natural reality is generally conceived. The social world is seen as hard, concrete, and independent of human perception. It is also seen as mechanistic and a "closed system." Moving to the left in the table, "Reality as a concrete process" is a category that continues to see the independent existence of the social world, but one that evolves through a relatively fixed or concrete *process* in the manner of an open system. "Reality as a contextual field of information" refers to a conception of social reality in constant and parallel evolution with the surrounding context or environment. "Reality as a realm of symbolic discourse" is the next position along the continuum

Reality as a projection of human imagination	Reality as a social construction	Reality as a realm of symbolic discourse	Reality as a contextual field of information	Reality as a concrete process	Reality as a concrete structure

FIGURE 3.1
Conceptions of social reality.

and focuses on the roles that language, symbols, and myths play in shaping and sustaining social reality. "Reality as a social construction" is a conception of social reality "created afresh in each encounter of everyday life as individuals impose themselves on their world to establish a realm of meaningful (and contingent) definition. "Reality as a projection of human imagination" is an extreme position that sees no reality outside oneself: "one's mind is one's world."

The categories described above overlap and seem to put too fine a point on some aspects of difference. The Figure 3.1 illustrates, however, that a wide range of conceptions of social reality exist. More importantly, what and how we can know about social reality varies with how reality is conceived. This variety has the potential to render agreement about the nature of relevant reality, the relevant and appropriate approach or approaches to knowing about the reality in question, and alignment around effective action unlikely or at least highly problematic.

Based on our work in organizations and consistent with our aim to provide an analysis with practical implications, we will propose an ontology that categorizes the common sense and relevant realities of organizational life. The starting point is the distinction that exists between natural and constructed reality. For us, the terms social and constructed reality are interchangeable and social reality is generally set against reality of a natural or physical type. The key points are that multiple realties have a bearing on life in organizations and how these realities are conceived and how knowledge about them is sought have practical consequences for organizations and individuals. From our perspective, it makes no practical sense to treat physical reality as anything other than independent and external to the perceptions of human beings and to treat nonphysical reality as constructed by humans, varying in degree by separation from independent existence. These realities are summarized in Figure 3.2.

Physical or Natural Reality

The universe of observable or at least measurable things and phenomena and the states of such things and phenomena belong to natural or physical reality. Examples include tables, apples, molecules, events, mountains, people, machines, the health of a person, the shape of a table or molecule, the ripeness of an apple, the setting and objective consequences of an event. The existence and character of that which is natural is revealed or directly inferred from information obtained in sensory experience. In our

Natural Reality	Constructed Reality		
Physical or Natural Reality	*Material Reality* (Internal and External)	*Non-Material Reality* (Internal and External)	*Conceptual Reality* (Internal and External)
Existence and states of *Physical or Natural* Objects and Phenomena	Money Performance Potentials Limits	Culture Functional/Political Structures Purpose Definitions e.g., Success/Failure	Ethics/Morality (Relevance, Application) Character of *the Whole* (Emergence, Gestalt)

FIGURE 3.2
Multiple realities of organizational life.

science-based intellectual tradition, natural or physical reality refers to that which can be determined empirically by observing, measuring, and recording phenomena which can be characterized as biological, physical, gravitational, electromagnetic, chemical, or quantum. While this definition of natural or physical reality would seem to be straightforward and uncontroversial, different cultures and groups have different assumptions about what constitutes external physical reality. For example, within some cultures, spirits, phantoms, or demons are conceived as real in a way that would challenge the sensibilities of members of our culture. Perhaps such examples properly refer to ambiguity about the boundaries of natural reality. Edgar Schein refers to experiences with the Indian shaman Don Juan and in the controversies that surround research on extrasensory perception. "At its core, physical reality is obvious; at its boundaries it becomes very much a matter of cultural consensus, raising the issue of social (or constructed) reality."[7]

Constructed Reality

It is clearly different to speak about the reality of an object in front of me with physical dimensions than to speak about the reality of law or potential or culture or an ethical position. There is no suggestion that constructed reality is not real in the sense of having existence and consequences. Constructed reality, however, differs from natural reality in terms of genesis and constitution and in its actual, if not perceived, existence as *independent* from human conception and society. Paradoxically, man is capable of producing a reality that he then experiences as something other than a human product. "It is important to emphasize that the relationship between man (the producer) and the social world (his product) is and remains a dialectical one." That is, man (not, of course in isolation, but collectively) and his social world interact with each other in a manner defined as three dialectal moments. "Society is a human product. Society is an objective reality. Man is a social product."[8]

Our analysis of constructed reality subdivides it into three categories, differing in composition and character and in the implications associated with seeking to know about them. Each subdivision or category may reflect internal (to the organization) or external (to the organization's environment) reality. We define material reality as that which is temporal and tangible yet non-natural (*not* existing as physical phenomena independent of human agency). Nonmaterial reality refers to nonmaterial manifestations of human behavior such as culture and patterns of conduct. Conceptual reality pertains to transcendence and embodies such concepts as equality, justice, good, bad, right, and wrong. Conceptual and nonmaterial realities can overlap and interact with each other more readily than either of these with physical or material realities.

Material Reality

John Searle in the *Construction of Social Reality* draws a distinction between "institutional" facts and "brute" facts. "Institutional facts are so called because they require human institutions for their existence. In order that this piece of paper should be a five dollar bill, for example, there has to be the human institution of money." The facts that Mount Everest has snow and ice near the summit or that hydrogen atoms have one electron, are brute facts; they exist independent of human conception and require no human institutions for their creation.[9] Our conception of material reality is a reality defined by institutional facts. As independently real as the ideas of money and property seem to be, they only exist as institutional creations, produced and sustained by human beings.

Institutions produce institutional facts and institutions come into existence through habitualization. All human activity is subject to habitualization when actions are repeated frequently and beneficially in a readily discernable pattern. Habitualization and, therefore, institutionalization supports important functional expediencies. Choices are narrowed and help establish a background of stable, routine and habitualized activity, opening a foreground for innovation and creativity.[10] Whenever we engage in a commercial transaction of any sort, we are able to go straight to the substance and dimensions of the transaction rather than be forced to decide whether bushels of corn or ounces of gold or some other agreed upon medium of exchange will be used for payment. The human and social context of the transaction, however, is meaningful. There are more than 150 forms of currency, from the Afghani to the Yuan, in use on our planet today.

Notions of tangible and other property and the rights, obligations, bases and terms of property ownership have evolved over hundreds of years. We know what property means in the twenty-first century but that meaning is vastly different from conceptions of property in fourteenth century feudal Europe. Local, regional, and national boundaries are conventions; they are essentially points on the compass institutionalized through the acts of other institutions working on behalf of collections of human beings. What we are able to do and what we are constrained from doing are proscribed by institutions of one type or other. We are able to work and own property, but we are not able to declare ourselves an independent state to avoid paying taxes. As massive and objectively real as the institutional world may appear to the individual, it is important to know that this reality is a humanly produced, constructed objectivity. It is also a fascinating and puzzling aspect of the human condition that virtually all the things we argue about and go to war over, for example, money, property, systems of belief, and boundaries, are our own inventions and have no existence other than the existence we give them.

Nonmaterial Reality

It is difficult if not impossible to count or locate the coordinates or measure the dimensions of non-material reality. That the various forms of nonmaterial reality exist, however, is rarely doubted. Culture is a form of nonmaterial reality that exerts enormous influence on behavior in general and on organizational behavior in particular. Culture exists on two planes or in two dimensions: 1) behavior and 2) the beliefs and assumptions that set behavior in motion.[11] We have observed the benefits of behavior patterns in organizations driven by knowledge, or true belief (beliefs and assumptions aligned with reality). We have also observed the unhappy consequences of behavior animated by illusion or beliefs which are out of phase with reality. The character, role, and dynamics of culture are vital to the themes of this book and will be fully explored in Chapter 9.

Although there are no meters or instruments to measure degrees of conflict or cooperation operating within a group of people, there can be little doubt that the relative dominance of one or the other of these states is observable and can be felt. Styles of verbal interaction, body language, and readable attitudes will lead us to conclude that a spirit of cooperation and collaboration animates the life of a specific group or, conversely, that a state of antagonism and struggle underpins its existence. Perhaps most significantly, the consequences of collective action will be influenced by whether conflict or cooperation frames the work of the group. Success and failure are states of being that may be defined in material terms. Wealth, in the case of individuals and the bottom line or the balance sheet in the case of organizations, are likely to be the most widely regarded indicators of success or failure. But nonmaterial reality may affect perceptions of success and failure as well. Organizations that develop and make use of limited resources in a sustainable manner, or comprehensively meet significant human need, or provide fair and living-wage employment while maintaining economic viability define success for some. The nonmaterial aspects of such conceptions of success are not easily quantifiable, but they have clearly observable consequences and are often embodied in organizational purpose. Other such existential forms of nonmaterial reality include the distribution of power and influence as reflected in the "politics" of an organization, the state of adaptation to external circumstances, states of relative satisfaction or dissatisfaction, or states of relative optimism or pessimism.

Conceptual Reality

The final category in our ontology or classification of realities for organizations is conceptual reality. While the separation of *conceptual* from *nonmaterial* reality may appear arbitrary and without substance, and although these realities may overlap, we will argue in this and in Chapter 4 that there are valid, operative reasons for the separation. Conceptual reality pertains to transcendence or the character of lying beyond ordinary (or even possible) experience. Under various headings, conceptual reality embodies such ideas as fairness, equality, beauty, justice, and excellence. The concept of ethical behavior incorporates notions of what is good and right, implying that effectual definitions of good, bad, right, and wrong exist. Ethics and morality are linked and tend to be sanctioned by individual or collective conscience or a divine or metaphysical source. Virtue, in its classical beginnings, pertained to strength and courage, but now tends to be understood as ethical or moral excellence. Ideals pertain to standards of perfection, beauty, or excellence and may only exist as a mental image or in human imagination.

We argue that an attribute of a certain kind of reality is that its character is not discernable by the sum of its parts. This reality, sometimes called a gestalt, possesses the quality of emergence, a quality which arises unexpectedly with the appearance of new characteristics at more complex levels and which cannot be fully predicted by an analysis of lower levels. "Some groups of things, particularly structured groups such as structures of cells as organs and structures of organs as organisms, clearly do have emergent properties—a person's capacity to think is not the aggregate of the thinking capacity of each of his cells, nor indeed is his capacity to run. It is looking to this kind of analogue for the relation between men and their groups that has been one historically potent source for the idea that societies as human collectives have emergent properties."[12] Emergence may be a beneficial or constraining force. The playing of Brahms's Fourth Symphony by the Berlin Philharmonic results in an experience that cannot be explained by the notes on the page, the playing of the individual instruments, and the tempo set by the conductor. On the other hand, "when the parochial and self-protective aspects of human nature become rooted and reinforced in the behavior of a group, the downside of emergence appears.... A kind of perverse gestalt is created where the whole of the set of defenses and hardened attributions among the individuals assumes an anti-learning and defensive character exceeding the sum of the traits of the individuals in the group."[13]

We have argued that *conceptual* reality is distinct from what we have called *nonmaterial* reality even though both belong to the larger category of constructed or social reality and both do not possess the attributes of what we have called *material* reality, which also belongs to the category of constructed reality. If nonmaterial and conceptual realities are different, we must understand how they differ in order to more fully comprehend the character of each. First, nonmaterial reality refers to observable and identifiable states of being or to context, as in conflict and cooperation or culture. Conceptual reality is not so readily observable and not so easily identifiable as representing states of being or operating contexts. The meaning of conceptual reality is subject to shades of emotion and nuance providing a filter on direct and unambiguous observation. Second, while manifestations of non-material reality are usually definable in terms of the characteristics of constituent concepts or entities, the same does not generally hold for representations of conceptual reality. The idea of emergence, for example, precludes reductionism or constituent analysis as a way to fully understand an emergent reality. Finally, and most importantly, the meanings of the manifestations of nonmaterial reality are generally not controversial and tend to be accepted by most individuals. On the other hand, the interpretation of instances of conceptual reality tends to be controversial with the potential for significant disagreement regarding meaning and implication. While the nature or character of the various realities bearing on organizational life is the subject matter of this chapter, approaches to knowing about these realities will be addressed in Chapter 4, Epistemology: Theory of Knowledge.

Mathematical Reality

We have described a set of realities pertaining to organizational life partitioned into the two larger categories of physical or natural and constructed or social. Is there a reality that is neither *natural* in the sense of existing independently and determinable empirically through experience or *constructed* in the sense of lacking the attribute of existence independent of human thought? The answer depends on whether we hold that there is an independent reality about which we can know without sensual experience through reason alone. For rationalists since Descartes, mathematics has represented a model of privileged reality knowable *a priori*. *A priori* refers to knowledge independent of all experience. Kant articulated a table of *a priori* concepts of understanding or categories encompassing mathematical and dynamical concepts. Dynamical concepts include cause and effect, existence and non-existence, possibility and impossibility.[14] The mathematical concepts of unity, plurality, totality, negation, etc., "give us a shining example of how far, independently of experience, we can progress in *a priori* knowledge.... It does, indeed, occupy itself with objects and with knowledge, solely in so far as they allow of being exhibited in intuition. Mathematical propositions, strictly so called, are always judgments *a priori*, not empirical, because they carry with them *necessity*, which cannot be derived from experience." That which is *necessary*, in contrast to contingent, holds in *all* possible worlds. The truths of pure mathematics have been almost universally supported as *necessary* in character. No other result than two as the sum of one and one is possible.[15] The Kantian view of mathematics and the potential for *a priori* knowledge in any context may be controversial. Whether or not we ascribe to the Kantian view, mathematics is how we deal with mathematical reality and this is not controversial.

Objective and Subjective Realities

The term *objective* in this context refers to that which exists apart from human consciousness and sensibility and at least appears to have an independent existence. The term *subjective* refers to the perceptions, ways of thinking, attitudes, emotions, motivations, and beliefs of individuals. Bearing on our ontology as developed earlier in this chapter, objective and subjective realities operate like templates that overlay the common sense and relevant realities in Figure 3.2 and shape perception and constitution of these realities. In other words, both natural and constructed realities have objective and subjective dimensions. That this would be true for constructed or social reality is not surprising; that it would also be true for natural reality, which we assume to exist objectively and independent of human perception and thought, is not immediately obvious.

"Objective" and "subjective" are different views of the same reality; they are two sides of the same coin. We will argue that to treat any reality as either exclusively objective or subjective is reductionism and will obscure the meaning of the whole. We defined reductionism in social science and for our purposes in our book *Beyond Reductionism: Gateways for Learning and Change*, as a process that reduces complex data and events to simple, even overly simple terms. It means reducing how we think about the whole to the components of the whole and the analysis of systems to their constituents. The biologist Stephen Rothman states that reductionism, "means that everything about the larger object can be attributed to its parts.... It argues that the whole has no properties beyond those of its component parts. Taken to this extreme, it maintains that the fact that we cannot describe humans, no less human society, in terms of their constituent atoms is simply a technical difficulty. There is nothing fundamental that stands in our way. However inconceivable this may seem, if we could specify the atoms completely, such a description would be provided."[16]

The most acutely felt aspect of reductionism in organizations pertains to how that which is perceived as objective is sharply demarcated from that which is seen as subjective. "Organizations exist for objective reasons and objective reality frames their existence. However, organizations are collections of human beings who have needs, imaginations, biases, idiosyncrasies, and egos. Organizations, therefore, embrace a reality that is both objective and subjective."[17]

Constructed reality, as a human product, has an obvious subjective dimension. As asserted earlier, however, it is paradoxical that humans are capable of *producing* a reality that is then *experienced* as objective, as something other than a human product. Institutionalization has been described as a powerful force in the process of turning a human creation into a reality with objective dimensions. Legitimation is the handmaiden of institutionalization in the process of turning social reality into objective reality. Legitimation is the process of explaining and justifying the institutional order by ascribing validity to its meaning.[18] Institutionalization and legitimation are clearly at work in material reality (e.g., pertaining to money and property), in nonmaterial reality (e.g., as in culture and purpose) and in conceptual reality (e.g., concerning ethics and virtue). Constructed reality as subjective reality has two strong features. The first is that humans, interacting with each other and reciprocally with evolving institutions, create constructed or social reality. The second is that when constructed reality is internalized by people, that which had become objective through institutionalization now becomes subjective, giving it enormous influence and power to endure and influence. It is worth revisiting the three dialectical moments in the interaction of humans and the social world previously described: society is a human product (externalization); society is an objective reality (objectification through institutionalization and legitimation); humans are shaped by society (internalization). It is useful to consider these dialectical moments and how we think about and make sense of the ideas of money, property, success and failure, and virtue.

We have described natural reality, using the term physical reality interchangeably, as that which can be determined empirically by observing, measuring, and recording biological, physical, gravitational, electromagnetic, chemical, or quantum phenomena. Natural reality is that which can be revealed or inferred from sensory experience. That natural reality is objective and exists independently of human perception and thought is not controversial, at least within the practical context of life in organizations. In other words, human perception and cognition have no influence whatsoever on the existence and character of natural or physical objects and circumstances. Given these assertions, where does subjectivity impact the objective reality of nature? We do not argue that human subjectivity alters the character of physical reality, but rather that human subjectivity shapes the character of individual and social apprehension of physical reality.

In science, which most of us take to be the exemplar of human institutions in terms of the objective comprehension of natural reality, Thomas Kuhn has opened a window on the role of subjectivity in the apprehension of physical reality. Kuhn's landmark study in the philosophy of science, *The Structure of Scientific Revolutions*, introduced the term paradigm to define the context of "normal science" within which pre-revolutionary science is done. The institution of science at any time within any discipline is framed by the relevant paradigm and, consistent with how institutions exert their influence, the paradigm becomes internalized and, therefore, subjective to members of the community. Kuhn painted a portrait of science as a series of such paradigms (held by different groups of scientists), supported by evidence and reason—often by substantial evidence and for good reason—but also in varying measure by biases, assumptions, suppositions, rationalizations, opinions, prejudices, fallacious reasoning, personal animosities, political considerations, and every other human trait imaginable. The paradigm represents a shared value judgment about nature and value judgments are rarely, if ever, the product of evidence and reason alone. In Kuhn's view, science was inescapably and unavoidably a social activity, as well as an analytic one.

The major shifts in our understanding, Kuhn argued, come about when the foundational tenets of a discipline are seriously challenged, when evidence is sought not to bolster a paradigm, but to dispute it. "Such an understanding comes about by sea change, by cataclysm, indeed by revolution, not by some smooth and reasoned process of gradualism."[19] Kuhn points to the revolutionary examples of Copernicus, Newton, Lavoisier, and Einstein, each of whom brought about the community's rejection of time-honored theories in favor of others incompatible with them.[20] The fact that the community initially rejected the new theories had nothing to do with the objective reality of these theories. Our everyday lives are less dramatic, but the subjective realities of our biases, worldviews, and patterns of socialization shape our comprehension of objective reality in ways that deny or corrupt its existence. Because we fail to understand an external threat due to our internalized images of how the world works, our lack of comprehension has no impact on the objective reality of the threat.

To the extent that subjective reality has been acknowledged, there has been a tendency in segments of organizational theory and the practice of management to separate objective and subjective realities. Perhaps at some level this flows from Descartes, who continues to be regarded by many as the father of modern philosophy, and his theory of dualism which argues that there are two fundamentally incompatible kinds of substance in the universe, mind and matter. If we aim for counter reductionism and an orientation to the whole of reality, however, we can look to Immanuel Kant, often regarded as the greatest modern philosopher, for his analysis and description of human subjectivity as fully a part of any reality we hope to comprehend. A cornerstone of our practice has been to seek to identify both the objective and subjective realities in any situation and to work to bring them into proper relation and reconciliation. We will describe such examples in Section II.

KNOWLEDGE IMPLICATIONS

How we conceive the character of reality plays a role in determining how we understand knowing in general and how we seek to know in particular. The coming together of conceptions of reality and ways of forming beliefs or seeking to know is explored in Chapter 5. Regardless of the reality about which we hope to know, an important implication of relevant knowledge pertains to its quality. Is knowledge absolute? Referring back to the standard definition of knowledge as *justified true belief,* are truth and justification binary values? Do we believe a proposition completely or not at all? While we can hope for a reality so compliant with our need for certainty, our knowledge of any reality is not absolute. Knowledge about nature or physical reality, which exists independently of human mediation, would seem to be absolute or very close to it. For most of us most of the time, our knowledge of the natural world appears to be unqualified and certain. We possess and manipulate certain physical objects or we don't; boiling water cooks eggs in 7 minutes; the desk top in front of me, as I see and touch it, is real. Yet, our knowledge of the physical world is based on our senses and our meaning-making apparatus. Insights from neuroscience, cognitive psychology, and philosophy point to the fallibility of our perceptive and cognitive mechanisms.

Knowledge of the natural world is most credibly and reliably made known to us through science. When we reflect upon what science teaches us about physical reality, however, it's important to remember that what we thought we knew about the natural world has changed over time. Consider how Einstein's and Heisenberg's understanding of nature differs from Newton's and how Newton's differs from Aristotle's. Our less than absolute and perfect knowledge is often good enough, however. We know that the ultimate physical reality concerning the natural world is not what drives most engineering practice. Engineering on a human scale is largely based on Newtonian physics. Yet we know that Newtonian physics is not a complete and fully accurate description of the natural world. Engineering is based on approximations of natural reality. It turns out that these approximations come close to objective truth, at least to the extent that we're able to build airplanes that fly, skyscrapers and bridges that withstand extremes of time and weather, chemicals that produce predictable reactions, and mechanical devices that perform functions reliably for decades.

The proposition that our knowledge about the natural world is fallible and less than absolute is controversial and will be disputed by some people based on theory and what looks like common sense. That knowledge about constructed reality is not absolute, however, is less likely to be contradicted. Although, especially regarding conceptual reality, there is a class of realism that sets forth the independent existence of "universals." Universals embody such concepts as good and bad, right and wrong, just and unjust. According to this view, conceptual reality is not constructed or socially contingent, but somehow given, as an aspect of the human condition, as an expression of some metaphysical reality, or as divinely revealed. We have argued, however, that constructed reality, including conceptual reality, is a human creation and has no existence independent of human perception and thought. As developed in this chapter, our conception of constructed reality encompasses categories or sub realities from material (property and money) to nonmaterial (culture and politics) to conceptual (ethics and morality). The character of constructed reality varies with time and place and it follows that what we know about such reality is by definition contingent, variable, and less than absolute. To contrast the problem of knowing about constructed reality in relation to knowing about natural or physical reality, Kant's perspective is admonitory. Kant is speaking specifically about the folly of seeking to know about social or constructed reality in the manner we would seek to know about natural reality. "For whereas, so far as nature is concerned, experience supplies the rules and is the source of truth—in respect of the moral laws it (experience) is, alas, the mother of illusion! Nothing is more reprehensible than to derive the laws prescribing what ought to be done from what *is* done, or to impose upon them the limits by which the latter is circumscribed."[21]

The degree of separation from the status of knowledge as certain and absolute intensifies as we move from the natural to the constructed realities identified in Figure 3.2, i.e., from natural to material to nonmaterial to conceptual. We argue that while knowledge is never absolute, relevant and actionable knowledge is achievable given that we speak in terms of 1) the reality about which we hope to know, 2) degrees of belief, 3) the quality of justification, and 4) the probability of truth. We have argued in this chapter, consistent with the foundational assertions summarized in Chapter 1, that there are multiple realities that affect and are affected by life in organizations. These realities pertain to natural or physical objects, to the human constructed yet material world of money, property, etc., to the constructed and nonmaterial world of culture, politics, etc., and to concepts such as ethics and virtue. To restate a central hypothesis, *the growth of knowledge is a function of the relevance and efficacy of the approach to knowing employed, subject to the nature of the reality about which we hope to know.* In support of this hypothesis, the following assertions, which set the stage for the next chapter, were made in Chapter 1. First, various theories of knowledge and approaches to knowing exist. All of these have something to say about belief, truth, and justification. These range from a complete reliance on experience to a complete reliance on reason and reflection. Second, no single theory and approach to knowing applies to all realities. For example, while theories based on realism may apply to the physical world but not to the nonmaterial or conceptual worlds; theories based on some form of idealism or constructivism may apply to the conceptual world, but not to the physical or material worlds.

REFERENCES

1. Berger, Peter L. and Thomas Luckman. 1967. *The Social Construction of Reality: A Treatise in the Sociology of Knowledge.* New York: Anchor Books, a Division of Random House.
2. Kant, Immanuel. 1963. *The Critique of Pure Reason*, Trans. Norman Kemp Smith. London: Macmillan and Co Ltd.
3. Berger, Peter L. and Thomas Luckman. 1967. *The Social Construction of Reality: A Treatise in the Sociology of Knowledge.* New York: Anchor Books, a Division of Random House.
4. Berger, Peter L. and Thomas Luckman. 1967. *The Social Construction of Reality: A Treatise in the Sociology of Knowledge.* New York: Anchor Books, a Division of Random House.

5. Williams, Michael. 2001. *Problems of Knowledge: A Critical Introduction to Epistemology.* New York: Oxford University Press.

6. Morgan, Gareth and Linda Smircich. 1980. The Case for Qualitative Research, *The Academy of Management Review* 5/4:491 - 500.

7. Schein, Edgar H. 1992. *Organizational Culture and Leadership*, Second Edition. San Francisco: Jossey-Bass Publishers.

8. Berger, Peter L. and Thomas Luckman. 1967. *The Social Construction of Reality: A Treatise in the Sociology of Knowledge.* New York: Anchor Books, a Division of Random House.

9. Searle, John R. 1995. *The Construction of Social Reality.* New York: The Free Press.

10. Berger, Peter L. and Thomas Luckman. 1967. *The Social Construction of Reality: A Treatise in the Sociology of Knowledge.* New York: Anchor Books, a Division of Random House.

11. Douglas, Neil and Terry Wykowski. 1999. *Beyond Reductionism: Gateways for Learning and Change.* Boca Raton: St. Lucie Press.

12. Harre, Rom. 1979. *Social Being: A Theory for Social Psychology.* Oxford: Basil Blackwell Publisher.

13. Douglas, Neil and Terry Wykowski. 1999. *Beyond Reductionism: Gateways for Learning and Change.* Boca Raton: St. Lucie Press.

14. Kant, Immanuel. 1963. *The Critique of Pure Reason*, Trans. Norman Kemp Smith. London: Macmillan and Co Ltd.

15. Kant, Immanuel. 1963. *The Critique of Pure Reason*, Trans. Norman Kemp Smith. London: Macmillan and Co Ltd.

16. Rothman, Stephen. 2002. *Lessons from the Living Cell: The Limits of Reductionism.* New York: McGraw-Hill.

17. Douglas, Neil and Terry Wykowski. 1999. *Beyond Reductionism: Gateways for Learning and Change.* Boca Raton: St. Lucie Press.

18. Berger, Peter L. and Thomas Luckman. 1967. *The Social Construction of Reality: A Treatise in the Sociology of Knowledge.* New York: Anchor Books, a Division of Random House.

19. Rothman, Stephen. 2002. *Lessons from the Living Cell: The Limits of Reductionism.* New York: McGraw-Hill.

20. Kuhn, Thomas S. 1962. *The Structure of Scientific Revolutions*, Second Edition. Chicago: The University of Chicago Press.

21. Kant, Immanuel. 1963. *The Critique of Pure Reason*, Trans. Norman Kemp Smith. London: Macmillan and Co Ltd.

4

Epistemology: Theory of Knowledge

ANTICIPATORY SUMMARY

Concerning any reality about which we hope to know, epistemology aims to answer the questions which inform and shape the central arguments and themes in this book. Epistemology is the branch of philosophy focused on the theory of knowledge. More precisely, epistemology is the study of the collection of theories pertaining to the character, scope, utility, and basis of knowledge.

While there may be controversy and disagreement among scholars about the ultimate aims and status of epistemology, from our perspective its purpose is nothing less than the improvement of knowledge and, therefore, the human condition. Beyond knowledge about everyday life and the subject matter that defines our roles and vocations in life, the human condition embodies a lack of knowledge about many of those things that most profoundly matter to us. We're interested in epistemology because, in the *real* world, knowing or forming true beliefs is *real* and consequential.

The subject matter of reality or ontology was explored in Chapter 3. In this chapter, we will explore approaches to knowing as these are defined by the various theories of knowledge. Various approaches to knowing may enrich our ability to know more fully, relevantly, and reliably; as we will see in Chapter 5, reality—specific approaches to knowing are "various" by definition.

Theories of Knowledge

Although epistemology is an esoteric-seeming, academic discipline, some concepts from epistemology have been acquired by the larger society. Most of us are comfortable with knowledge-related terms such as realism and idealism and make use of them.

Many other expressions from epistemology refer specifically to approaches to knowing that may not be generally understood. Nevertheless, these approaches describe *how* we form beliefs and seek to know, albeit unconsciously and intuitively in many cases, without awareness of implications and whether the specific approach is appropriate or relevant.

To view the various theories of knowledge as supplying alternative answers to the same questions is an oversimplification. They embody disagreements about what the real questions are and what counts as the answers. To help make sense of the array of "isms" that make up epistemology, a simple two-sided structure or dualism based on core assumptions about reality is developed in this chapter. A set of theories are surveyed and presented in this chapter and organized by alignment with one side or the other of the dualism.

The description and exploration of each theory addresses what it has to say about belief, truth, justification, and method. There is no claim that this list of theories is exhaustive, but within the framework of our experience and analysis, these theories offer the greatest potential relevance and application for pursuing the growth of knowledge in organizations.

EPISTEMOLOGY: THEORY OF KNOWLEDGE

Epistemology is the branch of philosophy focused on the theory of knowledge or, more precisely, on the study of the collection of theories of knowledge. Regarding any reality about which we hope to know, epistemology aims to answer the questions – *What* can we know? And, *how* do we know what we know? In the previous chapter under the heading *The Realities of Everyday Life*, we acknowledged that we know about all sorts of things as we go about daily living, from how to get to work and back to how to relate to people. We also know about subject matter. We know how to speak English or French or Chinese. We know about the Periodic Table of

Elements. We know about the three branches of government in the United States and about how parliamentary democracy works. We know how to fly airplanes and program computers and practice law. What we know, while sometimes less than perfect, serves our purposes for the most part as we live and work and interact day in and day out. However, beyond our awareness of the need to be taught and to learn how to do things, *how* we come to learn, believe, and know, as individuals, seldom captures our curiosity.

Descartes' epistemological inquiry in the *Meditations* begins with this question: What propositions are worthy of belief? In the *First Meditation* Descartes canvasses beliefs of various kinds he had formerly held as true and finds himself forced to conclude that he ought to reject them, that he ought not to accept them as true. We can view Cartesian epistemology as consisting of the following two projects: to identify the criteria by which we ought to regulate acceptance and rejection of beliefs and to determine what we may be said to know according to those criteria. Descartes' epistemological agenda has been the dominant agenda of Western epistemology to this day.[1] In formally theorizing about the dynamics of *knowing*, the discipline of epistemology seeks to identify the grounds, processes, and applications of knowledge.

Perhaps the central role that theories of knowledge have played in our intellectual history is normative, i.e., theories aim to either conform to or prescribe norms and standards that define "right" action. For Russell, "The problem for epistemology is not 'why *do* I believe this or that?' but 'why *should* I believe this or that?'"[2] Theories tell us which of the various processes of belief formation and justification we ought to be using. The "holy grail" of epistemology has been the development of a single, unified, and widely accepted theory of knowledge applicable to all classes of reality. The classical view held that such a universal theory would exist independently and prior to any specific theorizing, speculation, or experience; it was what Descartes called *first philosophy.* This historical quest of epistemology has not been successful—a single, unified, widely accepted theory has not been produced. This fact has led some theorists and scholars to conclude that epistemology is dead. At the same time, however, another (and larger) subset of scholars and champions of one theory or other, rather than seeing epistemology as having expired, tends to see near universal application of their own favored approach to knowing. Both groups continue to theorize and write about knowledge and how knowing occurs; neither group can be seen as having given up on epistemology.

While the practitioners of academic epistemology may disagree about the ultimate aims and status of epistemology, from our perspective its purpose is nothing less than the improvement of knowledge and, therefore, the human condition. Beyond knowledge about everyday life and the subject matter that defines our roles in life, the human condition embodies a lack of knowledge about those things that most profoundly matter to us. As we asserted in Chapter 1, we don't know how to live together without conflict and violence. We don't know how to accept our differences and take advantage of our diverse perspectives to improve our collective existence. We don't know how to create wealth and equitably distribute it at the same time. All too often, we don't know how to successfully collaborate and how to produce optimal solutions to problems. As individuals and collections of individuals, what we think we know about our common reality and how we come to believe and know about that reality seems to keep us from producing real knowledge. It is unlikely that a single, unified theory of knowledge will ever be developed. That probability, however, in no way diminishes the imperative and our duty to seek to know more and to know better.

In Chapter 1, an assumption pertaining to the foundations for this book was stated—that useful insights exist within the philosophical disciplines of ontology and epistemology pertaining to the character of reality and the growth of knowledge in organizations. While we agree with Rorty, the prominent contemporary philosopher and critic of epistemology, that there is no viable, single theory of knowledge, we disagree with his conclusion that since there have been a *variety* of answers (theories or approaches to knowing), there are *no* answers. We're interested in epistemology because we believe that in the *real* world, knowing is *real* and important. Various approaches to knowing may enrich our ability to know more fully, relevantly, and reliably and reality-specific approaches to knowing are "various" by definition. The subject matter of reality or ontology was explored in Chapter 3. In this chapter, we will explore approaches to knowing as these are defined by the various theories of knowledge. These theories refer to how beliefs are formed by individuals and collections of individuals and are also described as epistemic approaches or styles. In this chapter and the next, we will develop the concept of an "epistemic terrain," defined by the convergence of the reality about which knowledge is sought and the relevant approach or approaches to knowing about such reality.

THEORIES OF KNOWLEDGE

While epistemology is an arcane, academic discipline, some ideas and insights from epistemology have been acquired by the larger society. Most of us are comfortable with terms such as realism, idealism, and pragmatism and make use of them, even though we may not be able to precisely define them in philosophical terms. Many other concepts and terms, however, also potentially useful, have not made the journey from the world of academic specialty to everyday life. It turns out that there is a fairly extensive and daunting array of "isms" that make up the set of theories that define epistemology. Catherine Elgin writes, "Epistemological theories typically share an abstract characterization of their enterprise. Theories agree, for example, that epistemology is the study of the nature, scope, and utility of knowledge. But they disagree about how their shared characterization is concretely to be realized. So they differ over their subject's priorities and powers, resources and rewards, standards and criteria. To view them as supplying alternative answers to the same questions is an oversimplification. For they embody disagreements about what the real questions are and what counts as answering them."[3]

Some of these theories are very different from others, some are similar, some theories are subtly different; and sometimes the subtlety is such that a discussion of differences seems like a struggle to clarify the obvious or a debate over how many angels can dance on the head of a pin. Also, among the wide range of theories elaborated by thinkers from Plato to Russell, each seems to be framed and presented as representing a complete and stand-alone school of epistemic thought. This must be a result of the ancient quest to identify a single, unified theory for all purposes and all times. Rather than seeking to become dogmatically associated with any specific theory or family of theories, our aim is to look to the potential insights to be gained from each. Instead of adhering to one school of thought or another, our practical advocacy, as fully developed in Section II: Applications, is to seek to bridge differences and to match or fit the relevant and appropriate theory or theories (epistemic approach or approaches) to the reality about which we hope to know.

It is easy to discover, like those who have declared epistemology dead, that there is no single theory of knowledge that precedes experience and that can be applied to whatever reality about which we hope to know. There are many theories of knowledge and there are clusters of theories that share common traits. There are theories that spring from common ancestors and are woven together over time. There are theories that seek to address the central problems of knowledge, such as skepticism or method or value. A simplifying and organizing dynamic within the universe of theories and clusters of theories is a sort of categorical bifurcation, a duality that many specialists and nonspecialists see when they survey the field. The idea of this dualism was introduced in the previous chapter and will provide a context for exploring theories of knowledge. Each side of the dualism embodies a core set of assumptions pertaining to reality and the nature of knowledge. The general thought is that theories line up on one side of the dualism or the other depending on their attributes.

Dualism

The left side of the dualism pertains to the assumption of independent reality, sometimes referred to as "essentialism." The terms realism and positivism give further meaning to this category and the theories attached to this side of the dualism. Human mediation is the assumption regarding reality on the right side of the dualism. The terms idealism and constructivism apply to this category. The sociology of knowledge informs the meaning of the right side of the dualism by conceiving social reality as part of a human world, made by humans, inhabited by humans, and, in turn, making humans, in an ongoing historical process.[4]

Independent Reality/ Realism/ Positivism/Essentialism

Realism asserts that there is a reality, independent and external to human observers, and it is possible to know about this reality. Common sense realism says that ordinary things like chairs and trees and people are real. Scientific realism says that theoretical constructs like electrons and magnetism and quarks are equally real. Psychological realism says that mental states like pain and belief are real.[5] As noted earlier, a variant of realism even refers to the independent reality of such "universals" as justice and beauty. In *The construction of Social Reality*, John Searle argues: "Realism is the view that there is a way that things *are* that is logically independent of all human representations. Realism does not say how things *are,* but only that there is a *way* that they are."[6] For Michael Dummett, realism has a binary quality within the context of a certain class of statements. He writes, "The very minimum that realism can be held to involve is that statements in the given class relate to some reality that exists independently of our knowledge of it, in such a way that that reality renders each statement in the class determinately true or false, again independently of whether we know, or are even able to discover, its truth-value."[7]

Positivism is the doctrine that human sensory experience is the only object and source of knowledge. Positivism also represents the view that science is the only form of knowledge and that nothing can be known that cannot be scientifically known. Science in this context refers to formulation and testing of hypotheses through the collection of data by way of observation and experimentation.

Human Mediated Reality/Idealism/Constructivism

In common usage, the term idealism is taken to mean the practice of exemplifying ideals related to certain standards, e.g., of excellence, perfection, or justice. Philosophical idealism, however, has a different meaning. In this context, idealism refers to the view that reality is mediated by human subjectivity—that reality is mind-coordinated. There are various forms of idealism, from the extreme, which denies the existence of any reality apart from "cognizing minds" to moderate or "weaker" forms, which acknowledge the existence of independent reality, but denies our ability to know about it apart from our own subjectivity. For his analysis and description of human subjectivity as fully a part of any reality we hope to comprehend, Kant is largely responsible for our modern conceptions of idealism. According to Kant, "Our knowledge springs from two fundamental sources of the mind; the first is the capacity of receiving representations, the second is the power of knowing an object through (our concepts of) these representations. Through the first, an object is given to us, through the second the object is thought in relation to that representation. Intuition and concepts constitute, therefore, the elements of all our knowledge so that neither concepts without an intuition nor intuition without concepts can yield knowledge."[8]

Constructivism identifies the idea of the social construction of reality. Following Hegel and Durkheim, constructivism found an accessible and coherent voice in Peter Berger and Thomas Luckmann's 1966 book, *The Social Construction of Reality*. The constructivist perspective seeks to discover how individuals and groups interact to create their shared reality or, at least, to comprehend and interpret it. The appearance of an invented or interpreted reality as natural and self-evident is a key feature of social constructivism.

Theories

Theories of knowledge, organized by alignment with one side or the other of the dualism and indicated in Figure 4.1 below, will be explored in this section. There is no claim that the list in Figure 4.1 is exhaustive, but according to our analysis, these theories offer the greatest potential relevance and application for pursuing the growth of knowledge in organizations. We also acknowledge that our decision to parse certain theories into the left or the right side of the dualism may be seen as controversial or even wrong by some people. The rationale for our placing theories in one place or another is described in the material that follows.

The description and exploration of each theory will speak to what the theory has to say about truth, justification, and belief. In addition, antecedents or the "genealogy" of the theory and the methods pertaining to its application will be addressed.

Empiricism

Empiricism, one of the major theories of knowledge, asserts that experience is the source of all knowledge. It is usually contrasted with rationalism on the other side of the dualism; rationalism proposes that reason is the sole or primary source of knowledge. Empiricists grant that reason plays a secondary or supportive role in the growth of knowledge, but

Independent Reality/Realism/Positivism/ Essentialism	Human Mediated Reality/Idealism/ Constructivism
Empiricism	Rationalism
Foundationalism	Coherentism
Reliabilism	Pragmatism
Naturalized Epistemology	Hermeneutic Phenomenology

FIGURE 4.1
Theories of knowledge and conceptions of reality.

they see experience as primary and determinative. Empiricism's roots in theorizing about knowledge are ancient. From the Greek, *empeiria* means "experienced in," "acquainted with" or "skilled at." The Latin translation for *empeiros* is experiential or "experience."[9] Empiricism is closely linked with science and scientific methods. While empiricism posits that nothing can be known that is not revealed in experience or directly inferred from information gained in experience, it also argues that repeatable experience (as in experimentation) is the only way to confirm or disconfirm (and perpetuate or invalidate) knowledge claims. Although empiricists are realists through and through, they tend to be skeptical of the claims that universals such as justice and beauty are real.

John Stuart Mill, William James, Bertrand Russell, A. J. Ayer, W. V. O. Quine, and others have followed seventeenth and eighteenth century philosophers John Locke, George Berkeley, and David Hume as modern and postmodern advocates and sympathizers of empiricism. Locke and Hume use the term *sensation* to contrast sensory experience with any other potential basis for knowing. According to Locke, "The knowledge of the existence of *any other thing* we can only have by *sensation*: for there being no necessary connection of real existence with any idea a man hath in his memory.... For, the having the idea of anything in our mind, no more proves the existence of that thing, than the picture of a man evidences his being in the world, or the visions of a dream make thereby a true history."[10] Hume argued, "All the colors of poetry, however splendid, can never paint natural objects in such a manner as to cause the description to be taken for a real landscape. The liveliest thought is still inferior to the dullest sensation."[11] In the twentieth century, Quine critiqued traditional empiricism and argued that the grounding of natural science upon immediate experience in a firmly and logically deductive way is hopeless. Nevertheless, he asserted that two cardinal tenets of empiricism remain unassailable to this day. Quine wrote, "One is that whatever evidence there is for science is sensory evidence. The other is that all inculcations of meanings of words must rest ultimately on sensory evidence."[12]

In general, empiricism belongs to the set of theories of knowledge that conceives reality as independent of human influence and, as such, comprehends the truth of any proposition as corresponding to reality. The correspondence theory of truth is described in Chapter 2. Empiricism sits comfortably with the conventional definition or the "standard analysis of knowledge" as *justified true belief*, also described in Chapter 2. Ayer concludes, "that the necessary and sufficient conditions for knowing that something is the case are first that what one is said to know be *true*, secondly that one be sure of it (*believe it*) and thirdly that one should have the right to be sure (*justification*)."[13] (Parenthetical comments are the authors'.) At the same time, truth in empiricism is contingent. Because empiricism is grounded in experience, the extent of empirical truth in a general sense is bounded by the scope of relevant experience. In other words and this is a key point in understanding empiricism, that which has not been experienced cannot be fully known. Empirical statements cannot be certain in the way that *a priori* statements based on reason alone can be certain because they lack the attribute of *necessity*. That which is *necessary*, in contrast to *contingent*, holds in all possible worlds, not only those circumscribed by experience. A scientist and science administrator with whom we worked expressed the empiricist perspective in his definition of knowledge as contingent, having the best understanding (of the truth) of a set of circumstances at a certain time and in a certain place.

Empiricism seeks to know about specific reality through experience and to know about a wider reality through inference. Empiricism is based on induction, an important difference with respect to certain other theories on the left side of the dualism, especially foundationalism. In induction, nature's laws and mechanisms are inferred from observation; induction means moving from specific facts to general conclusions or, more precisely, making *probable* inferences (as opposed to *necessary* inferences in deduction, bearing in mind that necessary inferences hold in *all* cases). The methods of empiricism are those of science and thus characterized as observation, hypothesis, experimentation, and confirmation/disconfirmation. The problems of empiricism are the problems of induction or circular reasoning and the tendency to apply empiricism to incongruent realities. Induction generates hypotheses and theories. It does not prove them true. Inductively spawned hypotheses that come to be seen as not hypothetical at all, but proven aspects of nature are acts of circular reasoning.[14] The temptation to apply empiricism to the human sciences has produced reification in many instances. Reification is the process of regarding something abstract as a material or concrete thing. It is the apprehension of human phenomena in nonhuman terms; it is reductionism in the extreme.[15]

Foundationalism

Where empiricism asserts that experience is the source of all knowledge, foundationalism, as the name suggests, proposes that all knowledge flows from some set of foundational and uncontested beliefs. Where inference in empiricism is based on induction, inference in foundationalism is based on deduction. Like empiricism, foundationalism assumes an independent and knowable reality and is aligned, therefore, with the realist or left side of the dualism. "The core of foundationalism is a commitment to some special class of beliefs—so called basic beliefs—from which all justification derives. This (chain of justification) would be reflected in a J-rule system (a system or network of justification rules) that ultimately permits all other beliefs only by their relationship to members of this special belief class."[16] (Parenthetical comments are the authors'.) This quote from Alvin Goldman puts forward the idea that foundationalism is a theory of knowledge focused upon the structure of knowledge or the structure of justification. The structure in this case pertains to the system of justified beliefs held by a given individual and is divided into *foundation* and *superstructure*. *Foundation* refers to the *given* or to the set of basic beliefs; *superstructure* points to the modes or forms of inference or derivation of other beliefs grounded in the foundational beliefs. Basic beliefs are directly justified beliefs and these constitute the foundation upon which the superstructure of nonbasic or derived beliefs rests.

An obvious question is: From where do we get our foundations, our basic beliefs? The answer depends on what we're prepared to accept as unambiguous and certain. One class of answers pertains to that which is self-evident. According to Michael Williams, "Western epistemological ideas have been decisively influenced by the Greek discovery of the axiomatic method: the discovery, originally in geometry, that a rich variety of results, often far from obviously true, can be deduced from a small number of primitive propositions, each of which seems self-evidently and factually correct. On the view of knowledge that this discovery inspires, all genuine knowledge is demonstrative: to be known to be true, a proposition must be either immediately self-evident or deduced from such self-evident truths by a sequence of self-evidently valid steps."[17]

Another class of answers embodies beliefs about one's own state of consciousness. "I think therefore I am," Descartes' Cogito argument in which he extrudes certainty from the process of doubting is the classic example. Yet another class of candidates for foundational or basic beliefs is perceptual beliefs, which apart from the psychological implications of perception, brings us into contact with empiricism. Aristotle argued that the proper method of inquiry in science is to proceed from perceptual observations through induction until we reach experience, which is the best route to first principles. Paradoxically, the first principles of science for Aristotle were his candidates for foundational, self-justifying, basic beliefs upon which a rigorous structure of deduction could be constructed. Finally, a class of answers as to how basic beliefs are derived pertains to the existence of an authoritative source, which often affirms the independent existence of universals. In contrast to moderate forms of foundationalism, strong versions of this theory require the distinction that inferences be infallible and immune from error.

The superstructure of foundationalism is based on deduction. The essential idea in deductive reasoning is that conclusions by inference follow *necessarily* from foundational or general and universal premises. *Necessity* is the essential characteristic of deduction and means that no other conclusions are logically possible. As described above under empiricism, induction, on the other hand, is probabilistic; conclusions are contingent on context and other variables. The infinite regress argument is the historical appeal of foundationalism. Infinite regress refers to the problem of every belief inferred from some other inferred belief in a pattern of infinite regress. Foundationalism defeats this problem by ending the regress at basic, indubitable beliefs.

The corresponding and antithetical theory to foundationalism on the other side of the dualism is coherentism. Coherentism is the theory that justification and knowledge are determined by the coherence of a belief within a background system of beliefs. Ernest Sosa uses the two metaphors of the raft and the pyramid to draw the distinctions between coherentism and foundationalism. The coherentists ascribe to the view that "our body of knowledge is a raft that floats free of any anchor or tie . . . Repairs must be made afloat, and although no part is untouchable, we must stand on some in order to replace or repair others. Not every part can go at once." According to foundationalism, each piece of knowledge lies on a pyramid with each higher level supported by the lower levels, all of which rest on the base, which provides the foundation and support.[18]

There are two characteristics of a foundationalist perspective that will have meaning for us, especially in contrast to empiricism. First, within any setting of seeking to know, something will be taken to grant certainty or infallibility for some set of basic beliefs. That something may be the result of experience or observation as in empiricism, which, as argued earlier, is regarded by empiricists as inappropriate, or it may be something entirely different. Second, the inferences that follow under foundationalism are deductive in nature, giving them the character of necessity rather than contingency. There is little controversy surrounding the legitimacy of logical deduction. However, while there may be no dispute over granting foundational status to certain beliefs under certain circumstances, there most certainly will be controversy over granting such status to other beliefs.

Reliabilism

Empiricism and foundationalism are focused on the content and truth status of beliefs and related patterns of justification and thus are *content-oriented* theories. Reliabilism, in comparison, brings full attention to bear on *methods* associated with justification and knowledge. Reliabilism is seen by some theorists as an alternative to the *justified true belief* account of knowledge, or the standard analysis, by asserting that we are justified in believing something if we arrived at the belief by way of a reliable cognitive process. With attention brought to bear on cognitive processes, reliabilism looks to cognitive science, specifically to the psychological processes that cause or perpetuate belief. With respect to belief-causing processes, the notion of reliability pertains to the ability of such processes to produce high truth-ratio beliefs or a high proportion of true beliefs among the total set of beliefs generated by the process.[19]

In her paper "Revisiting Women's Ways of Knowing," B. M. Clinchy identifies "procedural knowing" as a reliabilism-like way of knowing. She writes, "Knowledge is a process. Knowing requires the application of procedures for comparing and contrasting and constructing interpretations, and the quality of the knowledge depends on the skill of the knower."[20] Like its companions on the positivist side of the dualism, reliabilism assumes a reality independent of human mediation and deduces the "knowability" of such reality given belief which is true, certain, and obtained by a reliable linkage to the truth.

There are multiple forms of reliabilism. Theories are first differentiated between *reliable indicator* and *reliable process* theories. The reliable indicator theory declares that a belief is justified if it is based on reasons that are reliable indicators of the truth; a dependable thermometer is often identified as a metaphor for such an indicator. The reliable process theory asserts that a belief is justified if a reliable cognitive process produces it.

An important distinction among reliable process theories is the *actual-counterfactual* distinction. *Actual*, in this case, refers to processes that relate to the proposition in question in a direct and positive way. *Counterfactual* processes, or those in opposition to actual processes, focus on how knowledge claims may be defeated. A variant of the counterfactual category is *relevant alternatives,* which sets forth the circumstance that the justification for claiming knowledge about any proposition must be sufficient to cause every alternative to be known to be false.

Since under reliabilism the critical causative agents of justification are psychological, belief-forming processes such as perception, memory, imagining, reasoning, and introspection, they are central to the theory of reliabilism. Taking perception to be what Goldman calls a "suitable starting point in exploring the interface between psychology and epistemology," it is generally agreed that perception is a mix of bottom-up and top-down processing. Bottom-up processing refers to the upward flow of information from smaller to larger units while top-down processing relates to the influence of background or higher-level beliefs on the interpretation of lower-level perceptual units. In our work with a cognitive style instrument and with individuals in organizations; however, we have seen a clear distinction between persons with dominant bottom-up versus top-down processing styles and how these individuals make sense of circumstances and form beliefs. Each style represents a reliable and personal justificatory cognitive process for the persons in question.

Naturalized Epistemology

Naturalized epistemology refers to a class of theories of knowledge that emphasize the continuity of theorizing about knowledge with natural science. Although there are exceptions, it is generally assumed that naturalistic approaches to knowing are descriptive, representing accounts of how knowing actually occurs, rather than normative in the sense of embodying views about how knowing *should* occur. In *Putting Naturalized Epistemology to Work*, Phyllis Rooney summarizes four relevant elements that naturalist epistemologists claim as necessary in theorizing about knowledge: "(i) what and how we actually know and specifically acquire and justify beliefs; (ii) what cognitive science tells us about how we know; (iii) (the state of) scientific knowledge and knowing; and (iv) what cognitive/social science tells us about scientific knowledge and knowing …We need to be more aware of the background assumptions about knowledge, epistemology, and science that are at work when various combinations of these—sometimes all four—are collapsed together."[21] Reliabilism, as described above, is a sort of link between traditional and naturalistic epistemology. Reliabilism is concerned with the validity and viability of natural or psychological processes, but does not disavow the normative attributes of such processes and the role of justification in claiming to know. We have located naturalized epistemology on the positivist side of the dualism because of its reliance on sensory experience to accurately represent independent reality and because of its affiliation with empiricism and natural science. A possible exception to this alignment with independent reality is the social science connection with naturalistic approaches and will be noted later in this section.

W. V. O. Quine's 1969 paper, "Epistemology Naturalized," either critically or approvingly, has become the point of departure for a range of naturalistic perspectives. Quine urges us to replace normative theories of cognition and knowledge with a descriptive science. He takes aim at induction and classical empiricism and "the impossibility of deducing theory from experience." He asks, "Why all this make-believe? The stimulation of his sensory receptors is all the evidence anybody has to go on, ultimately, in arriving at his picture of the world. Why not settle for psychology? Such a surrender of the epistemological burden to psychology is a move that was disallowed in earlier times as circular reasoning. If the epistemologist's goal is validation of the grounds of empirical science, he defeats his purpose by using psychology or other empirical science in the validation. However, such scruples against circularity have little point once we have stopped dreaming of deducing science from observations. If we are out simply to understand the link between observation and science, we are well advised to use any available information, including that provided by the very science whose link with observation we are seeking to understand. Epistemology, or something like it, simply falls into place as a chapter of psychology and hence of natural science—a conspicuous difference between old epistemology and the epistemological enterprise in this new psychological setting is that we can now make free use of empirical psychology."[22]

Making use of empirical psychology or, more broadly, making use of the concepts and methods of empiricism in epistemology *itself*, i.e., in the process rather than just the target or object of knowing, is the essential difference between classical empiricism and naturalistic approaches. Given this difference, there are other interpretations of naturalistic ideas, ideas less extreme than Quine's that don't seek to throw the epistemological baby out with the bath water. There are more modest conceptions of naturalism related to theories of knowledge that readily incorporate empirical results from psychology regarding how we remember, think, and reason within a framework of normative epistemology. Phillip Kitcher in his article "The Naturalists Return" asks, "How could our psychological and biological capacities and limitations fail to be relevant to the study of human knowledge?"[23] At the same time, theorists who adopt a modest conception of naturalism reject the reductionism that seeks to account for all knowledge in wholly natural and scientific terms with no concern for the standards we *should* adopt in striving to know. In its most expansive sense, naturalized epistemology reduces the processes and consequences of knowing to cognitive science and to the chemical, neuronal, and synaptic bases of brain function. While this reduction can be troublesome working at the level of the individual, it is highly problematic and controversial when the social dimension is introduced. Although some epistemological naturalists have sought to apply their orientation to the sociology of knowledge, there is much to suggest that the application is inappropriate and even that the sociology of knowledge is constructivist in nature and belongs on the other side of the dualism.

Evolutionary epistemology is a naturalistic theory of knowledge that sets forth an important connection between the growth of knowledge and biological evolution. Donald T. Campbell writes, "An evolutionary epistemology would be at a minimum an epistemology taking cognizance of and (being) compatible with man's status as a product of biological and social evolution." He argues that " Evolution—even in its biological aspects—is a knowledge process and that the natural-selection paradigm for such knowledge increments can be generalized to other epistemic activities, such as learning, thought, and science.... It is primarily through the works of Karl Popper that a natural selection epistemology is available today."[24]

Natural selection is characterized as proceeding through variation, selection, and retention. According to modern conceptions of evolution, genetic mutations provide the blind variation, the environment provides the screen of selection, and biological reproduction provides the retention. Campbell describes a theme recurrent in most knowledge processes:

a. A blind variation-and-selective-retention process is fundamental to all inductive achievements, to all genuine increases in knowledge, to all increases in fit of system to environment.
b. The many processes which shortcut a fuller blind-variation and selective-retention process are in themselves inductive achievements,

containing wisdom about the environment achieved originally by blind variation and selective retention.

c. In addition, such shortcut processes contain in their own operation a blind-variation-and-selective-retention process at some level, substituting for overt locomotor exploration or the life-and-death winnowing of organic evolution.[25]

Evolutionary epistemology can be seen as literal or analogical. The literal version conceives actual biological evolution as the principal cause of knowledge growth. The analogical version sees the governance of the growth of knowledge as a process analogous to biological natural selection. The following quote by Popper himself is an appropriate way to end this brief summary of evolutionary epistemology as well as this section on the positivist or realist side of the dualism. "Scientists should always remember, as I think Darwin always did, that science is tentative and fallible. Science does not solve all the riddles of the universe, nor does it promise to solve them. Nevertheless it can sometimes throw unexpected light even on our deepest and probably insoluble riddles.[26]

Rationalism

The great divide in epistemology has been represented by the chasm between empiricism and rationalism. William James speaks in terms of the rationalist and the empiricist tempers with "empiricist meaning your lover of facts in all their crude variety and rationalist meaning your devotee to abstract and eternal principles.... No one can live an hour without both facts and principles, so it is a difference rather of emphasis; yet it breeds antipathies of the most pungent character between those who lay the emphasis differently." He goes on to list his interpretation of traits. The rationalist is "intellectualistic, idealistic, optimistic, free-willist, dogmatical"; the empiricist is "deterministic, materialistic, pessimistic, pluralistic, and skeptical."[27]

The right side of our dualism expresses the conception of reality as mediated by human subjectivity. Through the belief that reason, independent of experience, is the primary source of knowledge, subjectivity is at the heart of the rationalist perspective. Rationalism lays the groundwork for exploring theories on the right side of the dualism because of its continuity with idealism and constructivism and the associated theories of knowledge.

Inference based on *deduction* supported by conceptions of *necessary* and *a priori* knowledge defines rationalism. The notions of necessity and contingency were introduced in this and the previous chapter. Necessary truths are those which must be true and whose opposite is *impossible*; contingent truths are not necessary and, therefore, their opposite is *possible*. In other words, a necessary truth applies to *all* possible worlds while a contingent truth applies only to *some* possible worlds. The rationalist grants the status of necessity to some propositions based on reason alone. Generally, *a priori* knowledge is independent of all experience and derives from our intuition, the meanings of our ideas and reason. We could say either that a truth is *a priori* knowable only if it is *necessary* or that a proposition is *necessary* only if it is *a priori* knowable.

In the *Critique of Pure Reason*, Kant set out to show that meaningful propositions are *a priori* knowable. To define *meaningful*, he drew a distinction between analytic and synthetic propositions. Analytic propositions are self-evident and uncontroversial. In analytic propositions, whatever is affirmed or denied regarding the subject belongs to the concept of the subject itself. The color "white is white" or the "value of 5 is 5" are analytic, self-evident, and essentially meaningless propositions. In synthetic propositions, however, whatever is affirmed or denied regarding the subject lies outside the concept of the subject. The propositions "causes produce effects" and "5 + 6 = 11," therefore, are synthetic in Kant's terms. Kant made his case for the possibility of synthetic *a priori* knowledge through the necessity reflected in the "Pure Concepts of Understanding" or the "Categories." His table of categories divided into mathematical and dynamical concepts. Mathematical categories included concepts such as unity, totality, and negation. Dynamical categories included cause and effect, existence, substance, and possibility/impossibility.[28]

The antecedents of rationalism are usually traced first to Plato and his conception of "forms," such as equality and justice as innate ideas or objects. In contrast to extreme realism and the independent existence of universals as previously described; however, knowledge in the proper sense of knowing cannot concern objects of the senses or experience under Plato's theory of forms. He believed that the abstract has more reality than the individual and particular concrete thing, and that knowledge was achieved by reasoning about first principles based on the truth of universal forms.[29] The thread of rationalism extends to Descartes, Spinoza, and Leibnitz through Voltaire and the enlightenment philosophers to Kant in an important if critical way. Although in the *Critique of Pure Reason*, Kant

Glass Bead Game

lays out the pitfalls and potential fallacies of reason and seeks to reconcile empiricism and rationalism; his exploration of the possibility of *a priori* knowledge and the distinctions between necessary and contingent truths set the stage for characterizing the essence of rationalism. The thread of rationalism continues to Hegel and the nineteenth and twentieth century idealists such as Husserl and Heidegger, to modern and postmodern interpretations.

To the present day, rationalists question the ability of the senses and induction to deliver knowledge, as in empiricism. Instead, inference based on deductions, logically and reasonably flowing from irrefutable and necessary propositions, given life by innate concepts and principles, is the dominant aspect of rationalist approaches to knowing. In common usage as well as in philosophy, rationalism brings forth ambiguous perceptions. To be rational is good; it suggests that one is guided by legitimate reasoning. To rationalize is not good; it uses reason inappropriately to provide plausible but untrue reasons for conduct. In philosophy, rationalism went through a period of pejorative usage. Anyone with a different and competing perspective was accused of being a rationalist. Circumstances have shifted, however, and rationalist approaches considered to be alive and well have emerged and been redefined.

Coherentism

Hermann Hesse's 1943 Nobel Prize winning novel *Magister Ludi* (or *The Glass Bead Game*) describes a future society and intellectual movement known as Castalia whose purpose is the growth of knowledge and understanding of the whole of reality. Castalia's members participate in its life through the mastery and play of the Glass Bead Game. The Glass Bead Game is a synthesis through which philosophy, religion, art, music, mathematics, and science are comprehended simultaneously. The organizing principles of the various disciplines are expressed in the game. Truths and holistic insights are developed as a result of the play, which flows from integration of the diverse elements and the coherent, systematic, and logical connections embodied in their collective existence.[30] On an imaginative and grandiose scale, the Glass Bead Game is representative of coherentism as a theory of knowledge.

Some people give little or no credence to the idea that basic or fundamental beliefs underpin knowledge, thinking instead that knowledge or the lack of it is a consequence of how beliefs or propositions relate to each other in either a coherent or an incoherent way. Coherentism and foundationalism (described on the other side of the dualism) are antithetical and usually rival theories of knowledge. Coherentism sees knowledge emerging from the mutual support among beliefs as the bricks in a building support each other and provide strength. Foundationalism conceives a foundation of basic beliefs upon which the "bricks" of deductive inference settle to produce knowledge. In *The Elements of Coherentism*, Laurence BonJour writes, "Coherence is a matter of how well a body of beliefs 'hangs together': how well its component beliefs fit together, agree, or dovetail with each other to produce an organized, tightly structured system of beliefs, rather than either a helter-skelter collection or a set of conflicting subsystems. It is reasonably clear that this 'hanging together' depends on the various sorts of inferential, evidential, and explanatory relations, which obtain among the various members of a system of beliefs, and especially on the more holistic and systematic of these."[31]

Coherentism emerged as a distinct theory in the nineteenth century. It looks to reason to understand and define the logical connections that produce holistic insights. Coherentism is related to rationalism and, like rationalism, traces its antecedents through the idealists to Kant and through the sixteenth and seventeenth century rationalists to Plato. Some empiricists gingerly embrace coherentism as an indirect approach to validate certain hypotheses pertaining to independent reality. Coherentism, however, is a distinctly different theory which takes account of subjectivity and belongs on the right side of the dualism. There are coherence theories of truth, justification, and belief, which come together in various ways to yield a theory of knowledge. The coherence theory of truth was introduced in Chapter 2 and is closely linked to the idea of logical truth. The coherence theory of truth asserts that beliefs, assumptions, or propositions are true if they fit into or cohere with a systematic body of known and accepted true beliefs, assumptions, or propositions. The ideas of meaning associated with logical context and meaning or purpose as a precursor of truth are compatible with coherentism and an aspect of postmodern thought, which has given rise to a revival of interest in coherence theories of truth. Coherence theories of justification are radically holistic. Michael Williams asserts, "For the coherence theorist, there is not a question of a belief's being justified by itself, as the foundationalist's basic beliefs are supposed to be. To be justified, a belief must fit into a justified system; and the system is more or less justified depending on how well it hangs together, when considered as a whole."[32] *How* the content of belief is formed is the central concern of

Coherentism	Foundationalism
Non-Linear: Justification depends on the density and character of interconnections and the properties of the system as a whole.	*Linear:* Justification proceeds step by step from premises to conclusions.
Holistic: Truth and knowledge are found in the nature of the whole set of beliefs or propositions.	*Atomistic:* Truth and knowledge are found in the character of the individual elements (beliefs, propositions).
Top-Down: Context and even relevant theory frame and influence knowing about sets of beliefs or propositions.	*Bottom-Up:* Starting with the first and primary item of knowledge, a system of beliefs is built up one element at a time.

FIGURE 4.2
Coherentism versus foundationalism.

coherence theories of belief. It is acknowledged that perception and even action triggered by belief influence the content of belief. In coherence theories of belief, however, the *manner* in which specific beliefs cohere within a network of beliefs shapes the content of belief. For example, patterns and rules of inference determine how beliefs develop and relate to each other and, therefore, are able to determine the content of belief.

The differences between coherentism and its rival foundationalism are summarized in the table in Figure 4.2.

Recognizing that beliefs are often not binary, either held completely or not at all, coherentists are naturally led to the idea of degrees of belief and, indirectly, to the ideas of degrees of justification and gradations of truth and knowledge. The logic of partial belief is the logic of probability or the ratio of the perceived likelihood of the truth of a belief to the total set of possible outcome states. Conclusions follow by *probability* in induction in contrast to *necessity* in deduction. Probability has been held to be the degree of belief a rational person ought to grant to a given proposition. Coherentists have argued that coherent degrees of belief should satisfy the rules of probability calculus.

A useful and widely accepted conception of probability is Bayes' Theorem, the application of which is Bayesianism or the Bayesian approach to epistemology. Bayesianism and probability theory in general are mathematically based approaches to epistemology. As such, the expectation would seem to be that numerical degrees of belief are the working material of Bayesianism and this seems, at first glance, to be far fetched; can people actually hold precise, numerical degrees of belief? The Bayesian approach, however, need not be committed to the literal existence of precise, numerical degrees of belief. For Paul Horwich, "The vital assumption is that there are belief gradations of some sort; their representation by numbers should perhaps be seen as nothing more than a heuristic device—something done for the sake of convenience (to learning and discovery), without commitment to its truth."[33]

Pragmatism

Pragmatism is regarded as an essentially American school of philosophy although, more precisely, it should be described as a theory of truth and knowledge. Its development in the nineteenth and twentieth centuries was chiefly the work of Americans, but Francis Bacon, Immanuel Kant, and others described its underpinnings. Although there are many forms of pragmatism, it is generally characterized by the "pragmatic maxim," according to which the meaning of a concept or proposition is to be sought in the practical consequences of its application. In Chapter 3, we described how conceptions of everyday reality and related knowledge are transmitted from generation to generation and how pragmatism is the driving force in the creation and preservation of such knowledge. Pragmatism, therefore, has a distinctly sensible and common sense spirit. That which produces useful and beneficial results is the standard for knowledge about everyday life. Pragmatism, as a philosophical movement with epistemological dimensions, however, seeks to address questions pertaining to knowledge in an all-encompassing way, beyond what we might call knowledge about everyday reality. Pragmatism speaks to the meaning of knowledge and the efficacy of belief and justification. As we described in Chapter 2, one of the three generally accepted theories of truth is the pragmatist view of truth. According to this view, truth is found in utility or the consequences of action. While truth adheres to good consequences, falsity is associated with results that exhibit little or no utility.

The sixteenth century English philosopher Francis Bacon argued that truth and utility are two sides of the same coin. It was the *practical* success of a theory which was for him the hallmark of its truth.[34] Pragmatists are critical of both empiricism and foundationalism and reject the notions that raw experience is the source of evidence for our beliefs and that foundational or basic beliefs can be justified solely on the basis of perceptual experience. Pragmatism is influenced by Kant's declaration that perceptions and ultimately intuitions regarding utility or anything else are blind without concepts. Therefore, Kant's scheme of categories, which catalogue and define concepts such as unity, causality, reality, and contingency, provide a framework for interpreting the world. Pragmatists part company with Kant, however, over his idea that the categories are immutable and *necessary*. Pragmatists believe, instead, that the categories are *our* creations and vary depending on the relevant interpretive framework, e.g., whether for everyday reality or for sociology or for physics. The American philosophers most closely connected with pragmatism are William James, John Dewey, and Charles Sanders Peirce. The best known of the contemporary adapters and revivers of pragmatism, the so-called neo-pragmatists, is Richard Rorty.

C. S. Peirce is usually credited with having coined the term *pragmatism* in the late nineteenth century and to have first articulated the argument that truth, justification, and knowledge are determined by the consequences of belief. Peirce did not, however, move away from the notion of independent reality and believed that the correspondence theory of truth was only incomplete and not in error. James' work popularized pragmatism and made it *the* American philosophy in the early part of the twentieth century.

Dewey, the third member of the American pragmatist trio, was influenced by James and made his reputation in the field of education. Although there are multiple forms of pragmatism, there are common themes. First, is the idea of the mutability of truth. To one degree or other, pragmatists believe that truth is subject to change. Second, pragmatists are anti-Cartesian. Although some pragmatists are more revolutionary than others in their separation from traditional epistemology, they all seek to establish distance between themselves and those who follow Descartes in the pursuit of certainty and incorrigibility. Third, pragmatism is oriented to action. For William James, pragmatism's only test of probable truth "is what works best in the way of leading us, what fits every part of life best and combines with the collectivity of experience's demands, nothing being omitted."[35]

It could be argued that pragmatism should be placed on the left, i.e., the realist or positivist side of the dualism. It could also be argued, as we have, that it belongs on the right side, which represents constructivist assumptions about reality. This range of perceptions about pragmatism suggests its potential usefulness as a bridging theory. We have placed it on the right side, however, based on our conviction that ideas about utility and what is "good and useful" are variable and, therefore, constructed. This view of pragmatism is consistent with a more revolutionary interpretation of James and Dewey.

In One Hundred Years of Pragmatism, Theo Anderson asserts, "James always insisted that that the human capacity to grasp reality is limited—that there is no God's-eye perch available to us. 'Objective evidence and certitude are doubtless very fine ideals to play with but where on this moonlit and dream-visited planet are they to be found.'"[36] Although pragmatism seemed to continue to be the American way of thinking, after Dewey, academic interest in pragmatism waned until the publication of Rorty's *Philosophy and the Mirror of Nature* in the later quarter of the twentieth century. Rorty's conception of pragmatism speaks to method and the role of community in constructing definitions of utility. "Our identification with our community—our society, our political tradition, our intellectual heritage—is heightened when we see this community as *ours* rather than *nature's*, *shaped* rather than *found*, one among many which men have made. In the end, the pragmatists tell us, what matters is our loyalty to other human beings clinging together against the dark, not our hope of getting things right."[37]

Hermeneutic Phenomenology

The meaning of hermeneutic phenomenology, a combination of phenomenology and hermeneutics, is far less threatening and off-putting than the name itself brings to mind. Phenomenology as an approach to research and learning and ultimately to knowing aims to bypass the presuppositions embodied in theories of one type or other in order to *describe* objects and situations precisely as they are experienced by a person, *the subject*. "This approach involves the practice of taking a fresh unprejudiced look—i.e., untainted by scientific, metaphysical, religious, or cultural presuppositions, or attitudes—at the fundamental and essential features of human experience in and of the world."[38]

The successors of Edmund Husserl, the acknowledged founder of the discipline of phenomenology, however, came to understand that human thought without presupposition is impossible and that interpretation is always required. The essence or spirit of phenomenology, therefore, was fused with the older discipline of hermeneutics, the art and practice of interpretation, to result in hermeneutic phenomenology. Briefly, phenomenology is *descriptive* and hermeneutics is *interpretive*. Hermeneutic phenomenology, as a combined discipline, is descriptive because it attends to how things appear, letting things speak for themselves, and it is interpretive because it seeks meaning and because of the claim that uninterpreted phenomena is inconceivable. Our interest is primarily in hermeneutic phenomenology, but we will briefly and separately survey phenomenology and hermeneutics below.

"To talk about phenomenology is the most idle thing in the world, so long as that is lacking which alone can give talk concrete fullness and intuitiveness, namely, the phenomenological *way of seeing* and the phenomenological *attitude*."[39] As indicated by this quote from Adolf Reinach, a pupil of Husserl who was noted for his ability to distill Husserl's thoughts with clarity, phenomenology is easy to define and difficult to explain. Phenomenology asserts that there is a *way things are* but that this *way* can only be grasped by taking account of how individual subjects make sense of this reality. In other words, our only access to the phenomena of physical objects, events, feelings, concepts, and circumstances is by human subjects experiencing them. Phenomenology, therefore, focuses on human consciousness. It seeks to discover the *essences* of the world as those who participate in them experience them; it is about the nature of human experience and the way these experiences are represented.

Phenomenology comes close to the realist view that reality is independent, but it criticizes empiricism for its failure to take subjectivity into account. Also, unlike empiricism, phenomenology is not a hypothesis-testing mode of learning and seeking to know, although hypotheses may emerge from phenomenological research. In terms of methods, "Husserl proposed that one needed to bracket out the outer world as well as individual biases in order to successfully achieve contact with essences. This is a process of suspending one's judgment or bracketing particular beliefs (presuppositions) about the phenomena in order to see them clearly."[40]

Phenomenology after Husserl, while retaining many of its ideas, moved in the direction of hermeneutics with Martin Heidegger, Hans-Georg Gadamer, Paul Rocoeur, and others and toward existentialism, a philosophy focused on the human condition, with Jean-Paul Sartre, Simone de Beauvoir, and others.

According to Richard Palmer in his book *Hermeneutics*, in the Greek pantheon, the wing-footed messenger-god Hermes is associated with "the function of transmuting what is beyond human understanding into a form that human intelligence can grasp." "Thus, traced back to their earliest known root word in Greek, *hermeneutikos*, the origins of the modern words 'hermeneutics' and 'hermeneutical' suggest the *process* of 'bringing to understanding,' especially as the process involves language, since language is the medium par excellence in the process."[41] Hermeneutics, then, is the study of the process or methodology of interpretation. Where phenomenology seeks to grasp the essence of reality free of preconceptions, hermeneutics asserts that we always bring prejudgments to interpretation of reality and these prejudgments involve our cultural backgrounds as well as our individual experience. The centering of the notion of interpretation in culture causes hermeneutics to be seen as connected with structuralism, the philosophical idea that all cultures have constant and durable structures, which the members of cultures hold unconsciously and prior to reflection.

Use of the name and principles of hermeneutics can be identified as early as the seventeenth century and connected with the process of Biblical interpretation. Hermeneutics broadened to include interpretation of nontheological literary texts and finally to interpretation of human actions, events, and circumstances. Richard Palmer's book *Hermeneutics* offers "six modern definitions" of hermeneutics as expressed by the leading thinkers on the subject, one of which is especially relevant for our purposes. Wilhelm Dilthey saw in hermeneutics "the core discipline which could serve as the foundation for all the disciplines focused on understanding man's actions, art, and writing." To interpret any expression of human life, whether it be an act, an event, a law, a literary work, or sacred scripture, "calls for an act of historical understanding," Dilthey asserted, "an operation fundamentally distinct from the quantifying, scientific grasp of the natural world; for in this act of historical (and cultural) understanding, what is called into play is a personal knowledge of what being human means."

Phenomenology, with all its rigor and richness of description, doesn't interpret. It doesn't speculate about essences or make inferences or draw conclusions; from a practical point of view, we have to ask, how can such an approach be useful? As noted above, our interest is brought to bear on the fusion of hermeneutics and phenomenology. As we will explore in Section II, we have relied in our work as consultants and authors on an approach to action research, and organizational analysis based on hermeneutic phenomenology. There are, however, tensions between hermeneutics and phenomenology. While one seeks to explain the world and how it is experienced free of bias and preconception, the other claims that bias and preconception are unavoidable in how humans contend with the world, including those humans engaged in research itself. Hermeneutics relies on a valid description of phenomena which a phenomenological approach provides, while hermeneutics provides an interpretation of the reality in question.

In terms of a methodology that embraces phenomenology *and* hermeneutics, hermeneutic phenomenology is an iterative approach to knowing best expressed through what is known as the hermeneutical circle. Palmer argues, "Understanding is a basically referential operation; we understand something by comparing it to something we already know. What we understand forms itself into systematic unities, or circles made up of parts. The circle as a whole defines the individual part, and the parts together form the circle. A whole sentence, for instance, is a unity. We understand the meaning of an individual word by seeing it in reference to the whole of the sentence; and reciprocally, the sentence's meaning as a whole is dependent on the meaning of individual words. By extension, an individual concept derives its meaning from a context or horizon within which it stands; yet the horizon is made up of the very elements to which it gives meaning. By dialectical interaction between the whole and the part, each gives the other meaning; understanding is circular, then. Because within this 'circle' the meaning comes to stand, we call this the 'hermeneutical circle.'"[42]

The idea of the hermeneutic circle has been applied to the relationship of the parts to the whole, as above, as well as to the relationship of preconceptions to the "things themselves." Speaking of the hermeneutical circle in *Truth and Method*, Gadamer describes Heidegger's disclosure of the fore-structure (set of the preconceptions and "fore-projections") of understanding. He states that a person trying to understand some phenomena is always projecting. "The process that Heidegger describes is that every revision of the fore-projection is capable of projecting before itself a new projection of meaning; interpretation begins with fore-conceptions that are replaced by more suitable ones (as the phenomenon itself is encountered). This constant process of new projection constitutes the movement of understanding and interpretation."[43] While hermeneutic phenomenology is not precisely a theory of knowledge, it is a theory of how knowing as understanding is possible and how such knowing can be achieved. Both phenomenology and hermeneutics assume construction of the social world, which makes clear why we placed hermeneutic phenomenology on the right side of the dualism.

REFERENCES

1, Kim, Jaegwon. 1988. What is Naturalized Epistemology? In *Philosophical Perspectives, 2, Epistemology*, ed. James E. Tomberlin, 381–405. Atascadero, CA: Ridgeview Publishing Company.

2. Russell, Bertrand. 1992. *An Inquiry into Meaning and Truth*. London: Routledge.
3. Elgin, Catherine Z. 1996. Epistemology's End. In *Considered Judgment*, 3–20. Princeton: Princeton University Press.
4. Berger, Peter L. and Thomas Luckman. 1967. *The Social Construction of Reality: A Treatise in the Sociology of Knowledge*. New York: Anchor Books, a Division of Random House.
5. Pettit, Philip. 1992. Realism. In *A Companion to Epistemology*, ed. Jonathan Dancy, Ernest Sosa, 420–424. Oxford: Blackwell Publishers, Ltd.
6. Searle, John R. 1995. *The Construction of Social Reality*. New York: The Free Press.
7. Goldman, Alvin I. 1986. *Epistemology and Cognition*. Cambridge: Harvard University Press.
8. Kant, Immanuel. 1963. *The Critique of Pure Reason*, Trans. Norman Kemp Smith. London: Macmillan and Co Ltd.
9. Reese, William L. 1996. *Dictionary of Philosophy and Religion: Eastern and Western Thought*. Atlantic Highlands, NJ: Humanities Press.
10. Locke, John. 1952. *An Essay Concerning Human Understanding*, Annotated by Alexander Campbell Fraser. Oxford: Oxford University Press.
11. Hume, David. 1952. *An Enquiry Concerning Human Understanding*. Ed. L.A. Selby-Bigge. Oxford: Oxford University Press.
12. Quine, W. V. O. 1969. Epistemology Naturalized. In *Ontological Relativity and Other Essays*, 69–90. New York: Columbia University Press.
13. Ayer, A. J. 1956. The Right to be Sure. In *The Problem of Knowledge*, 25–44. London: Penguin Books Ltd.
14. Rothman, Stephen. 2002. *Lessons from the Living Cell: The Limits of Reductionism*. New York: McGraw-Hill.
15. Douglas, Neil and Terry Wykowski. 1999. *Beyond Reductionism: Gateways for Learning and Change*. Boca Raton: St. Lucie Press.
16. Goldman, Alvin I. 1986. *Epistemology and Cognition*. Cambridge: Harvard University Press.
17. Williams, Michael. 2001. *Problems of Knowledge: A Critical Introduction to Epistemology*. New York: Oxford University Press.
18. Sosa, Ernest. 1991. The Raft and the Pyramid: Coherence versus Foundations in the Theory of Knowledge. In *Knowledge in Perspective*, 165–191. Cambridge: Cambridge University Press.
19. Goldman, Alvin I. 1986. *Epistemology and Cognition*. Cambridge: Harvard University Press.
20. Clinchy, Blythe McVicker. 2002. Revisiting Women's Way of Knowing. In *Personal Epistemology: The psychology of beliefs about knowledge and knowing*, ed. B. Hofer, P. Pintrich, 63–87. Mahwah, NJ: L. Erlbaum Associates.
21. Rooney, Phyllis. 1998. Putting Naturalized Epistemology to Work. In *Epistemology: The Big Questions*, ed. Linda Martin Alcoff, 285–305. Oxford: Blackwell Publishers Ltd.
22. Quine, W. V. O. 1969. Epistemology Naturalized. In *Ontological Relativity and Other Essays*, 69 – 90. New York: Columbia University Press.
23. Kitcher, Phillip. 1992. The Naturalists Return. In *Philosophical Review*, 101: 53–114.
24. Campbell, Donald T. 1987. Evolutionary Epistemology. In *Evolutionary Epistemology, Rationality and the Sociology of Knowledge*, ed. Gerard Radnitzky, W. W. Bartley III, 48–89. Chicago: Open Court Publishing Co.

25. Campbell, Donald T. 1987. Blind Variation and Selective Retention in Creative Thought as in Other Knowledge Processes. In *Evolutionary Epistemology, Rationality and the Sociology of Knowledge*, ed. Gerard Radnitzky, W.W. Bartley III, 48–89. Chicago: Open Court Publishing Co.

26. Popper, Karl R. 1987. Natural Selection and the Emergence of Mind. In *Evolutionary Epistemology, Rationality and the Sociology of Knowledge*, ed. Gerard Radnitzky, W. W. Bartley III, 48 –89. Chicago: Open Court Publishing Co.

27. James, William. 1975. *Pragmatism*. Cambridge: Harvard University Press.

28. Kant, Immanuel. 1936. *The Critique of Pure Reason*, Trans. Norman Kemp Smith. London: Macmillan and Co.

29. Reese, William L. 1980. *Dictionary of Philosophy and Religion: Eastern and Western Thought*. Atlantic Highlands, NJ: Humanities Press.

30. Hesse, Hermann. 1969. *Magister Ludi (The Glass Bead Game)*, Trans. Richard and Clara Winston. New York: Holt, Rinehart and Winston.

31. BonJour, Laurence. 1985. The Elements of Coherentism. In *Structure of Empirical Knowledge*, 87–110. Cambridge: Harvard University Press.

32. Williams, Michael. 2001. *Problems of Knowledge: A Critical Introduction to Epistemology*. New York: Oxford University Press.

33. Horwich, Paul. 1992. Bayesianism. In *A Companion to Epistemology*, ed. Jonathan Dancy, Ernest Sosa, 40–44. Oxford: Blackwell Publishers Ltd.

34. Rogers, G. A. J. 1992. Bacon, Francis, Lord Verulam. In *A Companion to Epistemology*, ed. Jonathan Dancy, Ernest Sosa, 40. Oxford: Blackwell Publishers Ltd.

35. James, William. 1975. *Pragmatism*. Cambridge: Harvard University Press.

36. Anderson, Theo. 2007. One Hundred Years of Pragmatism. *The Wilson Quarterly* XXXI-3:27–35.

37. Rorty, Richard. 1998. Pragmatism, Relativism, and Irrationalism. In *Epistemology: The Big Questions*, ed. Linda Martin Alcoff, 336–348. Oxford: Blackwell Publishers Ltd.

38. Moran, Dermot. 2002. Editor's Introduction. In *The Phenomenology Reader*, ed. Dermot Moran, Timothy Mooney, 1–26. London: Routledge.

39. Reinach, Adolf, 1969. Concerning Phenomenology, trans. Dallas Willard. *The Personalist* 50:194-224.

40. Laverty, Susann M. 2003. Hermeneutic Phenomenology and Phenomenology: A Comparison of Historical and Methodological Considerations. *International Journal of Qualitative Methods* 2(3):21–35.

41. Palmer, Richard E. 1969. *Hermeneutics: Interpretation Theory in Schleiermacher, Dilthey, Heidegger, and Gadamer*. Evanston: Northwestern University Press.

42. Palmer, Richard E. 1969. *Hermeneutics: Interpretation Theory in Schleiermacher, Dilthey, Heidegger, and Gadamer*. Evanston: Northwestern University Press.

43. Gadamer, Hans-Georg. 1989. The Hermeneutic Circle and the Problem of Prejudices. In *Truth and Method*, 2nd Revised Edition. London: The Continuum Publishing Company.

5

Exploring the Epistemic Terrain

ANTICIPATORY SUMMARY

How does the subject matter of Section I relate to the practical world of organizations, specifically to learning, the growth of knowledge, and the evolution of a knowledge enhancing culture? More to the point, what foundational topics remain to be explored to support the proposition that reliable and effectual practices exist for producing knowledge in contrast to mere belief?

Recognizing the need to begin to think in terms of real world situations involving different conceptions of reality and different ways of knowing, this chapter shifts the focus from theoretical and foundational subject matter to applications. In this chapter, we begin to survey what we have called the epistemic terrain or the field of convergence of conceptions of reality and theories of knowledge (epistemic styles or ways of belief formation and knowing).

Integrating Realities and Theories

The corollary to the argument that no single theory or approach to knowing applies uniformly to all realities is that certain theories are especially suited, in varying degree and sometimes in concert with other theories, to knowing about specific realities. In a negative sense, an inaccurate view of reality can result in the application of ways of forming beliefs suited only to the invalid conception of reality leading to the generation of false beliefs.

In Chapter 3, we argued that objects of belief vary; seeking knowledge, therefore, requires that we answer questions pertaining to knowledge about what? These answers led to a classification of realities that have meaning for life in organizations. In Chapter 4, we acknowledged that there are many theories of knowledge and examined the theories identified as the most relevant to organizational life. These theories determine *how* we form beliefs and seek to know as individuals and, ultimately, shape *what* we know.

This chapter summarizes and integrates the material from Chapters 3 and 4 and converges around multiple levels of diversity to be explored in this and subsequent chapters. This diversity pertains to 1) the reality or realities about which knowledge is sought, 2) the approach (specific theory) or approaches to belief formation or knowing that potential knowers bring to bear in seeking to know, 3) the degree of relevance between a defined reality and the application of specific theory, 4) the attributes of potential knowers as knowing subjects, and 5) the dimensions of organizational life that affect and are affected by the growth of knowledge.

Bridging Theories

Recalling the central argument that *how* we form the beliefs we hold influences *what* we believe and whether or not our beliefs are likely to be true, it follows that diverse and often divergent approaches to knowing play an influential role in the existence of contradictory beliefs and assumptions about common realities. Such divergent beliefs are likely to constrain effective learning and the growth of knowledge. It is argued that certain theories or approaches to knowing are potentially able to bridge or reconcile apparently incompatible approaches to knowing. The bridging and reconciling attributes of these theories are set forth and explored in this chapter.

EXPLORING THE EPISTEMIC TERRAIN

As we shift in this chapter from a focus on foundational subject matter to applications, there is a need to begin to think in terms of real world situations involving different conceptions of reality and different ways of knowing and the implications of these differences on the growth of knowledge and effective action. In this chapter we will begin to fully explore what we have called the epistemic terrain or the field of convergence of conceptions of reality and epistemic styles or ways of knowing. In any circumstance, conceptions of reality may vary from accurate to approximate to blatantly incorrect and by level from perceptions of the consequences of a deeper reality to the deeper reality itself, the latter representing the operative reality within which beneficial action may be taken. We have argued that reality is nonhomogenous and relevant approaches to knowing are generally reality specific.

Consider a circumstance defined by a set of indisputable facts about which a decision is required that will determine action to be taken. Consider further that members of the community or the decision-making group hold different perspectives and beliefs regarding the facts and make sense of them in different ways. In this circumstance, multiple choices can be made. Some choices are objectively better than others. What is the optimal among what could be a good set of choices? What is the least objectionable among what may be a bad set of choices? Which interpretation of the facts and the circumstance is the most meaningful and the most accurate? Which approach or approaches to knowing about this set of facts is most likely to produce the best answers and the most effective action?

If the facts at some level are indisputable, all the members of the group understand and agree on the reality in question, at least at the level of the facts. For example, consider the reality of an organization whose sales, revenue, and margins are down and costs are up. What do these facts mean and what do the members *believe* about the facts and the circumstance? *How* do they come to believe what they believe and how does this relate to *what* they believe? Do the differences in belief about the meaning of the facts create a barrier to reaching a decision? Does one of the beliefs reflect an approach to knowing more appropriate to knowing about this reality? Can the group agree on this approach? If not, is there a way to reconcile the divergent perspectives, beliefs, and bases for forming beliefs and does this reconciling approach result in the best answer? Or, does the dominant personality or politics or the path of least resistance carry the day?

Under a different circumstance, the facts themselves may be in dispute. However, given that facts have the character of verifiable objectivity, such disputes are usually reconcilable. Difficulties tend to arise when there is no contention over the raw facts, as in the example of an organization with declining financial performance in the previous paragraph, but the meaning of the underlying reality is in dispute. Is the underlying and operative reality defined by the competitors becoming stronger or the market contracting or the escalation of the costs of labor and materials or poor performance of the company's employees or some combination of these causes?

What are the factors underpinning the failure to comprehend the reality in question? In any circumstance, how can an inappropriate way of knowing about the reality in question be identified and isolated? Moreover, how can the dominant person or persons in the group with unjustified beliefs and inappropriate ways of knowing about the reality in question and who tends to strongly influence the group have their influence diminished?

In conflict situations, two or more individuals or groups look at the same circumstance and see two or more entirely different meanings and sets of implications. Beliefs and world-views differ and create conflict. Is there a way to look at the same reality and agree on what it is and what it means? Is there a way to bridge or reconcile different beliefs or, more importantly, is there a way to reconcile how the divergent beliefs are formed and sustained and taken to be knowledge for the purpose of resolving conflict?

There are important assumptions that bear on whether the questions raised above are worth asking. The first assumption pertains to good will. In asking such questions, there is an assumption that individuals and groups *want* to make the best decisions and take the most effective action and resolve conflict. Unfortunately, this is not always the case. In about 1500, Niccolo Machiavelli wrote, "It can be observed that men use various methods in pursuing their own personal objectives, such as glory and riches. And so, he should have a flexible disposition, varying as fortune and circumstances dictate—he should not deviate from what is good if that is possible but he should know how to do evil if that is necessary."[1] Machiavellians, now taken to be exemplars of behavior advocated by Machiavelli, are defined as deceitful and cunning—amoral, double dealing and unscrupulous—yet astute, shrewd and wily. Machiavellians say all the right things about common cause and teamwork and act in their own self-interest.[2]

The second assumption pertains to the existence of a cooperative as opposed to a competitive environment. Competition and cooperation coexist in society and in our organizations. There is clearly a place for competition, in games for example, although teams must be cooperative in order to compete effectively. There is a place for competition in identifying and nurturing finely honed skills and providing incentives to excel. Cooperation within a community or group, however, is necessary when the purpose of the group is problem solving, learning, enhancing knowledge, and acting collaboratively. Our social norms seem to favor and reward competition, but when competition within a group dominates cooperation, the growth of knowledge and the common good are the losers. Within such groups, when preconception-hardening debate focused on "winning" is tolerated and even promoted, dialogue, which can provide the opening to new perspectives that can lead to learning and the growth of knowledge, suffers.[3] As we will see in the chapters of Section II, the motivation to *know* is the imperfect but only remedy to "out of control" competition and the actions of Machiavellians and, therefore, the only consistent route to good will and cooperation.

In Chapter 1, we explored the profound consequences of knowing in contrast to believing falsely. We also took account of the growth of knowledge as primarily a matter of collective and cooperative effort. Section I: Foundations is comprised of Chapters 2 through 5, the current chapter. In Chapter 2, we addressed what it means *to know,* as knowledge is traditionally understood by looking at belief, justification and truth. In Chapter 3, we argued that seeking knowledge requires that we answer the question: knowledge about what? These answers led to the classification of realities that have meaning for life in organizations. Chapter 4 acknowledged that there are many theories of knowledge, which shape *how* we know as individuals and, ultimately, *what* we know and surveyed the theories identified as the most relevant to organizational life. How, then, does the subject matter of Section I relate to the practical world of organizations, specifically to learning and the growth of knowledge and the evolution of a knowledge enhancing culture? The purpose of this chapter is to summarize and integrate the content of Chapters 2, 3, and 4 and lay the groundwork for Section II: Applications.

A set of foundational arguments was introduced in Chapter 1 and used to frame the development of the chapters of Section I. The first three of these arguments are revisited below:

- There are multiple realities that affect and are affected by life in organizations. The whole of any circumstance may embody multiple realities.
- Various theories of knowledge or approaches to knowing exist. Each has something to say about belief, truth, and justification.
- No single theory or approach to knowing applies to all realities in the same way and to the same degree. Multiple approaches to knowing may apply to the same reality.

INTEGRATING REALITIES AND THEORIES

An ontology proposed in Chapter 3 categorizes the relevant realities of life in organizations and presents them in the table (Figure 5.1) restated below.

The essential meaning of this ontology is that multiple realities have a bearing on life in organizations and how these realities are conceived and how knowledge about them is sought have practical consequences for organizations. These realities are also multi-dimensional. There are objective and subjective dimensions to each of these realities, varying in degree and nature. The degree of objectivity and independence from human mediation diminishes while the degree of subjectivity increases moving from left to right in the table. The constructed realities have both internal and external dimensions. The internal dimension relates to the organization itself while the external dimension relates to the organization's environment.

The corollary to the argument that no single theory or approach to knowing applies uniformly to all realities is that certain theories are especially suited, in varying degree and sometimes in concert with other theories, to knowing about specific realities. Figure 5.2 integrates the theories of knowledge surveyed in Chapter 4 (with the exception of contextualism which will be described below) with the realities identified in Chapter 3 and summarized above in this chapter.

The theories connected to each reality are categorized by degree of relevance. The table is divided into two sections. The primarily relevant theories are represented above the dotted line; the remaining theories are

Natural Reality	Constructed Reality		
Physical or Natural Reality	*Material Reality* (Internal and External)	*Non-Material Reality* (Internal and External)	*Conceptual Reality* (Internal and External)
Existence and states of Physical or Natural Objects and Phenomena	Money Performance Potentials Limits	Culture Functional/Political Structures Purpose Definitions – Success/ Failure	Ethics/Morality (Relevance, Application) Character of the Whole (Emergence, Gestalt)

FIGURE 5.1
Multiple realities of organizational life.

Natural Reality	Constructed Reality		
Physical or Natural Reality	*Material Reality* (Internal and External)	*Non-Material Reality* (Internal and External)	*Conceptual Reality* (Internal and External)
Existence and states of Physical or Natural Objects and Phenomena	Money Performance Potentials Limits	Culture Functional/Political Structures Purpose Definitions - Success/Failure	Ethics/Morality (Relevance, Application) Character of the Whole (Emergence, Gestalt)
Highly Relevant *Empiricism* *Hermeneutic Phenomenology*	**Highly Relevant** *Pragmatism* *Hermeneutic Phenomenology*	**Highly Relevant** *Hermeneutic Phenomenology* *Pragmatism*	**Highly Relevant** *Coherentism* *Hermeneutic Phenomenology* *Pragmatism*
Relevant *Contextualism* *Reliabilism*	**Relevant** *Contextualism*	**Relevant** *Coherentism* *Evolutionary Epistemology (Analogical) Contextualism*	**Relevant** *Rationalism* *Foundationalism* *Contextualism*
Secondarily Relevant *Rationalism* *Coherentism*	**Secondarily Relevant** *Rationalism* *Coherentism* *Empiricism*	**Secondarily Relevant** *Rationalism* *Empiricism*	**Secondarily Relevant**
Possibly Relevant *Evolutionary Epistemology (Analogical) Naturalized Epistemology (Less Reductionist)*	**Possibly Relevant** *Reliabilism* *Foundationalism* *Evolutionary Epistemology (Analogical) Naturalized Epistemology (Less Reductionist)*	**Possibly Relevant** *Foundationalism* *Reliabilism* *Naturalized Epistemology (Less Reductionist)*	**Possibly Relevant** *Evolutionary Epistemology (Analogical) Naturalized Epistemology (Less Reductionist)*
Not Relevant *Pragmatism* *Foundationalism* *Naturalized Epistemology* *Evolutionary Epistemology (Literal)*	**Not Relevant** *Evolutionary Epistemology (Literal) Naturalized Epistemology (Reductionist)*	**Not Relevant** *Naturalized Epistemology (Reductionist) Evolutionary Epistemology (Literal)*	**Not Relevant** *Empiricism* *Reliabilism* *Evolutionary Epistemology (Literal) Naturalized Epistemology (Reductionist)*

FIGURE 5.2
Theories of knowledge and relevant reality.

shown below the line. We asserted in Chapter 1 and will argue in Section II that individuals tend to be predisposed to a dominant approach or a related set of approaches to knowing represented by these theories. Our parsing of the theories by reality and categorizing them by degree of relevance is our own assessment and has no bearing on what actual approaches to belief formation or knowing any specific individual may bring to any reality and knowledge-seeking situation. It should be noted that individual predisposition and variation is a matter of degree or dominance. For example, we are all foundationalists at *some* level—we all have basic beliefs that influence our beliefs about other things. We all learn from experience and are, therefore, empiricists to some degree. We are all rationalists to some extent when we exercise reason and logic although we may clearly not view reason as the source of all knowledge. The rationale for attaching theories to specific realities is described in the sections that follow.

Natural or Physical Reality

Natural reality includes the geology of petroleum reserves; the molecular structure of chemical products; the functional characteristics of catalysts and the labor required for a given output in a petrochemical company; the number, functional quality, duration, and patient outcomes associated with procedures; the labor per unit of patient service; infection rates and medication errors in a hospital; the functional specifications, product performance characteristics, and product failure rates in a software company; and the molecular character of compounds, efficacy in animal models, efficacy in humans, side effects in humans, and inputs and outputs of bioreactors in a biopharmaceutical company.

Highly Relevant Theories

Empiricism seeks to know based solely on experience and scientific methods and on the assumption that reality is independent of human mediation or subjectivity. Empiricism assumes that truth corresponds to this independent reality. Knowledge beyond that which is immediately experienced, however, is considered to be contingent since inferential necessity cannot be granted from experience alone. In other words, if experience is our only basis for knowing, that which has not been experienced can only be known conditionally. Inductive and probable inferences are made from the experience of observation, measurement, and comparison.

Hermeneutic phenomenology grants the possibility of the independent existence of objects and phenomena consistent with the character of physical reality, but also takes account of subjectivity. It is both descriptive and interpretive and, therefore, seeks to know about what exists and about what this existence means. It intends to blend a lack of theoretical bias in seeking to know with rules of interpretation and the perspective that knowledge of natural reality is only possible by way of our own subjectivity. This opening of the door to subjectivity may provide an opportunity to break the social bonds associated with established theories and procedures when these are inadequate for knowing about the whole of a natural or physical reality.[4] An opportunity may also be provided to take the active role of observation in shaping reality into account.

Observation of physical phenomena measurably alters the character of this reality at the quantum level. "There is no absolute truth at the quantum level. ...This is the really fundamental feature of the quantum world. It is interesting that there are limits to our knowledge of what an electron is doing when we *are* looking at it, but it is absolutely mind-blowing to discover that we have no idea at all what it is doing when we are not looking at it."[5] While discernible change in physical objects at the everyday or macro level due to observation is not usual, change of the reality of human (like quantum) phenomena as a result of observation is common.

Relevant Theories

Contextualism was not presented as a theory in Chapter 4 because it does not reject or conform to either side of the positivist/constructivist dualism developed in Chapter 4. In contextualism, the fundamental idea is that standards for justification and correctly attributing or claiming knowledge are not fixed but subject to circumstantial variation. Standards-related factors vary according to this circumstantial variation or context, including the relevant traits of persons making knowledge claims, and influence the status of knowledge claims and challenges to such claims. These standards-related factors have been classified under five main headings by Michael Williams. The first is *intelligibility*. Intelligible justification refers to the capability of knowledge claims to be understood or comprehended. More particularly, intelligibility pertains to the ability of persons claiming to know to cause others to make sense of such claims. Further, constraints associated with intelligibility have to do with the ability of the evaluators of knowledge claims to be able to credibly and reliably ask meaningful questions. The second factor exercising contextual constraints on justification pertains to direction of inquiry or *methodology*. "What we *are* looking into is a function of what we are leaving alone (or *not* looking into). We can no more inquire into everything at once than we can travel simultaneously in all directions." Direction of inquiry, therefore, limits the range and impact of the dubious and the irrelevant. The point of such methodological constraints is to make focused questioning possible.

Factors of the third type are *dialectical*. Given intelligibility and a certain direction of inquiry, the reciprocal influence of challenges, potential "defeaters" or alternatives and responses to such challenges shape the context and the results of dialogue. The epistemic or knowledge-related status of claims and beliefs change with developments within this dialectical context. The constraint of reasonability is labeled *economic* and identified as the fourth factor. The idea of benefits and costs associated with any process of justification helps to define context. "Anything we value is a benefit and anything we would rather avoid is a cost. I call these considerations 'economic' to stress the point that there is typically no purely epistemological (and non-contextual) answer to the question of what degree of severity or rigor in seeking to know is contextually reasonable." Severity and rigor are appropriate when being right about knowledge claims is highly important and less appropriate when the cost of being wrong is low.

Contextual factors of a fifth type are *situational*. Relevant settings or contexts are not exhausted by intelligibility, methodological, dialectical and economic considerations. Facts about the actual situations about which knowledge claims are offered or beliefs are held are crucial as well. Situational factors pertain to such facts and highlight the externalist element in contextualism.[6] (Parenthetical comments are the authors'.)

These five contextual factors converge around the idea of relevant alternatives. Keith DeRose has contended, "The most popular form of contextualism, I think it is fair to say, is what has been called the 'relevant alternatives' view of knowledge."[7] According to relevant alternatives, we need to qualify rather than deny the absolute character of knowledge. In order to know a proposition, our evidence need eliminate only the *relevant* alternatives, where relevant is determined by the standards. Relevant alternatives preserves the view of knowledge as an absolute concept but its absoluteness is relative to a standard (of justification); this is how contextualism differs from relativism.[8] As elaborated by Fred Dretske, consider the two similar but different concepts of flat and empty. Both appear to be absolute; however, their absolute character is relative to a standard. In the case of flat, there is a standard for what counts as a "bump"; in the case of empty, there is a standard for what counts as a "thing." Microscopic irregularities on the surface of a desk or the presence of dust in a warehouse would not deny the flatness of a desk or the emptiness of a warehouse. To be flat is to be free of *relevant* bumps. To be empty is to be devoid of *relevant* things.[9]

In summary, contextualism as a theory of knowledge pertains to identifying and potentially eliminating relevant alternatives or propositional defeaters to any knowledge claim through the application of contextual standards. Contextualism seems to provide an appropriate approach to knowing when there is a need, for example in interdisciplinary settings, to form true and justified beliefs about the *whole* of some multi-dimensional natural or physical reality. Such a nonreductionist approach would be expressed in recognition of circumstantial variation of standards. It could also be productively applied when there is a need to challenge established and fundamental assumptions associated with a natural or physical reality or with the processes for seeking to know about such a reality.

Reliabilism was first formulated as the assertion that a belief is knowledge if it is true, certain, and obtained by a reliable process.[10] Reliabilism is a process theory focused on cognitive or psychological processes that have reliably produced high truth-ratio results in the past. In addressing the subjective dimension of knowing about natural reality, reliabilism assumes an independent reality, which is compatible with the conception of independence associated with natural or physical reality. It also assumes something like a correspondence conception of truth, which is the basis for being able to claim results with a high truth-ratio.

Secondarily Relevant Theories

Rationalism asserts that reason, independent of experience, is the primary source of knowledge. The use of logic and reason clearly supports the formation of true and justified beliefs about natural or any other reality. However, rationalism's granting of *necessity* to inferences flowing from *a priori* notions of natural reality is inconsistent with the character of natural reality. A *necessary* truth applies to all possible worlds, not only those experienced and *a priori* knowledge by definition is independent of all experience. Rationalism, therefore, is inappropriate as a primary approach to knowing about physical or natural reality. Similarly, *coherentism* as a theory that looks to the manner in which a set of beliefs come together to express the truth of the whole supports knowing about natural reality. Nevertheless, the coherence of a network of beliefs about a natural reality does not primarily determine what we know about such a reality.

Possibly Relevant Theories

The analogical version of *evolutionary epistemology* and a subset of *naturalized epistemology* are possibly relevant to knowing about natural reality. Evolutionary epistemology is cognizant of and compatible with man's status as a product of natural selection, of biological and social evolution. As referenced in Chapter 4, "a blind-variation-and-selective-retention process is fundamental to all inductive achievements, to all genuine increases in knowledge, to all increases in fit of system to environment."[11] A problem with the analogy is that while variation is blind in biological evolution, variation is goal directed in intentional knowledge producing processes. Nonetheless, evolution as a metaphor for the growth of knowledge is thought to be illuminating and potentially engaging. Variation could be seen as the varied results of experiments and observation, selection as variation rendered valid by the ability to reproduce results, and retention as that which is institutionally sustained. Regarding naturalized epistemology, a modest, less reductionist form of a naturalized theory of knowledge is possibly relevant in seeking to know about natural reality. A theory that incorporates empirical results from psychology regarding how we remember, think, and reason within a normative framework is potentially useful in any growth of knowledge context.

Non-Relevant Theories

Pragmatism is focused on consequences. Its only test of probable truth associated with a proposition or action is what works best. Natural reality is poorly suited to the application of a pragmatic approach because natural reality exists in its own right irrespective of consequences. *Foundationalism*, while grounded on basic beliefs about an independent reality, is not an approach to knowing open to the existence of a circumstantial or provisional independent reality. Foundationalism can lead to the establishment of false premises and erroneous conclusions when contingent, empirical results are taken as necessary, basic beliefs.

The expansive form of *naturalized epistemology* and the literal variant of *evolutionary epistemology* seem to offer little practical value in seeking to know about natural or any other reality at this time. Reductionist and literal naturalism in epistemology seeks to describe the chemistry and neurobiology of learning and knowing and the evolution of these functions through natural selection. Based on understanding the actions of neurons and synapses, it aims to describe our uniqueness and diversity in *how* and *what* we know. "The brain is no longer an inaccessible black box." An ever-growing armory of experimental techniques such as the selective staining of neurons and their connecting pathways, electron microscopy, genetically modified mice, CAT scans, PET scans, MRI scans and functional MRI now provide us with an overlapping set of windows onto the brain's physical structure and neuronal activity.[12] For our practical purposes, however, until the arrival of a brave new world of instruments in the physical and virtual meeting spaces of organizations to measure and manipulate how and what we're coming to know, naturalized epistemology will be interesting but not very useful. Edward O. Wilson, the celebrated author and Harvard biologist, believes we are not yet there. In *Consilience: The Unity of Knowledge*, he argues, "the greatest enterprise of the mind has always been and will always be the attempted linkage of the sciences and the humanities." Wilson defines consilience as the linking of theories and facts across disciplines to create a common groundwork of explanation, writing "The belief in the possibility of consilience beyond science and across the great branches of learning is not yet science. It is a metaphysical worldview and a minority one at that, shared by only a few scientists and philosophers. It cannot be proved with logic from first principles or grounded in any definitive set of empirical tests, at least not by any yet conceived."[13]

Material Reality

Material reality is strongly institutional and objective. It is generally connected with currency or media of exchange and related indicators. Representations of material reality include money and associated ratios as expressed in internal financial reality, i.e., balance sheets, revenue, earnings, cost, and market share. External financial reality is expressed as the size of markets and the strength of competitors, property ownership and dimensions, material potential such as earnings and market capitalization, and material constraints such as debt and lack of investment capital.

Highly Relevant Theories

As described in Chapter 4, *Pragmatism* is characterized by the "pragmatic maxim," in which the meaning of a concept or proposition is to be sought in the practical consequences of its application. Regarding material reality as a constructed reality and in terms of knowing about what *is,* pragmatism evaluates consequences of reality to inform the nature of the reality itself; in terms of what *ought to be*, pragmatism looks to utility. In a normative sense, pragmatism looks to efficacy, potential, and limits to define the greatest good or utility among conceptual or propositional choices. *Hermeneutic phenomenology* is both descriptive and interpretive and is a highly relevant approach to knowing about the whole of an existing material reality. The methodology of hermeneutic phenomenology is iterative within the context of what has been described as the hermeneutical circle: "The whole receives its definition from the parts, and, reciprocally, the parts can only be understood in reference to a whole."[14] Hermeneutic phenomenology applies to the *apparent* (if not real) independence of both internal (to an organization) and external (an organization's environment) material realities.

Relevant Theories

Contextualism qualifies rather than denies the absolute character of knowledge. The contextualist asserts that what counts as knowledge (of the truth of some proposition) in some context depends upon the relevance or salience of the alternatives (alternative conceptions) in that context.[15] Based on the idea that standards for justification are not fixed but subject to circumstantial variation, the determination of whether alternatives are ruled out or defeated rests on the quality of justification in connection with relevant (to this context) standards. Another factor in establishing justification is an assessment of the degree to which something in the real world is at stake. To the extent that potential knowers care a great deal about the knowledge status of some proposition, standards for eliminating alternatives must be higher. Consider the proposition that an organization's material reality reflects the prospect of good, long-term financial health. In seeking to determine if this proposition counts as knowledge, a contextualist approach could suggest two things. First, the standard for justification would be defined within the context of some established meaning of good, long-term financial health, incorporating some combination of current and historical internal and external financial indicators. Second, given that a great deal of value could be associated with getting this assessment right, a high degree of rigor would be required to rule out alternative conceptions.

Secondarily Relevant Theories

In spite of the lack of harmony between *rationalism* and *coherentism* as a pair of theories on the one hand and *empiricism* on the other, these theories sit together as relevant approaches to knowing about material reality in a supportive or secondary way. In a manner similar to that associated with natural reality, the near or apparent independence of material reality causes rationalism and coherentism to be unsuitable as primary approaches to knowing about this reality. However, also as in the case of natural reality, the use of reason and logic (rationalism) and assessing the coherence of a system of beliefs (coherentism) in the process of seeking to know about material reality are highly useful, even required. Empiricism engenders skepticism regarding claims of good, useful, beneficial, productive, non-productive, etc., often associated with material reality, but the quantitative methods associated with empiricism are relevant to knowing about material reality, bearing in mind that material reality is constructed in spite of its appearing to be otherwise.

Possibly Relevant Theories

To the extent that psychological processes such as perception, memory, cognition, and introspection can be shown to have a normative influence on forming beliefs about an independently appearing yet constructed (material) reality, *reliabilism* could have possible relevance. However, reliabilism is oriented to subjectivity in the *process* of knowing about what is assumed to be an independent and objective reality, which paradoxically and by definition denies a subjective dimension to the reality itself. Reliabilism's relevance to knowing about material reality is, therefore, possible but conceptually problematic. *Foundationalism* is characterized as a commitment to a special class of beliefs, so-called basic beliefs. All other beliefs are permitted only by the nature of their relationship to this set of basic beliefs. With a strong emphasis on what *ought to be*, basic beliefs for some people, irrespective of how those beliefs are derived, define what is good or bad, right or wrong, where such characterizations give meaning to the idea of material reality. Nonetheless, the concept of necessary or deductive inferences flowing from basic beliefs regarding material reality speaks against the use of foundationalism. The analogical version of *evolutionary epistemology* as represented in the variation-selection-retention model is possibly relevant in seeking to know about material reality. Variation could be seen in the myriad ways material reality may be represented with selection as the alignment of specific representations with success, for example in pragmatic terms, and retention as that which is institutionally sustained. As indicated earlier, the modest form of *naturalized epistemology* is potentially useful in any growth of knowledge context.

Nonmaterial Reality

Broadly speaking, factors pertaining to culture define nonmaterial reality. Examples of nonmaterial reality include the attributes of culture, especially what organizational members believe about themselves and their environment; the character of operational and functional states within the organization; organizational purpose as internalized by members of the organization; political structures or the centers of power and influence; operative definitions of key terms such as success and failure; and the cultural, structural, and definitional characteristics of the external environment.

Highly Relevant Theories

Hermeneutic phenomenology, as both a descriptive and an interpretive approach to knowing, is ideally suited for this constructed reality with strong objective and subjective dimensions. Because hermeneutic phenomenology is oriented to both what exists and to the meaning of what exists, it is often equated with qualitative research. Briefly, qualitative research relies on qualitative rather than quantitative methods and emphasizes explanation through understanding rather than predictive testing. Culture is strongly reflective of nonmaterial reality and has been the central concern of social anthropology. A strand of hermeneutic phenomenology is structuralism which took an anthropological turn with Levi-Strauss and others and offers important insights in the study of culture. Structuralism is based on the idea that all cultures have constant and durable structures, which the members hold unconsciously and prior to reflection. Within the context of culture as nonmaterial reality, such structures pertain directly to the examples cited above, i.e., to systems of belief about the organization and its environment, the character of operational and functional norms, organizational purpose as internalized by members of the organization, crystallized definitions of important terms such as success and failure and political structures that define centers of power and influence.

Pragmatism postulates that the meaning of a circumstance or proposition is to be found in the practical consequences or outcomes associated with its existence or application. The consequences of hardened patterns of behavior and the collective beliefs that drive them are likely to be highly influential in the life of organizations. The practical effects of culture, in other words, may signal an organization's downfall or its long-term success. Pragmatism pertains to knowledge about culture in two important ways. First, an evaluation of organizational outcomes within the framework of the organization's operating environment can inform the character of culture itself. Is an organization's culture congruent with its internal and external reality and its aspirations? If culture needs to change because of its incongruence with reality, the second way of pragmatism provides an approach to knowing about what culture *ought* to be. It provides the basis for building from consequences to a culture whose attributes are consistent with reality and supportive of aspirations.

Relevant Theories

Coherentism is based on the argument that knowledge or the lack of it is determined by how beliefs relate to each other in a coherent or an incoherent way. Justification is found in the character of the whole as comprised of a system of logically linked and intelligible individual beliefs. Coherentism tends to focus on the objective reality of culture, but it is open to the idea of gradations of truth and knowledge through inductive logic and notions of probability. A high degree of coherence and interconnection among a set of actual (in contrast to espoused) beliefs about an organization and its environment comes together to produce a holistic conception of overall culture with a high probability of validity.

The analogical version of *evolutionary epistemology* is also oriented to the objective reality of culture. Application of the variation-selection-retention model as the mechanism for the evolution of culture, informs the character of culture itself and how culture can further evolve. *Contextualism* recognizes the objective aspect of culture, but also takes account of its subjective dimension. The contextualist asserts that knowledge about culture is subject to contextual variation and the proposition that standards for correctly claiming to know are not fixed but variable according to circumstances. Contextual variation, for example, could relate to whether the potential knower is embedded in the cultural reality or not. Depending on circumstances, contextual standards could be derived from pragmatism, coherentism, or hermeneutic phenomenology.

Secondarily Relevant Theories

Rationalism acknowledges subjectivity in knowing about anything and nonmaterial reality has a strong subjective component. It applies *a priori* rules of reason in establishing conditions of valid inference (noncontradiction, etc.) in the process of knowing about the beliefs and related actions that comprise nonmaterial reality. *Empiricism* is secondarily relevant simply because, at some level, experience plays a role in what we believe and potentially know about any reality including nonmaterial reality. It is important to note, however, that while nonmaterial reality has an objective dimension, it also has a subjective dimension and empiricism takes no account of subjectivity. The assumption of nonmaterial reality as independent and objective, therefore, creates a danger of reification in the application of empiricism. Reification, defined as the process of regarding something nonmaterial or abstract as a material or concrete thing, is reductionism in the extreme.

Possibly Relevant Theories

Foundationalism is not an approach to forming beliefs and knowing that is open to what actually exists. There is some peril, therefore, in the prospect of the predetermination of the character of nonmaterial reality by basic beliefs, as foundationalism requires. In other words, any set of basic beliefs underpinning foundationalism limits or circumscribes what can be positively learned about nonmaterial reality through descriptive, analytical and interpretive processes. Foundationalism is possibly (and arguably) relevant to knowing about nonmaterial reality by shaping the beliefs of some potential knowers regarding what *ought to be*. The danger in this context, however, is that basic beliefs may produce false premises and false conceptions of what *ought to be*.

By looking to the reliability of certain psychological processes in seeking to know, *reliabilism* is possibly relevant assuming some relatively objective standard of truth associated with nonmaterial reality can be defined. However, as in the case of material reality, the admonition regarding reliabilism and its possible relevance for nonmaterial reality is that even though its processes are subjective, it assumes an independent reality. Nonmaterial reality is unambiguously constructed by human belief and action. The less reductionist form of *naturalized epistemology* is possibly relevant in seeking to know about nonmaterial reality. As indicated earlier, empirical and normative results from psychology are potentially useful in any growth of knowledge context.

Conceptual Reality

Conceptual reality pertains to the ethical and moral concepts that have a bearing on the organization and its environment. Further, the validity, efficacy, and justification of a specific ethical or moral position contribute to an organization's conceptual reality. From another perspective, awareness of the character of the whole of an organization as emergent, as greater than (or less than) the sum of its natural, material, nonmaterial, and ethical realities, is an abstraction but also an expression of an organization's conceptual reality.

Highly Relevant Theories

Coherentism may productively apply to knowing about all aspects of this reality from relevant ethical or moral concepts to the validity of any specific ethical position to the coherence of collective beliefs about ethical behavior to the character of the organization as a whole. Coherence in this context refers to integrity among actual beliefs and between beliefs and actions as represented in the internal life of the organization. The impact on what *ought to be* (ethically and morally) is through the coherent alignment of beliefs. Gradations of truth and knowledge are informed by probability and inductive logic.

Hermeneutic phenomenology also addresses all aspects of conceptual reality through a reliance on both valid description and interpretation of phenomena in an iterative way using the concept of the hermeneutical circle. A degree of objectivity is acknowledged along with subjectivity's significant role in interpreting as well as shaping conceptual reality. *Pragmatism* looks to the consequences or potential consequences of behaving consistently with ethical or moral standards to define the validity, efficacy, and justification for such standards. Knowing about this dimension of conceptual reality is based on the potential or actual utility of one set of practices in relation to another. There is an emphasis in pragmatism to fit with external reality. By aligning belief and action with what produces the best results, there is an impact on what *ought to be*.

Relevant Theories

In terms of knowing about all aspects of conceptual reality, an approach which pairs *contextualism* with another relevant theory such as pragmatism or coherentism to establish context-specific standards of justification may eliminate relevant alternatives and result in a valid claim of knowledge about conceptual reality. *Rationalism* relies on universal ideas such as good and bad and right and wrong derived through reflection and reason. From such concepts, necessary truths are deduced and rationalism takes its place as a relevant theory with a strong emphasis on what *ought to be*. The relevance of *foundationalism* is also based on an emphasis on what *ought to be*. For some people, a basic set of beliefs, however derived, may define the ethical and moral issues and the relevant and appropriate positions and actions. Both rationalism and foundationalism have little to do with describing the actual character of the organization as a whole.

Possibly Relevant Theories

The analogical form of *evolutionary epistemology* is potentially relevant in knowing about conceptual reality. Such possible relevance would be due to the application of seeking to know about the evolution of ethical and moral concepts as a step in the process of defining such concepts and their implications. Evolutionary epistemology as expressed in the variation-selection-retention model, when understood analogically, produces a relatively objective view of aspects of conceptual reality. *Naturalized epistemology* in a modest and limited form is possibly relevant in seeking to know about conceptual reality. As indicated for other realities, a theory that incorporates empirically derived insights from psychology within a normative framework is potentially useful in any growth of knowledge context.

Non-Relevant Theories

Empiricism and *reliabilism* join the literal form of *evolutionary epistemology* and the reductionist version of *naturalized epistemology* as nonrelevant regarding conceptual reality. At some level, experience plays a role in what we believe about conceptual reality. However, subjectivity cannot be separated from conceptual reality and empiricism takes no account of subjectivity. Also, the assumption of reality as independent and objective in empiricism produces false premises and creates a risk of reification. Reliabilism, in looking to the reliability of certain psychological processes to produce high truth-ratio results, is similar to empiricism in assuming an independent and objective reality, which is distinctly out of phase with the constructed character of conceptual reality.

BRIDGING OR RECONCILING THEORIES

As developed and presented in Figure 5.2 and the previous segment of this chapter, some theories of knowledge are relevant to certain realities and appropriate to knowing about them and not to others. The degree and form of relevance also vary by theory from reality to reality. This is consistent with our argument from Chapter 1, restated earlier in this chapter: No single theory or approach to knowing applies to all realities in the same way and to the same degree, and multiple approaches to knowing may apply to the same reality. Revisiting another foundational argument from Chapter 1, individuals tend to be predisposed to one or a closely related set of dominant approaches to forming beliefs and seek to apply these approaches to knowing (or merely believing) to any reality.

At this point in the progression of this chapter, it is appropriate to refer to the hypotheses identified in Chapter 1:

- The growth of knowledge is a function of the relevance and efficacy of the approach to knowing employed, subject to the nature of the reality about which we hope to know.
- The growth of knowledge is influenced by the personal and subjective attributes of the individuals engaged in the process of coming to know, specifically including approach to knowing or belief formation.

- Within the work of groups, specific approaches to knowing can transcend and help to bridge or reconcile the diverse approaches to knowing of individuals.
- The essential task of leadership is to bring about and sustain an environment conducive to the growth of knowledge.

Coming into focus around the argument that individuals tend to be predisposed to specific approaches to belief formation and the hypothesis that there are theories or approaches to knowing that can bridge and reconcile differences, it will have been noted that *hermeneutic phenomenology* and *contextualism* are shown in Figure 5.2 as primarily relevant to all realities and *pragmatism* is shown as primarily relevant to all constructed realities. These theories are, therefore, offered as potential bridging theories. Regarding the differences to be bridged or reconciled, as noted before, these differences may only be in degree or emphasis, yet these differences may be severe and, to quote William James again, "breed antipathies of the most pungent character." Although theorists through the years have appeared to be wedded to their own favored approaches to knowing about *any* reality, reconciling diverse approaches to knowing has been a topic of interest in epistemology since Kant.

For example, Kant sought to reconcile empiricism and rationalism through his "transcendental deduction." His argument took shape as follows. There can be no *a priori* knowledge (gained through rationalism), except of objects of *possible* experience (the knowledge of which is gained through empiricism). "But although knowledge is limited to objects of experience, it is not all derived from experience. The pure intuitions and the pure concepts of understanding are elements in knowledge, and both are found in us *a priori*. There are only two ways in which we can account for a *necessary* agreement of experience with the concepts of its objects; either experience makes these concepts possible or these concepts make experience possible." The categories (concepts) contain the grounds of the possibility of all experience; hence the second supposition is, in fact, the only way, according to Kant.[16] (Parenthetical comments are the authors'.)

The bridging requirement pertains to reconciling multiple and often incompatible approaches to knowing within a single reality or within a circumstance comprising multiple realities. Consider the consequences of a person prone to empiricism and one inclined to rationalism seeking to know about a natural or physical reality where agreement and decisionmaking is required. The perspectives and beliefs about this reality produced by each individual, while potentially rich and interesting, will probably differ and, if they differ, render agreement unlikely. It may or may not be useful to point out to the rationalist, even though he may have valid concerns about empiricism within the context of this reality, that his primary approach to knowing about natural reality is inappropriate. However, the rationalist may be able to relate to an approach based on hermeneutic phenomenology while the empiricist may be able to be satisfied with such an approach as well. Consistent with the character of natural reality and the sensibilities of the empiricist, hermeneutic phenomenology grants the possibility of the independent existence of objects and phenomena, but also takes account of subjectivity and, therefore, may appeal to the concerns of the rationalist. It could be argued that the essence of Kant's "transcendental deduction" is captured in hermeneutic phenomenology.

Consider the potential to know about the whole of some natural, multi-dimensional reality among empiricists from different disciplines as well as among reliabilists and foundationalists. In this interdisciplinary setting, is there an integrative or non-reductionist approach to knowing that supports the challenge of inward looking and established, empirically-driven, discipline-based assumptions as well as the assumptions associated with reliable psychological processes and basic beliefs? Contextualism could provide such an approach based on its recognition of the independence of natural reality and its openness to circumstantial variation of standards of justification and elimination of relevant alternatives. Consider further a group comprised of rationalists, empiricists, foundationalists, and coherentists seeking to know about a situation with financial and cultural dimensions. The situation in question would embody material and nonmaterial realities. Given the knowing styles of the members of the group and bearing in mind the potential value of this diversity, coherentism is primarily relevant only to nonmaterial reality while empiricism and rationalism are not primarily relevant to either reality and foundationalism is likely to have no relevance for either reality. Regarding this situation, looking only at the practical consequences and outcomes (or potential outcomes) of the situation could lead the group members to pragmatism as an effective bridging and consensus building approach.

Although reconciliation did not occur, pragmatism or hermeneutic phenomenology could have provided the possibility of reconciliation between two groups in conflict we observed, each with obvious foundationalist tendencies. Members of both groups were engaged in ministries to support poor and marginalized people. While the members of both groups were of the same religious denomination, their approaches were vastly different, apparently driven by their basic beliefs about politics, the role of the church, and the nature of the support that should be provided. There was a high level of antipathy between these groups as expressed in their negative comments about each other and their stated intent to avoid being in the same room together. Bearing in mind that foundationalists find common ground and compromise difficult, an unambiguous focus on consequences or outcomes by both groups, as prescribed by pragmatism, could have transcended basic beliefs and produced useful action. Alternatively, the rigor of phenomenology applied to the description of the circumstances upon which both groups were focused, overlaid by the rules of hermeneutic interpretation, could have brought the groups together. Left to their own inclinations, however, any benefit from their collaboration was lost as well as the potential for good will among people *claiming* a common system of belief and the motivation to help people.

FRAMING SECTION II

Multiple levels of diversity frame application of the material developed and presented in Section I. This diversity pertains to 1) the reality or realities about which knowledge is sought, 2) the approach (specific theory) or approaches to belief formation or knowing that potential knowers bring to bear in seeking to know, 3) the degree of relevance between a defined reality and the application of specific theory, 4) the attributes of potential knowers as knowing subjects, and 5) the dimensions of organizational life that affect and are affected by the growth of knowledge. The set of foundational arguments from Chapter 1, identified below, also frame Section II.

- Human action is set in motion by belief. *Institutionalized* beliefs are embodied in organizational culture.
- Action is valid and has value when the belief that drives it is aligned with reality. The growth of knowledge in organizations is largely the result of learning to align belief with reality.
- Individuals and their collectives tend to be predisposed to one or a closely related set of dominant approaches to forming beliefs and

seek to apply these approaches to knowing (or merely believing) to *any* reality.

- Diverse approaches to knowing can facilitate or constrain creativity, problem solving and the growth of knowledge.
- Learning and the growth of knowledge is a collective matter resulting from the interaction of individuals in group settings. Four organizational dimensions influence the effective interaction of individuals for the purpose of learning and creating or extending knowledge. These dimensions are *individuals (as knowing subjects), groups, leadership and culture.*

The rationale for this book was described in Chapter 1, including the clear intent to be nonprescriptive, as in seeking to define some number of "easy steps" to the growth of knowledge. Nevertheless, variations of the following questions will be addressed in each of the chapters of Section II: Why do we *not* know and how can we know more fully?

REFERENCES

1. Machiavelli, N. 1961. *The Prince*. Harmonds Worth, Middlesex: Penguin Books.
2. Douglas, Neil and Terry Wykowski. 1999. *Beyond Reductionism: Gateways for Learning and Change*. Boca Raton: St. Lucie Press.
3. Barber, Benjamin R. 2007. The Lost Art of Cooperation. *The Wilson Quarterly* XXXI-4:56–61.
4. Kuhn, Thomas S. 1970. *The Structure of Scientific Revolutions*, 2nd ed. Chicago: The University of Chicago Press.
5. Gribbin, John. 1984. *In Search of Schrodinger's Cat: Quantum Physics and Reality*. New York: Bantam Books.
6. Williams, Michael. 2001. *Problems of Knowledge: A Critical Introduction to Epistemology*. New York: Oxford University Press.
7. DeRose, Keith. 1992. Contextualism and Knowledge Attributions. In *Philosophy and Phenomenological Research* 52:913-929.
8. Cohen, Stewart. 1992. Relevant Alternatives. In *A Companion to Epistemology*, ed. Jonathan Dancy, Ernest Sosa, Erest, 430–433. Oxford: Blackwell Publishers.
9. Dretske, Fred. 1981. The Pragmatic Dimension of Knowledge. *Philosophical Studies* 40:363–378.
10. Ramsey, F. P. 1931. Knowledge. In *The Foundations of Mathematics and Other Essays*, ed. R.B. Braithwaite, 258–260. New York: Harcourt Brace.
11. Campbell, Donald T. 1960. Blind Variation and Selective Retention in Creative Thought as in Other Knowledge Processes. *The Psychological Review* 67:380–400.
12. Churchland, Paul M. 2002. Inner Spaces and Outer Spaces: the New Epistemology. *Proceedings and Addresses of the American Philosophical Association* 76:25–48.

13. Wilson, Edward O. 1998. *Consilience: The Unity of Knowledge*. New York: Alfred A. Knopf, Inc.

14. Palmer, Richard E. 1969. *Hermeneutics: Interpretation Theory in Schleiermacher, Dilthey, Heidegger, and Gadamer*. Evanston: Northwestern University Press.

15. Zagzebski, Linda. 2006. Ideal Agents and Ideal Observers in Epistemology. In *Epistemology Futures*, ed. Stephen Hetherington, 131 – 147. Oxford: Oxford University Press.

16. Kant, Immanuel. 1936. *The Critique of Pure Reason*, Trans. Norman Kemp Smith. London: Macmillan and Co. Ltd.

Section II

Applications

Change is difficult. The truth of this maxim is rarely disputed. There are many reasons why change is resisted and some of them are justified when change merely for the sake of it is proposed. The question to be asked with some urgency is why, in the face of compelling reasons to change and adapt, is change so difficult to bring about? It is widely argued that the beliefs and assumptions we hold about how the world works and our place in it are responsible for our tendency to cling to the way things are. This level of analysis, however, falls far short of explaining why our beliefs and assumptions hold such sway and, more to the point, what can be done about it.

The chapters in Section II relate and apply the foundational material from Section I to practical, real world circumstances. The aims of Section II are to 1) assess the proposed set of hypotheses within the context of our experience and research; 2) develop our perspectives regarding the object, meaning, and dynamics of learning in organizations; 3) introduce new dimensions of diversity and potential with respect to individuals and groups; 4) explore an alternative conception of culture and culture change; and 5) develop the role of leadership in creating and sustaining an adaptive culture and integrating the human dimensions of organizational life.

The hypotheses restated from Chapter 1 are:

- The growth of knowledge is a function of the relevance and efficacy of the approach to knowing employed, subject to the nature of the reality about which we hope to know.
- The growth of knowledge is influenced by the personal and subjective attributes of the individuals engaged in the process of coming to know, specifically including approach to knowing or epistemic style.
- Within the work of groups, specific approaches to knowing can transcend and help to bridge or reconcile the diverse approaches to knowing of individuals.
- The essential task of leadership is to bring about and sustain an environment conducive to the growth of knowledge.

Organizational learning is equated directly with the growth of knowledge in all aspects of organizational life. Expressly, the growth of knowledge is explored in the chapters of Section II as an attribute of organizational culture and as a function of an integrated view of individuals as potentially knowing subjects and groups as the setting for the process of collective knowing and leaders.

Critically thinking individuals and groups able to engage in critical discourse are the twin pillars of collective learning in organizations. Leadership behavior, rarely neutral, either enhances or diminishes an organization's capacity for learning and knowledge growth.

6

The Knowing Subject

ANTICIPATORY SUMMARY

It is widely accepted that the shape and content of individual belief is a significant expression of diversity. It will be less commonly recognized that how we form the beliefs we hold and seek to know reflects an even deeper dimension of diversity. The diversity of attributes of individuals as belief forming and potentially knowing as well as reality shaping subjects is the focus of inquiry in this chapter.

In this connection, attention is brought to bear on the conjunction of the psychological or subjective reality of individuals and the reality of the world external to individuals. In particular, we will explore how individuals as unique and distinctive members of organizations play a role in both the growth of knowledge in organizations and in shaping the organization's reality.

Psychological and External Realities

We will take the uncommon view and argue that how we form beliefs and seek to know is a fundamental and influential aspect of individual diversity. A belief formation model, designed to frame the substance of this segment of Chapter 6, is presented. The essential concept expressed in the model is that beliefs (as potential knowledge) are comprised of two parts. Driven by *how* we form our beliefs, the first part pertains to the *structure* or the set of standards regarding what we believe and the second to the actual *content* of what we believe. The structure of what we believe shapes and sustains the content of our beliefs as informed by what we perceive and understand, remember, and feel. The content of our beliefs refers to what we hold to be real and true regarding life, the

125

world, our relationships, the meaning of events and circumstances, and the behavior of others.

The strength of the sustaining aspects of the structure of any belief determines how able we are to change and adapt with respect to that belief. For example, standards associated with belief characterized as fitness for some purpose, or contingent upon circumstances, or based on the application of reason enable openness of such beliefs to change consistent with a changed reality. Conversely, standards of belief defined as based on an authoritative source, or predetermined by a perceived cause and effect relationship, or grounded in a narrow subset of factors within a larger whole tend to cause beliefs to be hardened and less open to change.

The subject matter of Chapter 6 encapsulates two ideas: 1) individuals form beliefs and seek to know in different ways, varying from person to person and sometimes depending on the relevant reality about which a specific person is seeking to know; and 2) *how* individuals seek to know influences the growth of knowledge.

The Role of Individuals in the Growth of Knowledge

The essential matters of interest in this segment of Chapter 6 are the ability of individuals 1) to be motivated to form true beliefs, to know; 2) to become conscious of the psychological processes shaping their own belief formation; 3) to think critically in order to have the capacity to form true beliefs; and 4) to become positioned to interact and collaborate with others in efforts to enhance knowledge. While the ability of individuals to engage with each other in groups for the purpose of producing knowledge is the subject matter of the next chapter, it is necessary in this chapter to establish the premise that the counterpart of critical discourse or dialogue in groups is critical thinking in individuals.

Exploring the role of individuals in the growth of knowledge and critical thinking specifically comes into focus around two questions: Why do we *not* know and how can we come to know more fully? Responses to the first question are expressed in terms of constraints on critical thinking, including identification of systemic factors that pollute how we think. Responses to the second question are presented in terms that advance or promote the alignment of belief with reality.

THE KNOWING SUBJECT

Any successful effort to enhance learning and the growth of knowledge in organizations begins with individuals. "Primary individual epistemology" is the term Alvin Goldman associates with the identification and assessment of the role and limits of individuals in the quest for knowledge.[1] The processes associated with individual epistemology are *common* yet through development of the processes of cognition, perception, memory, attribution, and emotion, individuals become *diverse*. The diversity of attributes of individuals as knowing and potentially knowing subjects is the focus of inquiry in this chapter. In this connection, attention is brought to bear on the conjunction of the psychological or subjective reality of individuals and the reality of the world external to individuals. Specifically, we will explore how individuals as unique and distinctive members of organizations with both objective and subjective traits play a role in the growth of knowledge in organizations. Psychological processes are complex and many sided and the research and scholarship on human subjectivity is extensive and comprehensive. A definitive survey of all the factors and dynamics bearing on human subjectivity, therefore, is beyond the scope of this book. The limited intent in this chapter is to selectively focus on the significant factors that influence the formation and content of beliefs and the interplay among these factors.

Although individuals tend to be seen as passive receivers of stimuli defining external reality, individuals also actively shape reality. In other words, the role of individuals as knowing subjects not only pertains to receiving, processing, and making sense of reality, but also encompasses individuals as the source of the subjectivity that shapes the character of constructed reality. Material, nonmaterial, and conceptual realities were defined in Chapter 3 as categories of constructed reality. The objective and institutional character of constructed reality, along with the manifestations of natural reality are perceived and understood by individuals who, in turn, through interaction with others, influence the character of constructed reality and the ability to comprehend natural reality. Lorraine Code in the essay *Taking Subjectivity into Account* argues that, "objectivity requires taking subjectivity into account." She takes the position that objective reality exists, but our ability to know about such reality is limited once we seriously entertain the premise that knowledge is a construct produced by thinking individuals within the framework of specific social

...es and acknowledge the variability of such agents and practices across social groups and time.[2]

Beyond gender, race, and ethnicity, diversity is the expression of the extreme variability in the psychological reality of individuals. It will be readily acknowledged that belief is a significant expression of diversity and that diversity of belief is a function of the diversity of such factors as what we remember and perceive, how we attribute causes to events and circumstances, how we feel, and what motivates us. It will be less commonly acknowledged that how we think, more precisely how we *form* the beliefs we hold and how we seek to know, is an even more fundamental aspect of diversity. The relationship between *what* we believe and *how* we form our beliefs is a central connection within the context of this book as formulated in one of the hypotheses from Chapter 1: The growth of knowledge is influenced by the personal and subjective attributes of the individuals engaged in the process of coming to know, specifically including epistemic style or approach to knowing or forming beliefs. This hypothesis is underpinned by the foundational argument that individuals tend to be predisposed to one or a closely related set of approaches to knowing and seek to apply these approaches to knowing, or merely believing, to any reality. The term "predisposition" in the case of this argument refers to dominance or the default approach to knowing, in other words, the approach to knowing around which the potential knower will err. The combination of the hypothesis and foundational argument restated above encapsulates two ideas: 1) individuals form beliefs and seek to know in different ways, varying from person to person and sometimes depending on the relevant reality about which a specific person is seeking to know; and 2) *how* individuals seek to know influences the growth of knowledge.

PSYCHOLOGICAL AND EXTERNAL REALITIES

The model in Figure 6.1 is intended to schematically organize and frame our conception of the conjunction of the psychological realities of individuals and the world external to them. The model is a simple expression of function and information flows and is non-ideological with respect to any perception of primacy of epistemology or cognitive science or any specific aspect of human subjectivity. Further, the representation of distinct components and linearity in the model in no way suggests actual

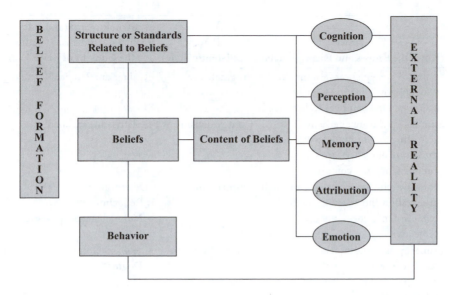

FIGURE 6.1
Conjunction of psychological and external realities in belief formation.

linearity or a reductive conception of subjectivity. It is acknowledged that the components of subjectivity dynamically interrelate and overlap and that the flows of information and influence should be read bidirectionally, vertically, and horizontally. The essential concept expressed in the model is that beliefs are comprised of two parts. The first part pertains to the *structure* or the set of standards regarding what we believe and the second to the actual *content* of what we believe.

Belief content takes the form of the assumptions we hold about the world, relationships, the meaning of events and circumstances, and the behavior of others. Belief formation is set in motion by cognition and results in the structure of what we believe. (See Figure 6.2.) The structure of what we believe shapes and sustains the contents of our beliefs as informed by perception, memory, attribution, and emotion and the content of our beliefs largely determines our behavior. It should be noted that *structure* of belief, given impetus by how we form beliefs and identified as a function of cognition, is a special class of belief *content,* also shaped by perception, memory, attribution, and emotion.

How (How One Knows and Forms Beliefs)	Theory (Epistemic Style)	Structure or Standards (Shapes, Informs, Sustains the Content of Belief)
Looks to consequences or utility to inform knowledge about "right" action and the nature of reality itself	Pragmatism	Utilitarian, Practical Focus
Eliminates relevant alternatives according to set of standards where the nature of reality varies by circumstance and context	Contextualism	Relativism, Qualified Realism
Primarily relies on experience through observation and scientific method, inductive inferences, not open to subjectivity	Empiricism	Determinism, Reductionism, Materialism, Skepticism
Primarily uses intuition and reason to relate to as well as to formulate core principals and ideas, deductive inferences	Rationalism	Idealism, Optimism, Dogmatism
Looks to the coherence and logical integration of beliefs pertaining to the reality in question	Coherentism	Intellectualism, Holism
Steps back, observes and interprets reality iteratively, taking account of objective as well as subjective factors	Hermeneutic Phenomenology	Holism, Comprehensiveness, Differentiative
Looks to psychological processes that have reliably produced true beliefs in the past	Reliabilism	Introspection, Qualified Realism
Primarily uses basic and unconditional beliefs from which deductive and necessary inferences are drawn	Foundationalism	Dogmatism, Fundamentalism

FIGURE 6.2
Structure or standards related to beliefs.

Cognition

One of the central arguments in this book is that *how* we form the beliefs we hold influences *what* we believe and whether or not our beliefs are likely to be true. The implication is that some ways of forming beliefs are more likely to produce knowledge than others, depending on the reality in question. As distinct from perception, cognition specifically involves judgment, reasoning, inference, and intuition. Cognition pertains to thought or, more specifically for our purposes, to the act or process of forming beliefs and knowing. Figure 6.2 pertains to the object or entity labeled Structure or Standards Related to Beliefs as depicted in the model in Figure 6.1. Figure 6.2 associates 1) *how* an individual may be predisposed to forming beliefs with 2) the related *theory* or underlying epistemic style with 3) the *structure or set of standards* the potential knower would be likely to apply to shape and sustain the contents of belief as fueled by perception, memory, attribution, and emotion. For example, the person inclined to pragmatism will tend to apply utilitarian standards to beliefs, emphasizing consequences or outcomes as indicating worthiness of belief, while the person prone to coherentism will seek to overlay a network of related beliefs to establish a standard of coherence. The empiricist will seek to form beliefs based on inductive logic and reduction of phenomena to objective or material constituents while the rationalist will look to intuition, reason, and deductive logic and seek to take subjectivity into account. The basic and inferred beliefs of the foundationalist will tend to be enduring and immutable while the beliefs of the contextualist will tend to be contingent or relative to circumstances.

It is sometimes argued that cognition, defined as the act or process of knowing or forming beliefs, differs from other psychological processes in that individuals are conscious of cognitive processes and not conscious of the others. In our experience and research, we find this argument not to be persuasive. How beliefs are formed and the effects of such processes on beliefs and behavior can be as unconscious and involuntary as processes associated with perception, memory, attribution, and emotion; and these latter processes, under certain conditions, can come to be as conscious as those related to cognition. Consciousness or awareness of psychological processes, however, is a crucial cognitive condition in the individual seeking to form true beliefs. In our perspective, the level and degree of consciousness and awareness is enormously influential in aligning belief with reality and is largely governed by developmental factors.

We surveyed developmental factors in our 1999 book *Beyond Reductionism: Gateways for Learning and Change* and wrote, "As consultants and managers, we have been struck by the apparent inability of many individuals to change. This inability is often present regardless of the strength of the argument for change and irrespective of what these individuals say about change."[3] Within the context and language of *this* book, the emphasis on ability to change has shifted to the ability to align belief with reality and participate in the growth of knowledge. We made the connection in the earlier book between consciousness of psychological factors and the ability to change and referenced constructive-developmental theory as both descriptive and potentially useful in change efforts. Ten years later, we are even more convinced that the dynamics associated with psychological development, as originally described by Jean Piaget as genetic epistemology and reformulated by Robert Kegan as constructive-developmental theory, are highly relevant in explaining the variability and diversity of cognition in individuals in the process of seeking to know. Regarding the relationship between individual development and the growth of knowledge, Robert Campbell asserted, "The core insight throughout Piaget's work is that we cannot understand what knowledge is unless we understand how it is acquired."[4]

For Kegan, the journey with Piaget was nothing less than a movement toward a new understanding of the development of the person. Kegan writes, "Much of what equipped Piaget to see so unusually will always be ineffable, but we do know that he brought together in one man a passion for both philosophy (the constructive theme) and biology (the developmental theme), and thus the psychology it leads to is a natural child of this distinguished marriage."[5] Constructive-developmental theory, then, represents the conjunction of these two "big ideas"—constructivism as the idea that certain circumstances represent a constructed reality and developmentalism as the idea that organic systems evolve through eras according to regular principles of stability and change. Piaget's studies with children demonstrated the now widely accepted set of views associated with cognition and behavior as varying according to developmental stages.[6] Piaget also put forward and described the central dynamic connected with stages of development through adult life and Kegan and others extended this understanding. This dynamic, common to both genetic epistemology and constructive-developmental theory, refers to the defining nature of the relationship between what an individual perceives as subject (characteristics and states internal to the perceiving person) and what is perceived as object (that which exists apart from the perceiving person) at each stage of development.

Constructive-developmental theory seeks to explain the developmental activity associated with the construction of meaning, which, for adults, is close to, or even the same as the concept of belief formation. According to this perspective, individuals are embedded or stuck in their beliefs and assumptions when those beliefs and assumptions cannot be separated from their essential being, their subjective selves. To the extent that individuals are able to separate *self* or their subjective being from their beliefs and assumptions, they can become fully *conscious* of them, able to examine them and evaluate their relevance and potentially able to realign them with reality if there is a need to do so. Kegan presented a schema in his book *The Evolving Self* representing six stages of development from infancy through adulthood. In the transition from each stage to the next, what was subject to the individual (part and parcel of 'self') becomes object (existing independently of 'self'). For example, in the stages beyond early childhood, needs, wishes, and interests as subject in stage 2 become object in stage 3; mutuality and interpersonal conceptions as subject in stage 3 become object in stage 4; identity and ideology as subject in stage 4 become object in stage 5. Where the stage 4 individual is defined and held by his sense of identity and his ideology, the stage 5 person *has* an identity and an ideology but *is not defined* by them.[7] The key insights relate to the dynamics of transition and the relation of subject and object at each stage. Consider how awareness of factors pertaining to identity and ideology at the putative stage 5 is influential in coming to understand how beliefs are formed and how this *consciousness* is a necessary precondition to the ability of an individual to align or realign beliefs with reality and, therefore, to know as opposed to falsely believe. As neat and tidy as this conception seems, the level of difficulty associated with developmental growth is significant and must not be underestimated.

Perception

For our purposes, the essential points pertaining to cognition were identified as the relationship between how we form beliefs and the structure of what we believe or know and the role of consciousness, as influenced by psychological development, in forming true beliefs. Perception was referenced in the model in Figure 6.1 as one of a set of psychological processes affecting the *content* of what we believe. Perception along with the other processes of memory, attribution, and emotion were identified in the model as influencing *structure* as well.

A standard approach to perception is to view it as largely involuntary pattern recognition and to view the output of perception as a classification or categorization of the stimulus. Cognitive psychology studies perception as a species of information processing, where information necessarily has content. In view of this, the dominant outlook in cognitive science describes the output of perception as the percept where the percept is a positive representation of the world, not a "contentless" bit of phenomenology.[8] Perceptual information is acquired through the senses. We're likely to assert that "seeing is believing" when we wish to define our evidence for something. Dretske writes, "We cross intersections when we see the light turn green, head for the kitchen when we smell the roast burning, squeeze the fruit to determine its ripeness, and climb out of bed when we hear the alarm ring." In each case we come to believe something by some sensory means.[9]

It could be argued that perception delivers objective input in the form of percepts to our subjectively shaped cognitive devices, which seek to rationally process and dispose of them. This idea pushes the information processing metaphor too far. In the first place, the process of perception itself has a subjective dimension. Carl Jung expressed the view that in perception, "besides the sensed object there is a sensing subject who adds his subjective disposition to the objective stimulus. ... If, for instance, several painters were to paint the same landscape, each trying to reproduce it faithfully, each painting will be different from the others, not merely because of differences in ability, but chiefly because of different ways of seeing indeed, in some of the paintings there will be a distinct psychic difference in mood and the treatment of colour and form. These qualities betray the influence of the subjective factor. The subjective factor is an unconscious disposition which alters the sense-perception at its source, thus depriving it of the character of a purely objective influence."[10] According to David Bohm, "another example would be a rainbow—everybody sees the same rainbow. ... There's a collective representation of the rainbow—we all have a consensus about it. But physics, which looks at things literally, says, 'No, there is no rainbow. There are a lot of droplets of water, the sun is in back of you and it's being reflected and refracted off the water and forming colors. In seeing this, each person is forming his own perception of a rainbow. It happens they all look very similar, therefore they all think they're all looking at the same rainbow'. The point is that a lot of our collective representations—a country, a religion, General Motors, the ego—are of the same quality as the rainbow. A great many things which we take as solid reality are very similar to the rainbow. The difficulty arises because we do not realize that this is happening, and we therefore give the representation the value of independent fact."[11]

While the idea that perception is preconceptual and precognitive is fairly widespread, it is also common in the literature on perception to see a distinction drawn between realist and constructivist theories of perception. Generally speaking, constructivism affirms that the mind frames and adds concepts to the incoming stimulus in the course of producing a percept, whereas realism denies any such preconceptual or precognitive activity. Goldman substitutes the term *stimulus* for *realist* based on the argument that internal processes are perfectly correlated with the sensory input and that what goes on internally is a direct function of the incoming stimulus. We might say, very roughly, that constructivist theories tend to postulate top-down processing, whereas stimulus theories postulate purely bottom-up processing. In bottom-up processing, information flows from little perceptual pieces to larger units built up from the individual pieces. We are only aware of patterns in bottom-up processing and such processing is assumed to be operative in recognizing words out of letters, sentences out of words, and so on.

When higher-level beliefs or background beliefs influence interpretation of low-level perceptual units, top-down processing is said to be operating. Goldman observes "Cognitive psychologists generally believe that perception uses a mixture of bottom-up and top-down processings."[12] While it seems to be clearly the case that perception is usually some combination of bottom-up and top-down processing, our experience with a psychometric instrument, as noted earlier, administered to hundreds of individuals in organizations suggests that dominance in either top-down or bottom-up processing is a fundamental aspect of diversity and plays a role in establishing an individual's dominant belief forming or epistemic style. Among many other variables, the instrument measures "intellectual styles" or problem solving styles, specifically, a linear versus a global orientation. A strongly linear style corresponds to bottom-up processing while a strongly global style is consistent with a top-down style. Individuals with radically different scores see the world in different ways and have trouble relating to each other. The global person sees forests and thinks the linear person only sees trees, while the linear person believes there *are* only trees and thinks the global person is too engaged in abstractions.[13]

Memory

Memory refers to the capacity to remember, to recall past experiences and to retain knowledge, or belief that was acquired in the past. We know or have beliefs about what we have seen and heard, about what we have experienced and felt. We also have beliefs about the future, about theoretical constructs, about ethical principals and universal generalizations.

The source of these beliefs could be perception or emotion or reason or attribution but regardless of the beliefs themselves and their source, they reside and persevere in memory. It follows that memory is a primary psychological factor when we think about the *content* of belief. Of course, memory can yield mistakes; beliefs may be true or false or somewhere in between. Consideration of "belief states" is a complex topic and the treatment here is admittedly brief and shallow. There are two general concerns to be raised, however, when we think about the content of our beliefs in terms of relative quality and veracity. The first pertains to the acquisition and storage of beliefs in the first place through cognition, perception, and other psychological processes. These were addressed in an earlier section pertaining to cognition and will be addressed in subsequent segments of this chapter. The second relates to the mechanisms associated with memory itself. Alvin Goldman in his book *Epistemology and Cognition* analyzes the mechanisms of memory in terms of activated and unactivated beliefs as two categories of "explicitly represented beliefs."

By equating percepts with a class of beliefs, Goldman begins his analysis of memory by excluding perceptual beliefs. Whether or not this exclusion is valid depends entirely on how perception is defined and the distinction he draws is not especially useful for our purposes. The lack of relevance associated with this distinction notwithstanding, Goldman's analysis leads him through at least two stages to another distinction, a very useful one in the later case. Goldman refers to two classes of memory-associated belief as dispositional belief, beliefs having a prevailing tendency or inclination, and occurrent beliefs, those beliefs occurring at a particular place and time. He argues that cognitive psychology shifts the focus from classes of belief, without losing the distinction, to the *duplex theory* of memory, according to which, the mind has two memories, long term and short term or active. "Long-term memory is a place where information can be stored for very long periods of time, perhaps indefinitely. Information in long-term memory decays very slowly. Short-term memory, by contrast, has a much faster decay period. There is also a big difference in the amount of information retainable in long-term memory as compared with short-term memory, which has a restricted capacity. Furthermore, whereas information lies dormant in long-term memory and is not capable of influencing cognitive activities, short-term memory is a sort of workplace where various operations and transformations can be performed on data and new items can be constructed. In order to utilize material stored in long-term memory, that material must be retrieved and copied into short-term memory. That's what it is to think of something one has previously known or believed."[14]

In what seems like a circular path, the duplex theory of memory has given way to the conception of activated and unactivated beliefs, all existing in long-term memory. Stated another way, all beliefs exist in memory with some in a state of activation and others not. Goldman refers to John Anderson's treatment of memory in the *Architecture of Cognition*. "Anderson views active memories not as events occupying a special location, but as activated states of long-term memory. Activation is something like a light bulb governed by a dimmer switch: Activation can take on a continuous range of levels, not just on and off."[15] For explanatory and predictive purposes, the activated/unactivated distinction is clearly vital, taking account of the fact that only activated beliefs are influential in decision making. The inferences an individual makes are determined by a relatively small number of activated beliefs and not by the enormous corpus of unactivated beliefs. "For example, at least a decade before Fleming's discovery of penicillin, many microbiologists were aware that molds cause clear spots in bacteria cultures; and they knew that a bare spot indicated no bacterial growth. Yet they did not consider the possibility that molds release an antibacterial agent. They apparently failed to activate these beliefs at a single time, juxtapose them, and then make a natural inference. Similar things occur in everyday life, when a person fails to 'put two and two together' to reach (what seems in hindsight) a natural conclusion. One belief lies dormant while the other is activated."[16]

Attribution

Attribution theory is a branch of social psychology that deals with how people explain and make sense of their own behavior and that of others. Attribution is both a process and an effect. As a handmaiden of perception, attribution plays an important role in feeding the content of belief. Faced with ambiguity in many if not most of our social interactions, attribution is how we "fill in the blanks" of the meaning we make of the behavior of other people. Miles Hewstone in his book *Causal Attribution: From Cognitive Processes to Collective Beliefs* surveys the major threads of development in attribution theory and concludes: "They all address the kinds of information that people use to determine causality, the kinds of causes that they distinguish and rules they use for going from information to inferred causes. ... Most important, all share a concern with common sense explanations and answers to the question 'Why?'"[17]

The study of attribution divides between automatic and so-called controlled attribution. Controlled attribution pertains to explanations flowing from logic and formal problem solving. For our purposes, controlled attribution belongs to cognition and will not be pursued here. Automatic attribution, however, is highly germane to our purpose. Automatic attribution pertains to those judgments and explanations that occur rapidly, unconsciously, and almost in a stimulus-response mode. Hewstone defines attributions as automatic to the extent that they fulfill three criteria: "1) They occur without intention; 2) they occur without giving rise to awareness; 3) they occur without interfering with ongoing mental activity."[18]

Our patterns of attribution play a significant role in how we perceive, assess, and deal with reality. All of us engage in the process of attribution and it can provide useful functions. It can help to make sense of the behavior of other people and to act efficiently, with an economy of effort. The process of attribution is also subject to error and can create consequences we don't intend. Hewstone identifies two significant consequences. The first pertains to selective memory, to how we remember. Our memory about people and events seems to be influenced by how clearly we are able to explain and attribute causes to events and the actions of other people. There is also evidence that we tend to discount those events and actions that threaten our beliefs, enabling our beliefs to persevere even when they are inconsistent with reality. Recalling the dynamics of memory from the previous segment, attribution appears to strengthen (or weaken) memories, affecting their ability to become both conscious and activated. Attribution also influences *what* we remember. When conflict between any two people is recalled by either party, each inevitably remembers it in different ways. Each person tends to remember what best explains the conflict for his or her own purposes. Another consequence of attribution is how we behave. How we behave is influenced by what we believe and what we believe is in some manner determined by how we explain and attribute causes to events and the actions of people. Of special interest is the part expectations of others and self-fulfilling prophecies play in the character of interpersonal relations through "behavioral confirmation." According to Hewstone, behavioral confirmation is the "idea that one's beliefs about another person might influence social interaction in ways that cause the behavior of that person to confirm one's prior beliefs."[19]

In a practical sense, we can perhaps learn most about the process of attribution by becoming aware of the generalized biases associated with attribution. Three of the most central biases in attribution have been identified as 1) the fundamental attribution error, 2) self-other differences, and 3) self-serving biases.[20] The fundamental attribution error is defined as the tendency for individuals to underestimate the impact of situational factors (factors pertaining to external circumstances) and to overestimate the role of dispositional factors (factors pertaining to temperament and personal characteristics) in making sense of the behavior of others. To cite Fritz Heider, one of the founders of attribution theory, "changes in the environment are almost always caused by acts of persons in combination with other factors." The tendency exists, however, to ascribe the changes entirely to persons.[21] Studies have shown that the tendency to inadequately account for external circumstances in the behavior of others is extremely widespread and is thought to be shared by almost everyone socialized in our Western culture.[22]

Another central bias in attribution is described as self-other differences. To cite Heider again, "the person tends to attribute his own reactions to the object world to circumstances apart from himself and those of another, when they differ from his own, to personal characteristics."[23] Stated another way and as confirmed by the fundamental attribution error, when conflict between individuals occurs, there is a tendency for individuals to attribute situational causes for their own behavior and causes related to personality and character traits for the behavior of the other person. We encounter this bias on a regular basis as we drive. When the driver in front of us crosses three lanes of traffic without a signal to exit the freeway, we attribute lack of intelligence and a flawed heredity to this "shameless" act. When we do the same thing, however, we tend to feel justified because we're late for a meeting, or a scheduled flight departure, or the conspiracy of the other drivers in failing to give way to our legitimate needs. Self-serving biases help satisfy a requirement for support of self-esteem. There appear to be two biases. The first of these, a self-enhancing bias, operates to assign internal causes to success. Such causes include hard work, competence, ambition, and character. The second, a self-protecting bias, attributes failure to external causes such as timing, the recession, unfair competition, etc.

Emotion

Emotion is implicitly connected with the content of belief. David Hume's conception of this connection and the difference between what we imagine and what we feel continues to inform and broaden our understanding of it. David Hume writes, "Nothing is more free than the imagination of man; and though it cannot exceed that original stock of ideas furnished by the internal and external senses, it has unlimited power of mixing, compounding, separating, and dividing these ideas, in all the varieties of fiction and vision. It can feign a train of events, with all the appearance of reality, ascribe to them a particular time and place, conceive them as existent, and point them out to itself with every circumstance that belongs to any historical fact, which it believes with the greatest certainty. Wherein, therefore, consists the difference between such a fiction and belief? It lies not merely in any peculiar idea. We can, in our conception, join the head of a man to the body of a horse; but it is not in our power to believe that such an animal has ever really existed. It follows, therefore, that the difference between fiction and belief lies in some sentiment or feeling, which is annexed to the latter, not to the former, and which depends not on the will, nor can be commanded at pleasure. ... It is evident that belief consists not in the peculiar nature or order of ideas, but in the manner of their conception, and in their *feeling* to the mind."[24]

Beliefs by definition have an emotional component and emotions play an important role in our ability to form and sustain true beliefs. It follows that our ability to be at our cognitive best, perceiving reality and reasoning accurately is, in part, a function of avoiding emotionally laden reactive or defensive attitudes and behavior. Defensiveness is the result of largely unconscious mental processes and serves to protect the individual from threat. Defensive beliefs are largely set in motion by the emotions of fear and anxiety—fear of loss of control over circumstances, anxiety associated with potential loss of self-esteem or advantage over others. As our defenses engage, our potential for producing flawed perceptions and beliefs increases.[25] The mode of thinking which Chris Argyis calls defensive reasoning functions to sustain our beliefs whether or not they conform to reality. When individuals are reasoning defensively, their assumptions and beliefs remain hidden, the processes by which they reach conclusions are unexpressed, and their conclusions tend to be untested. According to Argyis, "Defensive reasoning is self-serving, anti-learning and over protective."[26] The defensive behavior of one individual can trigger reciprocal defensive responses in another, which can, in turn, strengthen the defensiveness of the first individual creating a downward spiral in the learning character of the relationship between the two individuals. Such patterns of defensiveness can become the norm in groups and seriously constrain the growth of knowledge in organizations.

Emotions play a role in the content of belief associated with perception and attribution. David Chalmers in his book *The Conscious Mind* describes how emotions often have distinctive experiences associated with them. "The sparkle of a happy mood, the weariness of a deep depression, the red-hot glow of a rush of anger, the melancholy of regret: all of these can affect conscious experience profoundly. These emotions pervade and color all of our conscious experiences while they last."[27] Goldman contends that there will be an enhanced tendency to perceive stimuli in high affect or emotionally laden circumstances and shape belief, even if belief is fleeting. "For example, a young child who has a strong desire to see her mother will recognize lots of women in the distance as her mother. The parent in the shower, listening for its infant's cry in the next room may hear such a cry when in fact it is only the noise of the shower."[28] According to Hewstone, Russell Weiner has made an important distinction between two kinds of achievement-related affects: "outcome-dependent" and "attribution-linked" affects. "Outcome-dependent affects refer to the very general, even primitive emotions that are experienced following success and failure outcomes. These emotions include 'happy' following success and 'frustrated' or 'sad' following failure; they are labeled outcome-dependent because they depend on attainment or non-attainment of a desired goal, not on causal attributions given for the outcome. Attribution-linked affects, in contrast, are influenced by the specific causal attribution for the outcome. Especially if an outcome is negative, unexpected or especially important, one makes causal attributions in order to make sense of it." The combination of causal attributions (e.g., ability, effort, character) and their underlying properties (e.g., internal versus external, stability, controllability) generate highly differentiated emotions (e.g., surprise, joy, satisfaction, disappointment).[29]

THE ROLE OF INDIVIDUALS IN THE GROWTH OF KNOWLEDGE

The essential matters of interest in this segment of the current chapter are the ability of individuals 1) to be motivated to form true beliefs, to know, 2) to think critically in order to have the capacity to form true beliefs, and 3) to become positioned to interact and collaborate with others in efforts to enhance knowledge. While the ability of individuals to engage with each other in groups for the purpose of producing knowledge is the subject matter of the next chapter, it is necessary in this chapter to establish the premise that the counterpart of critical discourse or dialogue in groups is critical thinking in individuals. We will argue in the next chapter that the growth of knowledge is largely a communal affair and that groups are in some way responsible for most of what we know. It will become self-evident, however, that productive discourse and learning in groups is not achievable without critically thinking individuals as members of such groups.

Various terms have been introduced in recent years to identify the individual or personal faculty we refer to as critical thinking. These terms include the *rhetoric of reason* and the *theory of argument*, both of which are based on pragmatic rhetorical theory with attention brought to bear on written reasoning and how such reasoning is involved in creative discovery and clarification of ideas. The term *dialectical thinking* conveys the idea of techniques associated with exposing false beliefs and eliciting truth, which is precisely the meaning we associate with critical thinking. For our purposes, we will stay with the conventional term *critical thinking* and seek to give it additional meaning.

Traditionally, critical thinking has been taken to mean comprehensive and accurate thinking for the purpose of producing relevant and reliable knowledge about the world. Critical thinking is focused on what to believe about multidimensional and complex situations where the beliefs of others and options for action vary. It may be helpful to consider what critical thinking is *not*; it does not refer to the capacity to process information and determine that stopping at a red traffic light or carrying an umbrella in the rain are useful acts. Such low order thinking, expedient though it may be, is sufficient only for basic personal survival and comfort and most individuals are fully able to achieve it. Critical thinkers, on the other hand, exhibit higher order thinking shaped by knowledge, skills, attitudes, and habitual ways of behaving. Critical thinkers use evidence skillfully and impartially; they organize their thoughts and articulate them concisely and coherently, stripping out irrelevancies. They understand the differences between reasoning and rationalizing and the validity of a belief and the intensity with which a belief is held. They distinguish between logically valid and invalid inferences and attempt to anticipate the probable consequences of alternative actions. Critical thinkers understand the idea of degrees of belief; they habitually question their own views and attempt to understand both the assumptions and implications pertaining to those views. They are aware of the fact that their own understanding is always limited and fallible and influenced by subjective factors.[30]

Consistent with the themes and language of this book, critical thinking at the level of the individual equates with forming true beliefs or aligning belief with reality. As described earlier in this chapter under the heading Cognition, consciousness is a crucial condition in the individual seeking to form true beliefs; consciousness, therefore, is the first and essential requirement in critical thinking. Chalmers in the *Conscious Mind* asserts "Conscious experience is at once the most familiar thing in the world and the most mysterious. There is nothing we know about more directly than consciousness, but it is far from clear how to reconcile it with everything else we know. Why does it exist? What does it do? How could it possibly arise from lumpy gray matter? We know consciousness far more intimately than we know the rest of the world, but we understand the rest of the world far better than we understand consciousness. The *International Dictionary of Psychology* does not even try to give a straightforward characterization: 'Consciousness – The having of perceptions, thoughts, and feelings; awareness. (Circularly), the term is impossible to define except in terms that are unintelligible without a grasp of what consciousness means.'"[31]

As difficult as consciousness is to define, it is universal in human beings. However, many, if not most, human beings are not very good at critical thinking so what is the level of consciousness required for thinking at this level? It is clear that critical thinking as described above and as developed in the remainder of this chapter requires consciousness at a high level, embracing awareness of one's beliefs, assumptions, worldviews and epistemic style or approach to forming beliefs and knowing. Peter Senge in his highly acclaimed 1990 book *The Fifth Discipline: The Art and Practice of the Learning Organization* argues in various ways and contexts that suspending assumptions is a fundamental requirement for individuals aiming to participate in individual and collective learning.[32] Attention must be called to the more fundamental argument, however, that it is impossible for an individual to suspend assumptions if he or she is unaware of them. And further, that the ability to become fully conscious of beliefs and assumptions is a function of psychological development and rarely able to be influenced by simple exhortation.

The topic of the role of individuals in the growth of knowledge and critical thinking specifically comes into focus around two questions: Why do we *not* know and how can we come to know more fully? Responses to the first question are expressed in terms of constraints on critical thinking, including identification of systemic factors that pollute how we think; responses to the second question are presented in terms that advance or promote the alignment of belief with reality.

Why Do We Not Know?

We fail to understand the relevant reality. We developed the arguments in Chapter 3 that multiple realities frame and influence life in organizations and that the perception and treatment of these realities have practical implications. Briefly, these realities were first partitioned into two domains—natural and constructed. The universe of observable and measurable physical phenomena was defined as belonging to the category of natural reality while the domain of constructed reality was further subdivided into material, nonmaterial and conceptual realities. Individuals may misconceive reality and, in their misconception, become constrained in their capacity for critical thinking. Such constraint may cause belief to be misaligned with reality with the result of ineffective decision making and problem solving. As individuals, we are perhaps most inclined to misunderstand reality by failing to take account of the dual dimensions of any reality, i.e., internal/external and objective/subjective, especially the latter.

The objective dimension of reality refers to that which exists apart from human consciousness and sensibility and appears to have an independent existence. The subjective dimension, as defined in this chapter, refers to the beliefs and assumptions of individuals as shaped by perception, cognition, attribution, emotion, and motivation. Because individuals, interacting with each other and with evolving institutions, create constructed reality, such reality has an obvious subjective dimension. When we fail to reckon with the human dimension of an ethical reality or the financial reality of a circumstance influenced by human subjectivity, we fail to understand the character of the reality in question. On the other hand, the constitution of a constructed reality takes on an objective dimension through the process of institutionalization and the passage of time. The failure to comprehend the objective dimension of this reality will also lead to failure to understand its character. For most of us, it is also obvious that natural reality is objective and exists independently of human perception and thought. While we don't suggest that human subjectivity alters the character of natural or physical reality, we do assert that subjectivity shapes the perception of such reality. When we fail to take account of our own subjectivity in our efforts to grasp the characteristics of any natural reality, we are likely to fail to understand it.

Our beliefs are incongruent with reality. Within the framework of the model in Figure 6.1, this is primarily a *content* of belief problem. We argued earlier in this chapter that attribution is a handmaiden of perception and plays an important role in providing the content of belief. Especially with regard to relationships, generalized biases associated with attribution shape and sustain beliefs, irrespective of reality. We tend to systematically underestimate the influence of situational factors and over-estimate factors pertaining to temperament and personal characteristics in forming and sustaining beliefs about other people. Other biases connected with attribution lead us to believe that hard work and competence are responsible for our successes while external causes such as the economy or the acts of others are responsible for our failures. Still other biases, closely related to attribution, are connected with confirmation and causal explanations. Under the heading *Belief Perseverance*, Goldman describes how people tend to recognize the relevance of circumstances that confirm prior beliefs more readily than circumstances that disconfirm such beliefs. Concerning casual explanations, beliefs based on events and situations that can be explained, even if the explanations are weak, are considered to be more likely true than those that cannot be explained.[33]

As described in the preceding segment on emotion, fear, anxiety, and perception of threat can lead to defensive thinking and false beliefs. In our experience, we have observed many examples of competent and psychologically healthy individuals forming and sustaining flawed beliefs through reactive or defensive attitudes, thought styles and behaviors. The Birkman Method, the psychometric instrument we have used extensively in our practice, is useful in many ways, especially in identifying the dynamics associated with defensiveness in individuals. The behavioral segment of the instrument assesses needs, usual or productive behavior, and stress or reactive behavior associated with eleven specific components. The components include esteem, acceptance, structure, authority, advantage, activity, challenge, empathy, change, freedom, and thought. The logic of the instrument can be briefly summarized as follows: All of us have needs in connection with each component although they may vary widely. When our needs are met, our attitudes, thought processes, and behaviors will tend to be productive and positive although different from one person to the next. When our needs are not met, our attitudes, thought processes, and behaviors will vary, but will tend to be defensive. For example, for the "esteem" factor and any given person, the nonreactive attitudes and productive behavior associated with the states of "lack of self-conscious feelings" or "supportiveness toward others" shifts to "downplaying the needs of others" or "over-sensitivity to criticism" when the person experiences stress and becomes defensive. Concerning the "advantage" factor, the positive styles associated with "trusting and team-oriented" or "opportunity minded and resourceful" turns into "becoming impractical and overly idealistic" or "self promotional and distrusting" under stress. The defensive modes of thought responsible for these stress behaviors propel the formation and perpetuation of false beliefs.[34]

We fail to challenge our incongruent beliefs and apply inappropriate approaches to forming beliefs and knowing. With reference again to the model in Figure 6.1, this failure is chiefly a *structure* of belief problem. One of the central arguments we have pursued and will continue to pursue in this book is that *how* we form the beliefs we hold influences *what* we believe and whether or not our beliefs are likely to *be* and *remain* true. With reference also to the table in Figure 6.2, a relationship is drawn between *how* an individual may be predisposed to forming beliefs and the *structure* the individual would apply to shape and sustain the content of belief. As indicated in the table in Figure 6.2, some ways of forming beliefs are open to challenge and others are significantly less so. To the extent that structure of belief is deterministic, reductionistic, or dogmatic, beliefs are hardened and embedded and critical thinking is constrained. "Deterministic" refers to the content of belief necessarily or inevitably caused by preceding events, circumstances, or natural laws; "reductionistic" pertains to belief content based on oversimplification and loss of conception of wholes; "dogmatic" relates to belief content founded on authoritative but often insufficiently grounded premises.

How Can We Come to Know More Fully?

Define the implications of knowing. Thinking critically for the purpose of forming true beliefs, aligning belief with reality, is difficult and sometimes threatening work. It's easier and perhaps more satisfying to form beliefs about any specific set of circumstances that confirm our broader beliefs and then to cause them to persevere. This component of coming to know more fully pertains to the desire to know—a desire that can overwhelm the constraints on critical thinking and our natural tendencies. In other words, this component relates to wanting to know and generating the internal motivation to overcome all the reasons why we often fail to know. We argued in Chapter 1 that knowledge accounts for our progress as human beings and that the action we take, or fail to take, based on what we know, will align what we do with reality and be likely to produce desirable and beneficial effects. To the extent that individuals comprehend the growth of knowledge as purpose, the idea of personal leverage can provide the motivation and the emotional commitment to know. If we think of the growth of knowledge as our work, our resources as our knowledge-producing potential, and the increments of knowledge as the output of our work, our perspective on personal leverage from *Beyond Reductionism* is germane. Douglas and Wykowski assert, "By leverage we mean creating the greatest good per unit of invested resource. Without a definition of good, leverage makes no sense. Therefore, without a clear sense of purpose and relevant output equated to good, leverage is a meaningless concept. Leverage relates to output per activity and can be thought of as a multiplier where relatively small investments of time, energy, and capital can yield large results. The seeking of leverage compels us to sustain an intimacy with purpose or goal or destination and the consequences of effort. As individuals, the single most important resource and perhaps the only resource we truly possess is our time. It is the one absolutely finite resource we are granted. Given the motivation to achieve, individuals can maximize their investment of time and their contribution through the creation of personal and positive leverage."[35]

Define the relevant reality. For individuals in organizations, the critical assessment of relevant reality in any circumstance is a matter of asking and seeking to answer a set of questions. Does the reality belong to the class of observable and/or measurable physical, chemical, biological, electromagnetic or quantum things, and phenomena? Does the reality pertain to money, property or recognized boundaries? Is the reality defined by culture or politics or perceptions of such states of being as success and failure? Does the reality pertain to conceptions of virtue, beauty, or ethics? Does the reality in question pertain to circumstances internal to the organization or to the world outside the organization? What are the objective dimensions of this reality; what are the subjective dimensions? Does the relevant reality embody multiple realities and dimensions? Whatever else we may say about critical thinking, it must always settle on some, at least provisional, version of reality.

Identify the valid approaches to knowing about the relevant reality. We have argued that individuals tend to be predisposed to one or a set of closely related approaches to knowing and seek to apply these epistemic approaches or styles to any reality. We have also argued that epistemic style is a fundamental aspect of diversity. These views were formed through our collective work with individuals in organizations over a period of more than fifteen years. We have also observed a loose correlation between Birkman Method results and the dynamics of belief formation. In connection with our preparation for this book, we undertook a simple program of research to validate these arguments. We recognize that reliably assessing something as fluid and dynamic as epistemic style among a set of individuals is very difficult and we encourage others to take up this research. Therefore, in seeking only to confirm that there is an array of approaches to forming beliefs that individuals apply and that they tend to favor certain approaches without apparent regard to relevant reality, we make no sweeping claims based on this research. The table in Figure 6.3 is the informal instrument we asked our research participants to complete.

Under Degree of Agreement, for each entry, participants were asked to record a number from 1 to 5 where 1 means complete disagreement with the statement(s) and 5 means full agreement. Any number may be recorded for any entry, irrespective of others.

How My Beliefs Are Formed	Degree of Agreement
1. What I believe is primarily influenced by what works (that which produces the best practical result).	
2. My beliefs are subject to situational factors. What is true within one set of circumstances may be untrue within another.	
3. My beliefs are based on the facts as I experience them or as others in whom I have confidence have experienced them.	
4. My beliefs flow from my own intuition and reason and the meaning (to me) of ideas and principles.	
5. Whatever I believe is a part of some network of beliefs that "hold together," and form a coherent whole.	
6. Dispassionate observation and interpretation of what I observe are the tools I use to shape my beliefs.	
7. I rely on my own internal thought processes for forming beliefs that have reliably produced true beliefs for me in the past.	
8. Whatever I believe is unconditional and is inferred from deeper, basic beliefs about which I have no doubt.	

FIGURE 6.3
Belief formation instrument.

The theories or approaches to knowing associated with the belief statements in the instrument are (1) pragmatism, (2) contextualism, (3) empiricism, (4) rationalism, (5) coherentism, (6) hermeneutic phenomenology, (7) reliabilism, and (8) foundationalism. The responses to the instrument were highly variable with all theories receiving a significant quantity of aggregate numerical responses. Figure 6.4 summarizes the responses in terms of percentages associated with each set of pairs as follows: For the pair Highest and Lowest, the percentages indicate the proportion of responses for each theory representing the highest and lowest responses given by the individuals in the group. For example, 8 percent shown in the highest column for pragmatism indicate that pragmatism was the closest to complete agreement for 8 percent of the responses while 21 percent shown in the lowest column indicate pragmatism as the theory closest to complete disagreement for that percentage of the responses. The highest responses for coherentism were 19 percent while only 4 percent of responses for coherentism were shown in the lowest column. The columns headed 4s and 5s and 1s and 2s set the theories with the highest aggregate numerical scores, ruling out the neutral 3s, against the theories with the lowest such scores. For example 14 percent of the highest scores went to coherentism while 13 percent of the lowest went to reliabilism. Finally, considering only responses of 5 and 1, the percentage entries reflect the proportion of total respondents who recorded either 5 or 1, indicating complete agreement or complete disagreement for one or more theories. For example, 5 percent of the individuals recorded complete agreement with pragmatism while 21 percent each of the individual responses recorded complete agreement with both contextualism and coherentism. An insignificant number of 1s

Theory/Approach to Knowing	Highest %	Lowest %	4s and 5s %	1s and 2s %	5s Only %	1s Only %
1) Pragmatism	8	21	12	16	5	
2) Contextualism	19	12	14	9	21	
3) Empiricism	8	0	11	12	11	
4) Rationalism	7	0	18	3	5	
5) Coherentism	19	4	14	3	21	
6) Hermeneutic Phenomenology	8	21	10	22	11	
7) Reliabilism	19	13	14	13	10	
8) Foundationalism	12	29	7	22	16	

FIGURE 6.4
Summary of belief formation results.

were recorded for any of the theories, but of those lowest level responses, pragmatism, contextualism and foundationalism were represented.

There were a fairly high number of responses at levels 3 and 4 suggesting that either respondents felt compelled to answer in an affirmative way because of the positive way the statements were worded, or they were taking different realities into account (although no questions regarding character of reality were raised), or they couldn't decide. Regarding the approaches to knowing that have been proposed as bridging styles, i.e., pragmatism, contextualism, and hermeneutic phenomenology, the collection of these styles recorded very high scores for some people and very low for others.

As described above, if defining the relevant reality is an important step in the process of coming to know more fully, it should be understood that *how* I seek to know can shape what I take reality to be. In other words, the reality most closely aligned with my most dominant epistemic style is likely to be the reality I will tend to see. For example, if empiricism is my dominant belief forming or epistemic style, I will have a tendency to see any reality as unaffected by human influence and able to be understood by the methods of natural science. If my dominant style, on the other hand, is pragmatism, I will be inclined to see any reality as fluid and open to interpretation. An important step for thinking critically and coming to know more fully, therefore, is to become aware of how I am inclined to form beliefs and seek to know. We have argued that no single theory or approach to knowing applies uniformly to all realities and further, as a corollary to this argument, certain theories are especially suited, in varying degree and sometimes in concert with other theories, to knowing about specific realities. Attention is called to the table in Figure 5.2 of Chapter 5, which integrates the theories of knowledge surveyed in Chapter 4 and summarized in Figures 6.3 and 6.4 with the realities initially described in Chapter 3.

REFERENCES

1. Goldman, Alvin I. 1986. *Epistemology and Cognition*. Cambridge: Harvard University Press.
2. Code, Lorraine. 1993. Taking Subjectivity into Account. In *Rhetorical Spaces*, 23–57. London: Routledge, Inc.
3. Douglas, Neil and Terry Wykowski. 1999. *Beyond Reductionism: Gateways for Learning and Change*. Boca Raton: St. Lucie Press.

4. Campbell, Robert L. 1997. Jean Piaget's Genetic Epistemology: Appreciation and Critique. Paper presented at the Institute of Objectivist Studies Summer Seminar, Charlottesville.

5. Kegan, Robert. 1982. *The Evolving Self: Problem and Process in Human Development.* Cambridge: Harvard University Press.

6. Piaget, Jean. 1954. *The Construction of Reality in the Child,* Trans. by Margaret Cook. New York: Basic Books.

7. Kegan, Robert. 1982. *The Evolving Self: Problem and Process in Human Development.* Cambridge: Harvard University Press.

8. Goldman, Alvin I. 1986. *Epistemology and Cognition.* Cambridge: Harvard University Press.

9. Dretske, Fred. 1992. Perceptual Knowledge. In *A Companion to Epistemology,* ed. Jonathan Dancy, Ernest Sosa, 333–338. Oxford: Blackwell Publishers Ltd.

10. Jung, C. G. 1974. *Psychological Types,* A Revision by R.F.C. Hull of the Translation by H. G. Baynes. Princeton: Princeton University Press.

11. Bohm, David. 1996. *On Dialogue.* New York: Routledge Classics.

12. Goldman, Alvin I. 1986. *Epistemology and Cognition.* Cambridge: Harvard University Press.

13. Birkman, Roger. 1995. *True Colors.* Nashville: Thomas Nelson Publishing.

14. Goldman, Alvin I. 1986. *Epistemology and Cognition.* Cambridge: Harvard University Press.

15. Anderson, John. 1983. *The Architecture of Cognition.* Cambridge: Harvard University Press.

16. Goldman, Alvin I. 1986. *Epistemology and Cognition.* Cambridge: Harvard University Press.

17. Hewstone, Miles. 1989. *Causal Attribution: From Cognitive Processes to Collective Beliefs.* Oxford: Blackwell Publishers.

18. Hewstone, Miles. 1989. *Causal Attribution: From Cognitive Processes to Collective Beliefs.* Oxford: Blackwell Publishers.

19. Hewstone, Miles. 1989. *Causal Attribution: From Cognitive Processes to Collective Beliefs.* Oxford: Blackwell Publishers.

20. Hewstone, Miles. 1989. *Causal Attribution: From Cognitive Processes to Collective Beliefs.* Oxford: Blackwell Publishers.

21. Heider, F. 1944. Perception and Phenomenal Causality. *Psychological Review* 51:358–374.

22. Nisbett, R. E. and L. Ross. 1980. *Human Inference: Strategies and Shortcomings of Social Judgment.* Englewood Cliffs: Prentice-Hall.

23. Heider, F. 1958. *The Psychology of Interpersonal Relations.* New York: Wiley.

24. Hume, David. 1952. *An Enquiry Concerning Human Understanding,* ed. L.A. Selby-Bigge. Oxford: Oxford University Press.

25. Douglas, Neil and Terry Wykowski. 1999. *Beyond Reductionism: Gateways for Learning and Change.* Boca Raton: St. Lucie Press.

26. Argyris, Chris. 1990. *Overcoming Organizational Defenses: Facilitating Organizational Learning.* Boston: Allyn and Bacon.

27. Chalmers, David J. 1996. *The Conscious Mind: In Search of a Fundamental Theory.* Oxford: Oxford University Press, 1996.

28. Goldman, Alvin. 1986. *Epistemology and Cognition.* Cambridge: Harvard University Press.

29. Hewstone, Miles. 1989. *Causal Attribution: From Cognitive Processes to Collective Beliefs*. Oxford: Blackwell Publishers.
30. Nickerson, Raymond S. 1986. Why Teach Thinking? In *Teaching Thinking Skills: Theory and Practice*, ed. J.B. Baron, R.J. Sternberg, 29–30. New York: W. H. Freeman and Company.
31. Chalmers, David J. 1996. *The Conscious Mind: In Search of a Fundamental Theory*. Oxford: Oxford University Press.
32. Senge, Peter, M. 1990. *The Fifth Discipline: The Art and Practice of the Learning Organization*. New York: Doubleday/Currency.
33. Goldman, Alvin I. 1986. *Epistemology and Cognition*. Cambridge: Harvard University Press.
34. Birkman, Roger. 1995. *True Colors*. Nashville: Thomas Nelson Publishing.
35. Douglas, Neil and Terry Wykowski. 1999. *Beyond Reductionism: Gateways for Learning and Change*. Boca Raton: St. Lucie Press.

7

Collective Knowing

ANTICIPATORY SUMMARY

The growth of knowledge is widely regarded as a communal affair, as directly or indirectly social. The character of life in organizations is interdependent and groups representing an array of beliefs, predispositions, job specialties, and differentiated tasks are the framework for the playing out of organizational life. While the individuals that come together in groups are diverse and groups themselves reflect varied dynamics, the success of an organization or any group depends on its collective ability to accurately comprehend reality. The focus in this chapter is on aligning collective belief with the whole of relevant reality through the processes associated with collective knowing.

Bridging from Individuals to Groups

Individuals can enhance or reduce the quality and results of group interaction. Reciprocally, groups can cultivate or diminish the quality of individual contribution. This segment of Chapter 7 explores both the dynamics of individuals in groups and the emergent or "collectivist" properties of such groups as well as the circumstance that there is no bright line that separates individual dynamics and emergent properties.

The Quality of Discourse

The quality of discourse, or the level and nature of interaction and communication, largely determines the learning and knowledge enhancing potential of a group. Dialogue in groups is critical discourse and the counterpart of critical thinking in individuals. Groups engaged in dialogue are

153

seeking to comprehend reality as completely and accurately as possible. Dialogue, however, is far easier to talk about as an abstraction and an ideal than it is to achieve.

It is widely acknowledged that the ability to suspend assumptions or beliefs is fundamental to the ability of individuals to engage in dialogue for the purpose of collective learning. The simple admonition to suspend assumptions, however, is inadequate. It is argued in this segment of Chapter 7 that it is impossible to contend with our collective beliefs if we are unaware of them. And, more importantly, that the ability to become fully conscious of our beliefs is a function of awareness of how they were formed in the first place.

The art of dialogue as a practical means to learning and the growth of knowledge in groups is also explored in this segment by considering the motivations, preconditions, and methods associated with effective dialogue.

The Role of Groups in the Growth of Knowledge

Through the work of groups, the potential exists to go beyond the limitations of individuals and to take advantage of their diverse perspectives for the purpose of knowing more fully. In the later third of this chapter, two questions and their proposed answers with examples frame the exploration of the role of groups in the growth of knowledge. These questions are: Why do we *not* know as groups and collections of individuals? And how can we know more fully through the work of groups?

COLLECTIVE KNOWING

Groups of individuals either working contemporaneously and in the same physical space or separated by time and geography are responsible for most of what we know. The growth of knowledge is widely regarded as a communal affair. Werner Heisenberg, a formulator of the uncertainty principle in modern physics, looking back on conversations with Pauli, Einstein, Bohr and others, argued, "Science is rooted in conversations."[1] "Truth," said the Scottish philosopher, David Hume, "springs from arguments among friends." Cardinal John Henry Newman in his Dublin Discourses asserted, "Truth is wrought out by many minds working together freely."[2]

Michael Williams refers to the insights developed in Thomas Kuhn's *The Structure of Scientific Revolutions* as exemplifying what it describes—a new paradigm and a way of thinking about epistemological questions that does not put skepticism and individualism first.

The problem of skepticism refers to the issue of whether it is possible to obtain knowledge at all. At least during the modern or post-Cartesian period, attempts to address the problem of skepticism center on the ability or inability of individuals to know. Williams continues, "The skeptical problem of our knowledge of the external world apparently forces us to seek the foundations of knowledge within: in the contents of our minds, conceived as an inner arena of irreducibly private happenings." Breaking with such notions of individualism, "We can see knowledge for what it is (and always has been): a socially shared and transmitted achievement, where entitlements are passed on by testimony and where not everyone needs or can reasonably aspire to know everything there is to know. ... We can even see knowledge as a social construction, provided we detach this conception from the skeptical thought that there is no such thing as worldly (or physical) constraint, and that knowledge is therefore just what some group or other says it is."[3]

Revisiting one of our foundational arguments from Chapter 1, learning and the growth of knowledge is largely a collective matter resulting from the interaction of individuals in group settings. The meaning of this argument is that an enormous portion of what we know or believe we know is directly or indirectly social. Concerning our belief-generating thought processes, the renowned physicist David Bohm maintained, "A key assumption that we have to question is that our thought is our own individual thought. ...Now to some extent it is. We have some independence. But we must look at it more carefully. We have to see what thought *really* is, without presuppositions. I'm trying to say that most of our thought in its general form is not individual. It originates in the whole culture and it pervades us."[4]

A June 2005 Public Broadcasting System television program based on historian David Bodanis' book $E = mc^2$: *A Biography of the World's Most Famous Equation* explored the ancestry and the legacy of Einstein's great insight. The pioneering efforts of earlier scientists that helped make Einstein's epiphany possible were described by deconstructing the equation: $E = mc^2$ (energy equals mass times the speed of light squared). Before the mid 1800s, there was no overarching notion of energy. Michael Faraday's work helped the scientific community to understand energy and to see that every form of energy is connected. Before Antoine-Laurent Lavoisier, there was no coherent and integrated notion of material substance or mass. Lavoisier was instrumental in demonstrating and describing the law of the conservation of mass, one of the great scientific achievements of the 1700s. The speed of light is designated by c (celeritas is Latin for swiftness). Before Einstein could have possibly thought of using c, someone had to confirm that light travels at a finite speed, the discovery in which Galileo, Faraday, James Clerk Maxwell and, especially, Roemer of Denmark played significant roles. Emilie du Chatelet, an early 18th-century French woman was highly influential in the story of how a factor "squared" came to be seen as deeply significant. With her colleagues, including Voltaire, building on the work of Leibnitz, Du Chatelet found the decisive evidence that velocity squared yields improved accuracy within the framework of the established view that an object's energy is in some way the product of its mass times its velocity. Over time, velocity squared times mass became the accepted indicator of energy. Einstein's insight in $E = mc^2$ was that energy and mass are interchangeable; they are different forms of the same thing. Under the right conditions, energy can become mass and vice versa. The ideas and experimentation that shaped Einstein's understanding of mass, energy, light, and velocity were separated by time and space yet the influence of collective thought is unmistakable.[5]

Most of what we believe seems to be derived from our families, our schools, our books, our cultures, our social settings, our work lives, our professional disciplines. Sometimes we are simply recipients of belief. Many of these beliefs are never questioned and to the extent that we accept them as justified and true, as knowledge rather than mere belief, we are passive receivers of these beliefs. Sometimes, when we place our own perspectives into the mix with other perspectives, we participate in the formation of our own beliefs and the beliefs of others. When we validate our beliefs within the context of some relevant reality without respect to how we came to hold these beliefs in the first place, we participate not only in belief formation and justification, but also in the growth of what we and others *know*.

The character of life in organizations is interdependent and groups representing an array of beliefs, interests, styles, predispositions, skills, job specialties, and differentiated tasks are the framework for the playing out of organizational life. Through the work of groups, we are able to go beyond the limitations of individuals and use to advantage their diverse perspectives for the purpose of knowing more fully. Formal groups are deliberately created in organizations for a variety of purposes. Examples include management teams, work units established to perform complex and interdependent tasks, staff groups providing specialized services, standing committees set up to deal with policy or ethics, and project teams organized to solve problems and address specific issues.

Groups may be vertically oriented, providing a basis for association within a function, a department, or a discipline. Groups may also be horizontally structured, crossing functional boundaries when broadly based coordination is required as in strategic planning and product development. Formal groups may be permanent or they may come and go depending on circumstances. Informal groups arise out of a combination of objective factors and human needs. Informal groupings may coincide with and/or overlap with formal ones, or they may exist independently from them. Informal groups may meet the social needs of individuals within an organization and, while such groups are often ignored, they can wield significant influence, for good or ill, on learning and objective achievement.[6]

In general, it is undeniable that the success of an organization or any group depends on its ability to comprehend reality as it is. As described in Chapter 3, multiple realities have a bearing on life in organizations and how these realities are conceived and how knowledge about them is sought have practical consequences for organizations. These realities are also multi-dimensional. There are objective and subjective dimensions to each of these realities, whether natural or constructed, varying in degree and character. Groups themselves have objective and subjective realities and often have subjective as well as objective functions. The constructed realities (material, nonmaterial, and conceptual) have both internal and external dimensions relating to the organization itself and the organization's environment respectively. The whole of any circumstance may embody multiple realities and dimensions. Truth is manifested in the whole of relevant reality where the whole pertains to the life of the organization or the group and whatever circumstances confront it. The focus in this chapter is on aligning collective belief with the whole of relevant reality through the processes associated with collective knowing.

BRIDGING FROM INDIVIDUALS TO GROUPS

Individuals can enhance the quality and results of group interaction or detract from the character and outcomes of such interaction. Reciprocally, groups can cultivate or diminish the quality of individual contribution. The philosopher Rom Harre is a leading voice in the growth of a genuinely scientific social psychology. He investigates the ways an individual can act as a competent member of a collective in his book *Social Being* and states, "The longest running, and perhaps the deepest philosophical issue in the theory of the social sciences has to do with the metaphysics of the groups in which human beings associate." He goes on to assert that any discussion of this persistent and enduring area of interest must take account of the collectivist and the individualist positions.

The extreme collectivist position holds that each human being is wholly constituted as a social person by the collective properties of the society or group in which he or she participates as a member. "These collective properties are not themselves constituted of individual properties but rather are the very structural properties which are the basis of the properties of the collective. …Such a theory effectively denies any autonomy or creativity to an individual." On the other hand, "the extreme individualist thesis, that is the theory that each individual is wholly autonomous and could exist as a person wholly independent of the collectives to which he or she belongs, is a reflection of the theory that the relations which a person has to his collectives are wholly external and consequently quite contingent." In other words, the relations of a person to the groups to which he or she belongs are of little or no significance.

In rejecting both extremes, Harre says, "It is fairly easy to show, simply by drawing attention to uncontroversial facts available to anyone, that many properties of fully developed human beings are dependent upon that person being a member of a collective." However, he continues, "there is an observable autonomy and creativity shown by individual human beings, so that the collectivist thesis in the extreme form is simply wrong."[7] Harre charts a course between these extremes and our experience in working with individuals and groups in organizations points to the soundness of a middle perspective. Individuals *do* act with autonomy and creativity yet the dynamics of groups play a significant role in the behavior of individuals in organizations. We have observed the existence of a mutual influence between individuals and groups and further, that groups tend to be the primary context for the expression of individual creativity.

While groups are obviously comprised of individuals and group perception and action breaks down to the level of the individual, groups themselves bring something extra that contributes to or detracts from the lives of individuals and organizations; the "something extra" associated with the attributes of a group is defined as the emergent properties of the group. The sections that follow explore both the dynamics of individuals in groups and the emergent or "collectivist" properties of groups as well as the circumstance that there is no bright line that separates individual dynamics and emergent properties.

Individuals in Groups

The extreme individualist perspective supposes that the nature of a group is defined as nothing more or less than the sum of the traits and beliefs of the individuals that make up the group. In rejecting this extreme perspective, it is nevertheless necessary to affirm that the diverse attributes a collection of individuals brings to groups, not the least aspect of which is diversity in how such individuals seek to know, plays a role in shaping the character and dynamics of the groups themselves. It is common to observe how a single person either added to or removed from a group affects the disposition of the group in either a positive or negative way. We bring our complete selves to group encounters, whether or not we reveal all aspects of ourselves. We bring our positive and our less than positive traits to our groups. We bring our objective selves, our knowledge, our skills, and our accomplishments. And we bring our subjective selves, our beliefs, our epistemic styles, our blind spots, and our psychological baggage.

The objective character of a group reflects its functional competence, experience, and expertise. The argument that the objective character of a group can be assessed based on the accumulation of the objective-only traits of the individuals in the group seems reasonable on the surface. Consideration of the *subjective* traits of the individuals, however, leaves us in an entirely different place. To a significant degree, subjectivity determines whether and to what extent the objective traits of individuals are expressed. In Chapter 6, we explored individual diversity in terms of cognition, perception, memory, attribution, and emotion as elements of subjectivity. We considered how the content of our beliefs and our belief-forming processes shape what we see as well as how we behave in either a productive or defensive manner. Surrounding these factors associated with belief formation and sense-making, we considered the dynamics of development and argued that, while groups can shape individuals, the process of individual growth and change is largely a one person at a time process. How the interaction of individuals in groups produces expedient or disadvantageous group dynamics is illustrated by the following pair of circumstances, the first comparatively productive and the second relatively counterproductive.

Under an ideal and productive set of group conditions, the relevant beliefs held by individual group members would be accurate or at least held loosely and open to challenge. The individuals coming together in this ideal setting would respect each other and appreciate the diverse styles and perspectives represented in the group. The attributions made by members would be routinely tested and understood for what they are, i.e., the results of naturally occurring human processes that are determinedly wrong much of the time. Nondefensive norms would exist and productive reasoning would shape the group's collective thought. Individual motivation would be consistent with the purpose of the group, which would serve to keep the individuals aligned, collegial, and willing to transcend differences. Under these conditions, the collective behavior of the group would reinforce the positive traits of the individuals in the group leading to a virtuous cycle, or a circumstance that would bring out the best qualities of the individual members of the group.

At the other end of the spectrum, under a less than ideal set of conditions, the subjective nature of individuals would be in play as well. One member of this group might hold the belief that certain other members have no legitimate place in the group. These members would tend to be out of place and essentially invisible to the first member. A commercially oriented member of the group might believe the technologists in the group to be naïve and tend to discount their assertions while the technologists, resentful of this attitude, could view the business people as unable to grasp the essence and dimensions of problems. Another member might hold the belief that those in authority are always right and should not be challenged while another might believe that those who always yield to leaders are weak and superficial. The leader of the group could believe that conflict is bad group behavior and a sign of poor leadership and, therefore, might seek to terminate and avoid conflict whenever it occurs. The members of this group will behave defensively. They will hear assertions as affronts whether or not they are. Their responses will either be subdued or argumentative and will trigger defensive responses in others. The general defensive patterns, called "defensive routines" by Argyris, will ensure that the underlying dynamics of the group will be covered up and bypassed to avoid threat and embarrassment.[8] The negative dynamics in this group will reinforce negative subjectivity among the group members thereby creating a vicious cycle resulting in a manifestation of the least positive attributes of the individuals in the group.

Having briefly considered the dynamics associated with individuals in groups at both ends of the effectiveness spectrum, we have seen how groups as simply collections of individuals turn back on themselves either virtuously or viciously, creating situations that begin to look very much like emergent properties.[9]

Emergent Properties of Groups

The attributes of group belief and behavior, not describable as simply the collective attributes of the individuals who make up the group, constitute what Harre calls emergent properties. Such properties arise from the natural coming together of individuals who need each other to act and represent the added dimension or something extra to which we have referred. Emergence may produce positive or negative effects and groups almost always exhibit some degree of either beneficial or inexpedient emergence.

Emergence in groups is an expression of gestalt or the idea that *the whole is greater than (or less than) the sum of its parts.* Consider the examples of a sports team comprised of good players but because of spirit or some other undefined quality becomes a great team, or conversely, a team made up of great individual players that never rises above the level of mediocrity. Groups in organizations that are required to think insightfully and take creative and coordinated action may tap the intelligence of many minds and become collectively more intelligent than any one mind. This kind of beneficial emergence is uncommon. Based on laboratory experiments, Michael Argyle reports that problem solutions arrived at by groups are usually better than those of the average individual, but not as good as those of the best group members. Further, regarding creativity, when the results of groups are compared with those of individuals, they have usually been found to be inferior.[10]

When the parochial, self-interested, and self-protective aspects of human nature become rooted and reinforced in the behavior of a group, the downside of emergence appears. A kind of perverse gestalt is created where the whole of the set of defenses and hardened attributions among the individuals assumes an anti-learning and defensive character exceeding the sum of the traits of the individuals in the group. Group performance is reduced to the lowest common denominator or worse, and the very existence of the group becomes counter-productive. The salient feature of such groups is their highly developed ability to obscure reality and deal in untested and often false beliefs.[11]

Positive emergence is possible, however. An example of such beneficial emergence comes from our work with a group of physicians and clinical and basic scientists. The members of the group included the department chairman and the section chiefs within a large academic department. The members of the group had been engaged in a process of seeking to set the strategic research and clinical agenda for their department. The process had been less than satisfactory having produced only a consolidated list of initiatives matching the interests of the individual members of the group. Although the scientific and clinical reality surrounding this department represented significant opportunity for breakthroughs through collaboration, each section viewed itself as virtually autonomous. The results of the process did not include an expression of clinical and basic science outcomes associated with the initiatives, foreclosing any ability to assess strategic importance and discriminate among the initiatives.

While the individual members of the group were highly regarded clinicians and researchers, strong, negative, subjective factors influenced the work of the group as a whole. Unresolved conflict, lack of trust, and attribution of inappropriate motives to the chairman and others had resulted in a general pattern of false belief and defensiveness. Work with this group focused on the subjective factors. These factors were catalogued, assessed in terms of consequences, presented to the group, and validated by the members of the group. Working with individuals, pairs of individuals, and the group as a whole, conflict was brought to light and resolved or mitigated, attributions were tested and more often than not, shown to be inaccurate, and the effects of negative perceptions were minimized. It would be inaccurate to suggest that all negative subjective issues were resolved and the group lived happily ever after. The defensive dynamics of the group changed, however, and what was collectively at stake for the group became clear.

The group developed the ability to challenge each other's beliefs and collectively learn about their potential as a department, even when some members would potentially lose status and budget allocations. The group developed and became aligned around a statement of direction, embodying a purpose larger than the collective purpose of the individuals, which spelled out the outcomes in objective terms that would represent significant achievement and growth for the department. The complete array of proposed initiatives was then evaluated in terms of how each initiative did or did not relate to the objective direction of the department. More importantly, a level of creativity developed in the group wherein collaborative efforts were identified, old initiatives were enhanced and new and more relevant ones were introduced. Because of the altered subjective chemistry of the group and the heightened awareness of their collective purpose, something greater than and different from the sum of the work of the individuals emerged. The work of the group as a group created results that a disconnected collection of individuals, irrespective of their individual traits, simply could not have produced.

THE QUALITY OF DISCOURSE

We have argued that the growth of knowledge largely occurs in groups. Given that groups don't always, or perhaps even usually, enhance knowledge, we could modify the argument to assert: the growth of knowledge occurs in groups except when it doesn't. Given that groups engage in verbal interchange or discourse, we will argue, moreover, that the quality of discourse largely determines the learning and knowledge enhancing potential of a group. We will argue further that the nature and influence of subjectivity, especially the processes and content associated with collective belief, shapes the dynamics of a group in either beneficial or detrimental ways and, therefore, shapes the quality of discourse. Individuals bring intelligence, knowledge, unique perspectives, and diverse epistemic and personal styles to their groups. The quality of discourse in these groups refers to the level and character of interaction or communication among the members. A precondition to effective communication and beneficial group dynamics will have been met when the individuals in a group, through a collective motivation to *know*, are able to hold their beliefs as hypotheses or propositions open to either validation or invalidation and to manage their potential defensiveness. Under the influence of this precondition, fundamental constraints on collective creativity will have been mitigated and attention can turn to productive modes of collective thought and discourse.

The aims of effective discourse are nothing less than learning and truth. Given our need to *know* rather than to believe falsely or incompletely, it would seem that we would strive for effective discourse as a norm in our encounters with each other. Unhappily, high quality discourse does not seem to be a feature of life in our times. Examples of poor communication and suboptimal discourse are ubiquitous from business to politics to multidisciplinary science, to religion to public policy to interactions within our organizations. Conclusions are drawn from untested hypotheses; inconsistent and unjustified beliefs, unchallenged assumptions, and faulty attributions are allowed to hold sway; muddled inferences pass for acceptable thought and debates are decided based on the loudest and most persistent arguments and those that strike some emotional chord. As complexity, the consequences of technology, and interdependence in our collective lives accelerate, we appear to be less and less able to think and interact critically, creatively, and effectively. As well-educated as we have become in ever more narrow fields of study, our education seems to leave us woefully unprepared to learn in a broader context and from each other. Reductionism in our intellectual lives has been in the ascendancy for generations. As we have mastered technology and vastly diverse specialties, we have learned much and come to know much, but we seem to have lost the ability to learn about wholeness, beyond limited and bounded subject matter. The biologist Edward O. Wilson contends in his article "Back From Chaos" that most of the problems and issues that vex humanity can only be solved by integrating knowledge from the natural and social sciences and the humanities. He writes, "Only fluency across the boundaries will provide a clear view of the world as it really is, not as it appears through the lens of ideology and religious dogma, or as a myopic response solely to immediate need."[12]

Trivium

The mediaeval syllabus in education consisted of two components, the trivium and quadrivium. The trivium pertained to the foundations or tools for learning; the quadrivium was composed of subject matter. The trivium consisted of three parts: grammar, dialectic, and rhetoric. The quadrivium encompassed arithmetic, geometry, music, and astronomy. Dorothy Sayers described the trivium in a paper delivered at Oxford University in 1947. The whole of the trivium, she said, was intended to teach the proper use of the tools of learning before the pupil began to apply them to subjects. In grammar, the student learned the structure and use of language. Dialectic embraced logic and disputation. In the study of dialectic, the student learned how to define terms and make accurate statements, how to construct an argument and how to detect fallacies in his own arguments and those of others. In rhetoric, "He learned to express himself in language: how to say what he had to say elegantly and persuasively." The trivium conceived dialectic and rhetoric as two sides of the same coin. Speaking about the study of rhetoric, Sayers continued, "At this point, any tendency to express himself windily or to use his eloquence so as to make the worse appear the better reason would, no doubt, be restrained by his previous teaching in dialectic. If not, his teacher and his fellow pupils, trained along the same lines, would be quick to point out where he was wrong; for it was they whom he had to seek to persuade."[13] Socrates' alternative to pointless and unedifying debate was good conversation or dialectic. "To converse originally meant to turn toward one another, in order to find a common humanity and to move closer to the truth of something. Dialectic, in other words, is decidedly not about wining or losing, because all the conversants are ennobled by it. It is a joint search."[14]

It is our loss that dialectic languishes while rhetoric and grammar in support of rhetoric thrive in our modern and economic, political, ethical, and everyday lives. It is as if we're often traveling without a compass or flying without instruments, without the ability to test our direction and alter our course when circumstances change. Without dialectic as a means of creating balance in our rhetoric, attention is solely on winning arguments and not on accessing the truth. "As the disciplined search for truth, dialectic includes all of logic. It is concerned with every phase of thought: with the establishment of definitions; the examination of hypotheses in light of their presuppositions and consequences; the formation of inferences and proofs; the resolution of dilemmas arising from opposition in thought." Consistent with Plato's conception in the Dialogues, dialectic is "the art which deals with inferences and definitions and divisions and is of the greatest assistance in the discovery of meaning ... Dialectic, in other words, is divorced from the practical purpose of stating and winning an argument and given theoretical status as a method of inquiry. Rhetoric, on the other hand, is not to be used so much for ascertaining meaning as for setting forth meaning when it has been ascertained."[15]

As children we are exemplary learners in the broadest possible sense, but progressively as we grow into adulthood, our training and socialization slots us into ever-narrower sets of learning options. As adults, therefore, we have few skills in collective learning outside relatively fixed frames of reference. Although the notion of learning from the past, especially the European Middle Ages, is not especially congenial to twenty-first century minds, the skills to successfully engage in collective discovery and creativity are rooted in the trivium. The language of the trivium is also somewhat unnatural and off-putting to modern ears and sensibilities; therefore, the term dialogue will be substituted for dialectic in the remainder of this chapter.

The term dialogue in current usage is generally and merely taken to mean a conversation between two or more people. It should be borne in mind, however, that dialogue and dialectic are from the same Greek root meaning discourse, which itself means orderly thought. For our purposes, the definition of dialogue more specifically will be conversation and reasoning as a method of intellectual investigation and learning.[16]

Dialogue

Dialogue in groups is critical discourse and is the counterpart of critical thinking in individuals. In dialogue as a substitute term for dialectic, there is a spirit of back and forth and mutual influence—between contradictory ideas or between ideas that vary slightly but significantly, between proposition and counterproposition, between a concept and its opposite, between thesis and antithesis. The principles of dialogue become the principles of change when change itself is perceived as progress or evolution from lower to higher, from part to whole, from analysis to synthesis. As a mode of communication, dialogue aims for the development of meaning in contrast to simply conveying information or knowledge from one person to another. David Bohm, the quantum theorist with a life long interest in dialogue, defines it this way: "Consider a dialogue, when one person says something, the other person does not in general respond with exactly the same meaning as that seen by the first person. Rather, the meanings are only similar and not identical. Thus, when the second person replies, the first person sees a difference between what he meant to say and what the other person understood. On considering this difference, he may then be able to see something new, which is relevant both to his own views and to those of the other person. And so it can go back and forth, with the continual emergence of a new content that is common to both participants."[17]

Dialogue is the collective art of seeking to know, of seeking to comprehend reality, and of seeking to move from belief to knowledge through logical discussion and collective effort. In dialogue, diverse perspectives and cognitive or epistemic styles are joined to gain deeper understanding and a new synthesis. In dialogue, we explore complex issues from many points of view and seek to move from contradiction to clarity and reconciliation.

To return to David Bohm's view of dialogue, "the picture or image is of a stream of meaning flowing among and through and between us.... This will make possible a flow of meaning in the whole group, out of which may emerge some new understanding. It's something new, which may not have been in the starting point at all. Contrast this with the word 'discussion,' which has the same root as 'percussion' and 'concussion.' It really means to break things up. It emphasizes the idea of analysis, where there may be many points of view, and where everybody is presenting a different one— analyzing and breaking up. That obviously has its value, but it is limited, and it will not get us very far beyond our various points of view."[18]

In dialogue, the opportunity exists to move beyond one person's understanding to enable the growth of knowledge and to produce qualitatively better results. While the quote from Bohm captures the spirit of dialogue, it also conveys an idealized or utopian feeling of an equality or symmetry of perspectives, any one of which is as potentially good as any other, which is not consistent with our perspective. For us, some perspectives or beliefs are more *right* than others; in dialogue, there *is* a reality about which we are seeking to know and the "new understanding" is simply that which is closer to the truth.

The Mechanics of Dialogue

Groups engaged in dialogue are seeking to comprehend reality as completely and accurately as possible. Dialogue, however, is far easier to talk about as an abstraction and an ideal than it is to achieve. In this section, the art of dialogue as a practical means to learning and the growth of knowledge in groups will be explored by considering the preconditions and certain methods associated with dialogue. The core ideas embodied in our conception of how dialogue can be achieved are 1) the existence and function of individual and collective beliefs and assumptions, 2) the role of purpose as the motivation for individuals in groups to engage in dialogue and 3) the proposition that there is a reality associated with the work of groups, the knowledge of which has important implications for the lives of the group and the organization. As a leading theorist and supporter of dialogue, David Bohm's perspectives are influential and we are grateful for his insights. Our analysis beyond the essence or spirit of dialogue, however, diverges from his path, especially as related to preconditions and methods.

Beliefs and Assumptions

The facts that individuals bring their beliefs and assumptions to group settings and that groups themselves can form collective beliefs through emergence bring about circumstances that may act as constraints to dialogue. The beliefs that produce such constraints are not trivial; they often have to do with conceptions of good and bad, individual self-interest, organizational success, proper and inappropriate roles, and the meaning of effective action. Bohm's prescription is to suspend beliefs or assumptions and, in the process, to become open to other more relevant beliefs or assumptions.[19] Bohm wonders, however, "Does the difficulty not originate in some more subtle way?" Our perspective is that there *is* a more subtle difficulty, expressed in two ways as developed in Chapter 4. First, while Husserl's phenomenology, laying the groundwork for views such as Bohm's, proposed suspending one's judgments or particular beliefs about phenomena in order to see them more clearly, the fusion of hermeneutics with phenomenology suggests that suspending beliefs is practically impossible because our making sense of any reality is based on our frames of reference, including our beliefs and preconceptions. Second, our best hope to transcend our beliefs and develop our ability to hold them as hypotheses and not be held by them, rests on our ability to be acquainted with how we formed the beliefs in the first place and to match the relevance of our belief-forming processes or epistemic styles with the character of the reality in question.

Purpose

Dialogue is often perceived as unnatural, difficult, and possibly unable to serve the interests of individuals. A precondition to dialogue pertains to the willingness of individuals to engage in dialogue and the preparedness of group members to grant colleagueship to each other. Willingness relates to being willing to make the effort and colleagueship refers to trust and the idea that we're better as a group than we are as individuals. The motivation to succeed resulting from a clear and shared sense of purpose is the only way we know to develop the ability to deal with hardened patterns of perception, attribution, belief formation, self interest, and defensiveness in order to satisfy this precondition. We separate company with Bohm again over his conception of dialogue as having no purpose by definition. Bohm argues that there is no place in dialogue for authority and hierarchy and we should hope to be free of these influences. "But in dialogue, insofar as we have no purpose and no agenda and we don't have to do anything, we don't really need to have an authority or a hierarchy. Rather, we need a place where there is no special purpose—sort of an empty place, where we can let anything be talked about."[20] While purposeless dialogue may be possible and interesting as a game or as an academic exercise, dialogue without purpose as a useful and practical mode of discourse in organizations is unrealistic and not worth the effort.

Methods

Given willingness and colleagueship and the ability to hold beliefs and assumptions as hypotheses, the ability to produce and sustain dialogue seems to turn on the availability of methods to engage group members in effective exposition (rhetoric) and reconciliation (dialectic) of divergent perspectives. Some useful methods from our experience are described below:

- Definition of Terms—Definition of terms is a straightforward and universal convention in the crafting of coherent and productive arguments, yet it is frequently not met. The clear definition of categories or classes of objects, concepts, and terms associated with arguments provides a fundamental and crucial building block of coherent interaction surrounding those arguments. When opposing arguments are in disagreement concerning the essence of objects or concepts central to the arguments, there can be no basis for common ground. It is an all too common occurrence, in organizations as well as in the public arena, to hear irreconcilable positions argued concerning apples on the one hand and oranges on the other with no attempt having been made to identify and define the objects of argument and difference.

- Formulation of Inferences—Inference is the process of deriving conclusions from premises. It is the process of passing from one proposition or statement considered as true and justified to another whose truth and justification are believed to follow from that of the former. Inference is a feature of all epistemic styles or approaches to forming beliefs and knowing and good argumentation requires that inferential steps be described and made explicit. As described in Chapters 4 and 5, there are generally two kinds of inference, inductive and probabilistic on the one hand and deductive and necessary on the other. Epistemic styles tend to embody one or the other type of inference. The concept of necessity holds that what is necessary cannot be otherwise; necessary truths are those whose opposite is impossible. Approaches to knowing such as foundationalism and rationalism, which are based on notions of *necessity* of basic beliefs and deductive inference are poorly suited to dialogue since they preclude holding beliefs as contingent or hypothetical. Depending on the nature of the reality in question, approaches to knowing or epistemic styles embodying patterns of inductive and contingent inference such as empiricism, coherentism, pragmatism, contextualism, and hermeneutic phenomenology are well suited to dialogue.

- Hermeneutical Circle—The methodology of hermeneutic phenomenology is iterative within the context of what has been described as the hermeneutical circle. Paraphrasing the description from Chapter 4, the whole of any circumstance or object receives its definition from the parts and, reciprocally, the parts can only be understood in reference to the whole. The hermeneutical circle refers to a method that can support the collective understanding of the nature of the reality facing a group and around which dialogue is sought as a mode of discourse. However, the concept of the hermeneutical circle involves a logical contradiction. According to Frederich Schleiermacher, the German philosopher who undertook a project to define General Hermeneutics, "If we must grasp the whole before we can understand the parts, then we shall never understand anything. Yet we have asserted that the part derives its meaning from the whole. And surely, on the other hand, we cannot start with a whole, undifferentiated into parts. Is the concept of the hermeneutical circle therefore invalid? No, rather, we must say that logic cannot fully account for the workings of understanding. Somehow, a kind of 'leap' into the hermeneutical circle occurs and we understand the whole and the parts together. With its spatial image, the hermeneutical circle suggests an area of shared understanding. Since communication is a dialogical relation, there is assumed at the outset a community of meaning shared by the speaker and the hearer. This seems to involve another contradiction: what is to be understood must already be known. But is this not the case? Is it not vain to speak of love to one who has not known love, or of the joys of learning to those who reject it? One must already have, in some measure, a knowledge of the matter being discussed."[21]

- Linguistic Devices—A primary challenge in bringing about dialogue for the purpose of learning and the growth of knowledge is to stimulate individual minds and bring them together in relation to a relevant reality. Paradox, metaphor, allegory, and parable are figures of speech and linguistic constructs that provide color and drama, illuminate conflict and dilemma, and provide frames of reference. Looking specifically at paradox, most of the dilemmas we encounter in life are paradoxical. The opposing perspectives that define a dilemma and tend to polarize and harden perspectives usually define the two sides of a paradox. Some paradoxes in modern life are: How do we achieve a challenging and rewarding professional life and maintain a satisfying and rich personal and family life at the same time? How do we gratify ourselves in the short-term and postpone gratification for long-term benefit at the same time? In organizational life, how can we be big in some ways and small in others? How can we sustain differentiated work units yet become integrated around the larger organization? How can we maintain control over organizational units and empower them at the same time? Paradoxes are not often resolved in ways that make them go away. The best we can usually hope for in paradox is to find a way through it, bringing both sides into some degree of congruence where winning and losing doesn't occur.[22] The "third perspective" is a tool for thinking about effective ways through paradox. Charles Handy in *The Age of Paradox* describes how "Trinitarian thinking or third angle thinking is always looking for solutions which can reconcile or illuminate the opposites." Handy describes the motto of the French Revolution—"Liberty, Equality, Fraternity"—as the best known example of trinitarian thinking. Liberty cancels out equality and vice versa. The two can only survive in any sort of harmony if there is fraternity. "If we care for one another, we will not press our demands for individual liberty so far that it intrudes on our equal right to be free, nor will your pressure for equality be pushed so far that it denies me my liberty."[23]

Preconditions for Dialogue and (Steps to Satisfy Preconditions)
Willingness
(Define Purpose)
Colleagueship
(Mitigate Defensive Patterns)
Beliefs as Hypotheses
(Identify Operative Beliefs/Assumptions and Approaches to Knowing/Belief Formation)
Engagement in Exposition and Reconciliation of Divergent Perspectives
(Methods)
(Definition of Terms)
(Formulation of Inferences)
(Hermeneutic Circle)
(Linguistic Devices)

FIGURE 7.1

Figure 7.1 summarizes our conceptions of the preconditions for dialogue and the steps that may be taken to satisfy the preconditions.

THE ROLE OF GROUPS IN THE GROWTH OF KNOWLEDGE

Two foundational arguments from Chapter 1 apply to the role of groups in the growth of knowledge, especially as they pertain to the quality of discourse. The first of these states: *Individuals and their collectives tend to be predisposed to one or a closely related set of dominant approaches to forming beliefs and seek to apply these approaches to knowing (or merely believing) to any reality.* The second argument is as follows: *Diverse approaches to knowing can facilitate or constrain creativity, problem solving and the growth of knowledge.* The role of groups in the growth of knowledge comes into focus around two questions: *Why do we not know as groups or collections of individuals, and how can we come to know more fully through the work groups?*

Why Do We Not Know as Groups or Collections of Individuals?

Collectively, we fail to recognize and understand the relevant reality. Organizations confront multiple realities, from physical to material to nonmaterial to conceptual, embodying objective and subjective dimensions. Material, nonmaterial, and conceptual realities have internal and external dimensions relating to the organization itself and the organization's environment. The whole of any actual circumstance may embody multiple realities and dimensions. When we fail to grasp the relevant reality, we seek to know about the wrong set of circumstances. Our consequential actions, while possibly valid in an absolute sense, may be ineffective or worse within the context of the actual reality. This is analogous to carefully planning and executing the steps to travel from point A to point B when the required destination is point C. Purpose and reality are tightly linked concepts. When reality is misinterpreted or individual and collective beliefs result in imputing false characteristics to reality, purpose becomes difficult or impossible to clearly define and articulate. In the absence of a clear purpose, the motivation to *know* among group members is imperiled.

Our collective beliefs are incongruent with reality and our groups fail to support substantive challenge to these beliefs. Given the presence of relevant reality, how are our collective beliefs incompatible with this realty? The members of a group may share a set of beliefs, which could have emerged through the existence and work of the group, or the members may hold individual and diverse beliefs. In either case, if the group *acts* based on what it believes and thinks it knows, it is acting in accord with some belief or set of beliefs whether or not they are shared or representative of a dominant belief among one or more dominant members. Reality is what it is, even taking account of the circumstance that the group may be helping to shape the relevant reality. But if this reality is not seen and comprehended for what it is, the actions of the group will be based on what it falsely believes rather than what it knows.

The model in Figure 6.1 of Chapter 6 pertains to individuals. Shifting the meaning of this model from individuals to groups, the fact that collective beliefs are incongruent with reality is a *content* of belief problem. In contrast to *structure* of belief, such beliefs as "the earth is flat" or "we hold our employees in high regard" when the evidence is otherwise, are examples of (false) belief content. The degree of intransigence associated with our collective beliefs pertains to the *structure* of our beliefs. We can be certain that learning, the growth of knowledge, and effective, group inspired action will not occur when our beliefs are false and when the structure of our beliefs causes us to fail to challenge and realign them with reality. It seems unlikely that the character of relevant reality and the *content* of related belief could be fully understood as incongruent, yet the group would resist bringing such beliefs into question. It seems more likely that the *structure* of a group's beliefs (characterized as, for example, dogmatic, reductionistic, or deterministic) would inhibit understanding reality and collectively comprehending related belief as first order concerns in the process of seeking to know.

We collectively apply inappropriate or invalid approaches to knowing about the relevant reality. One of the central themes of this book is that, given an understanding of the nature of the reality in question, certain epistemic styles are more relevant than others and some are not relevant at all. Although the individual members of a group bring diverse ways of knowing to the group, through emergence the group may evolve a collective way of knowing that holds the group in its grip. An example of the downside of emergence is groupthink. Groupthink represents a special class of group incompetence through emergence and results from too much cohesiveness and conformity. According to Michael Argyle, groupthink occurs when "a group comes to see itself as invulnerable; there is rationalization of blind spots; it ignores ethical issues; stereotyped outgroups are seen as evil, weak or stupid; a lot of pressure is put on dissenters who are regarded as disloyal; any doubts are not voiced and there is an illusion of unanimity.[24] In groupthink the members of a group become so identified with the group that any threat to the group is a threat to the members and a mode of defensiveness becomes the norm. Even though the individual members may know better, the group adopts a kind of collective *foundationalism* in its approach to reality based on basic beliefs about the group and reality. As we have seen, foundationalism as an epistemic style is anathema to dialogue. It is an inappropriate way of knowing about any but a few phenomena and will tend to ensure that the group will fail to question what it thinks it knows. One of the better-known early twenty-first century examples of groupthink on a large scale is Enron, the failed energy company that went from being a Wall Street darling to a criminally bankrupt organization based on its flawed basic and foundational belief that "We're the smartest guys in the room."

We became acquainted with the work of Marco Polo, a project team so named within one of the major business functions of an international manufacturing and services company. The project team was conceived, organized, and set to work to design and implement new work processes to support globalization of the function and to bring about improvements in efficiency. The project team had failed to produce a credible plan, it had alienated key internal customers and stakeholders, taken dubious actions, and caused embarrassment and anxiety for the general manager of the overall function. This team had failed to comprehend the relevant reality and, on several levels, had failed to know what it needed to know. Various conceptions of the relevant reality existed within the team. The global reality of the overall organization was represented, along with the local realities associated with the Americans, the Asians, and the Europeans. There were also conceptions of reality associated with the manager of the project, the dominant member of the project team and the primary internal customer. Some members of the team held unjustified beliefs about other members of the team that shaped their beliefs about the reality facing the team. Some members' conceptions of reality took account of human factors to such an extent that objective factors were under considered. Others gave no credence to the notion that subjectivity was a part of the relevant reality.

As asserted before, purpose and reality are tightly linked concepts. The heart of Marco Polo's difficulty as a team was that it had not conceptualized its role and produced a coherent purpose for the project around which team members could become aligned and committed. Groupthink was distinctly not this group's problem. The epistemic styles or approaches to knowing in this group were varied. They ranged from an extreme, objectively oriented empiricism to rationalism to foundationalism, none of which was suited to knowing about the complex reality facing the group. Related to its existence and its work, the team simply did not know what was operative and real. In the absence of a common perception of reality and common sense of purpose, no path to reconciling the diverse ways of knowing represented in the group had been identified and pursued.

How Can We Come to Know More Fully Through the Work of Groups?

Collectively identify and define the implications of knowing and not knowing. This part of our answer regarding the positive role of groups in the growth of knowledge pertains to the *desire* to know. When something important and unambiguous is at stake in knowing versus believing falsely, there is a motive for the members of a group to defeat the many reasons why we often fail to know. Purpose is a primary motivating factor for individuals and frames collective aspiration and shared commitment in groups. Objective purpose is *why* groups, formed for a wide range of functions, exist; a sense of common cause clarifies the implications and consequences of knowing and not knowing. A recent news story featured two interviews, one with a prominent Harvard biologist and agnostic and the other with the pastor of a large church and president of the Association of Evangelicals in the United States. The two leaders of their respective communities are working together to find common ground between science and religion on the issue of climate change induced by human activity. The scientific and religious communities are traditionally very far apart on an array of issues and operate from profoundly different worldviews. In spite of their differences, however, the need for knowledge and action to respond to the reality of climate change facing both communities provided the common cause to transcend their differences. Both individuals spoke about being good stewards of the environment and how science can provide the knowledge about climate change and how the churches can provide the people, able to be educated, and positioned to act.

Collectively identify and define the reality in question. Without clarity about reality, clarity in relation to purpose will be impossible. Therefore, this and the previous part of our answer to the question pertaining to how to know more fully are not serial steps and cannot be separated. Without comprehension of the reality of climate change, the creation of purpose or common cause and the collaboration referenced above would have been unachievable. Although various members of a group may have different ideas about the reality confronting the group, the group as a whole must ultimately identify, define and agree about the character of this reality. The greatest threats to understanding reality are fragmentation (the breaking of reality into pieces and losing a sense of the whole in the process) and reductionism (reducing a complex reality into simplistic or contrived and often numerically measured terms). The preconditions for dialogue and the methods associated with dialogue are essential to the effective work of groups in defining relevant reality.

Identify and define the collective approaches to knowing being brought to bear on the reality in question. When the group has identified and characterized the reality facing the group, it becomes necessary to know how the various members of the group will seek to form beliefs and, potentially, to know about this reality. It has been argued throughout this book that epistemic style is a fundamental aspect of individual diversity and that we tend to apply the style or styles most natural and comfortable to us to any reality we face. We have argued further that, given the relevant reality, some approaches to knowing are appropriate and others are not. This aspect of diversity puts up walls and separates people. We have suggested that it is a deeper and more influential dimension of our individuality than the beliefs or assumptions we hold. As a precondition to the next part of our answer to the question of how we know in groups, it is necessary to be able to become collectively aware of the approaches to knowing being brought to bear on the reality in question and the implications and consequences of these differences.

Identify and develop consensus around the valid and/or reconciling approaches to knowing about this reality. The ability of individuals as group members to think critically and the capacity of the group to engage in dialogue converge to enable the group to apply a valid approach to knowing about the reality in question. Given that any group may contain members who tend toward approaches to knowing as diverse as, for example, empiricism, reliabilism, rationalism, and coherentism, any one of these may be valid for the relevant reality and able to be agreed upon. The development of consensus around one of these epistemic styles, however, may not be possible. When such consensus fails to result from the work of a group, it will be useful to recall one of the hypotheses from Chapter 1 of this book: Within the work of groups, specific approaches to knowing can transcend and help to bridge or reconcile the diverse approaches to knowing of individuals. Hermeneutic phenomenology and contextualism were offered in Chapter 5 as approaches to knowing that relate to all realities and combinations and dimensions of reality and offer reconciling features to those individuals who hold divergent epistemic styles. For the realities we have defined as constructed, pragmatism was put forward as a potentially valid and reconciling approach to knowing.

The question on the minds of the leader and the members of an operations management team with whom we worked was how can we "ruthlessly prioritize" what we do? Corporate management had high expectations for this unit and its management. There were more opportunities in an expanding market and more ideas to take advantage of the opportunities than the organization could effectively pursue. There were also physical constraints on the production capacity of the organization. The members of the team felt compelled to develop all the good ideas and remedy all the constraining factors. At the same time, they felt overworked, pushed to the limit and worried about achieving the financial goals. At one level, this was the group's reality and the group's efforts to make sense of this reality had produced no beneficial change in its operations. What did the members of this group need to know that they did not know? At a deeper and more influential level, what was the reality facing this group? With the exception of the leader of the group, most members understood their reality to be purely physical and material and their approaches to knowing about this reality, consistent with this view, were primarily empiricist and foundationalist.

A process of qualitative research to understand and interpret the dimensions and meaning of this organization's reality was undertaken based on the principles and methods of hermeneutic phenomenology. What the members of the group did not know was identified in the research and expressed in these questions: What are the most relevant, important, and leverage-producing outcomes for this organization? In other words, what are the results we can achieve that will produce the greatest good for this unit and the larger organization? What are the characteristics of the subjective reality of this unit and how do these factors affect objective reality and performance? What are the attributes of the existing culture and how does culture affect behavior within this organization? The process of answering these questions framed a period of dialogue, which resulted in the collective understanding that the reality facing the organization was material and nonmaterial and in no part natural or physical. Further, the group came to understand that its need for a more planned and long-term orientation was being thwarted by the organization's culture, which elevated "firefighting" as a desired way of being. The members of the group saw that there was a collective belief that firefighting was good based on the fact that the members received a great deal of psychic reward from behaving in this manner, even though it was counterproductive for the team and the organization. Representing pragmatism as a collective epistemic style, an orientation to outcomes emerged as a method for achieving "ruthless prioritization" and was adopted by the group. Based on the "felt" need of the members of the group, the motivation to know was clearly present and the group was able to define its relevant reality and ultimately to *know* and to act in such a way as to improve its performance and achieve its goals.

REFERENCES

1. Heisenberg, Werner. 1971. *Physics and Beyond: Encounters and Conversations*. New York: Harper and Row.
2. Newman, John Henry. 1946. *The Living Thoughts of Cardinal Newman*. New York: David McKay Company.
3. Williams, Michael. 2001. *Problems of Knowledge: A Critical Introduction to Epistemology*. New York: Oxford University Press.
4. Bohm, David. 1996. *On Dialogue*. New York: Routledge Classics.

5. Bodanis, David. 2005. $E = mc^2$: *A Biography of the World's Most Famous Equation.* Presented as: Einstein's Big Idea. Public Broadcasting System.
6. Douglas, Neil and Terry Wykowski. 1999. *Beyond Reductionism: Gateways for Learning and Change.* Boca Raton: St. Lucie Press.
7. Harre, Rom. 1979. *Social Being: A Theory for Social Psychology.* Oxford: Basil Blackwell.
8. Argyris, Chris. 1994. *Knowledge for Action: A Guide to Overcoming Barriers to Organizational Change.* San Francisco: Jossey-Bass.
9. Douglas, Neil and Terry Wykowski. 1999. *Beyond Reductionism: Gateways for Learning and Change.* Boca Raton: St. Lucie Press.
10. Argyle, Michael. 1989. *The Social Psychology of Work*, 2nd ed. London: Penguin Books.
11. Douglas, Neil and Terry Wykowski. 1999. *Beyond Reductionism: Gateways for Learning and Change.* Boca Raton: St. Lucie Press.
12. Wilson, Edward O. 1998. Back from Chaos, *The Atlantic Monthly* March 1998:41–62.
13. Sayers, Dorothy. 1947. *The Lost Tools of Learning.* London: Methuen and Co. Ltd.
14. Arguing to Death: Socrates in America. 2009. *The Economist* December 19:61–63.
15. Dialectic. 1952. In *The Great Ideas: A Syntopicon of the Great Books of The Western World* 1, 345–352. Chicago: Encyclopedia Britannica, Inc.
16. Douglas, Neil and Terry Wykowski. 1999. *Beyond Reductionism: Gateways for Learning and Change.* Boca Raton: St. Lucie Press.
17. Bohm, David. 1996. *On Dialogue.* New York: Routledge Classics.
18. Bohm, David. 1996. *On Dialogue.* New York: Routledge Classics.
19. Bohm, David. 1996. *On Dialogue.* New York: Routledge Classics.
20. Bohm, David. 1996. *On Dialogue.* New York: Routledge Classics.
21. Palmer, Richard E. 1969. *Hermeneutics: Interpretation Theory in Schleiermacher, Dilthey, Heidegger, and Gadamer.* Evanston: Northwestern University Press.
22. Douglas, Neil and Terry Wykowski. 1999. *Beyond Reductionism: Gateways for Learning and Change.* Boca Raton: St. Lucie Press.
23. Handy, Charles. 1994. *The Age of Paradox.* Boston: Harvard Business School Press.
24. Argyle, Michael. 1989. *The Social Psychology of Work*, 2nd ed. London: Penguin Books.

8

Leaders

ANTICIPATORY SUMMARY

Leadership behavior, rarely neutral, either enhances or diminishes an organization's capacity for knowledge growth and adaptive change. Among the functions of both formal and informal leaders, the argument is made that the foremost function is providing and sustaining an environment hospitable to truth, enabling the creation and extension of a set of conditions conducive to learning and the growth of knowledge.

A set of leader-influenced factors that either constrain or facilitate the growth of knowledge is proposed. If and how leaders mitigate the barriers or the constraints to the growth of knowledge as well as how they support or fail to support the factors that facilitate the growth of knowledge are explored in this chapter.

Factors That Constrain the Growth of Knowledge

The factors that constrain the growth of knowledge are barriers that operate sometimes subtly and sometimes not so subtly to inhibit and restrict learning. The barriers that emerge as primary centers of interest are 1) reductionism, 2) organizational politics, and 3) culture. Reductionism masks the true character of reality and renders attempts to *know* shallow and incomplete. Negative political dynamics suggest an environment of defensiveness where individuals protect vested interests and pursue hidden and private agendas. The aspects of culture that constrain the growth of knowledge are those that perpetuate an anti-learning status quo.

Factors That Facilitate the Growth of Knowledge

Three important factors associated with establishing and sustaining the conditions required for the growth of knowledge are 1) perception of the proper relation among the objective and subjective dimensions of any reality, 2) clarity of purpose, and 3) the salutary attributes of a progressive culture. Treating any reality as either exclusively objective or exclusively subjective obscures the meaning of the whole. The collective motivation to know, to hold beliefs that are both justified and as close to true as possible, is provided by purpose. In addition to the positive influence of these factors in their own right, they help overcome the barriers to the growth of knowledge.

Leaders and the Growth of Knowledge

Effective leaders bring about and sustain a culture oriented to hypothesis rather than belief. They identify and manage processes to reconcile divergent perspectives and ways of forming beliefs and knowing within the context of an accurate and shared conception of reality.

The functions of leadership and the influence of constraints and factors that facilitate the growth of knowledge come into focus around the essential responsibility of leaders to align the institutional beliefs of an organization with reality. The implications of this central responsibility, the related functions of leadership, and the influence of barriers and facilitators are examined within the framework of the questions: What role do leaders play in *not* knowing and what role do leaders play in knowing more fully?

LEADERS

In any aspect of organizational life, the behavior of leaders is seldom neutral and without consequences. The subject matter of this chapter is how leaders behave to either enhance or diminish the capacity for knowledge growth. Our conception of leadership within the context of this book is broad. It relates to the proposition that through their ideas, expertise, example, persuasion, and authority, individuals as leaders have an uncommon effect on the life, work, and results of organizations. The term leader may be applied to virtually anyone with influence—to the engineer with innovative product ideas, the physician with special knowledge and skills, the creative designer, the highly respected nurse, the dedicated teacher, the staff assistant whose spirit encourages others, the project manager with a record of success, the general manager with the ability to foster teamwork, or the chief executive officer with a clear vision of the organization's successful future. The fundamental meaning of leadership does not define difference across this arbitrary spectrum of roles. Rather, the difference potentially lies in the effects of an individual's actions and the proportion of time and energy an individual allocates to producing results through other people. The central idea in our conception of leadership is leverage. Our use of the term leverage in relation to leaders pertains to taking action that produces multiplier effects, especially in the results of the work of other people. Such action may be direct and formal as in the case of the exercise of authority, or persuasion, or indirect and informal as in the application of expertise or personal example or a combination of both. With the actions of leaders as rarely neutral, they tend either to add value through positive leverage or reduce value through negative leverage. In other words, based on the simple idea of leverage as a multiplier, an action leading to greater advantage for the organization is an example of positive leverage while action leading to disadvantage or impediment illustrates negative leverage.

Informal leaders influence others and create leverage. The material presented in this chapter, therefore, pertains to individuals in both informal and formal leadership roles. Calling attention for the moment, however, to formal leadership, these roles exist solely for the purpose of adding value to the work of other people. It is obvious that leaders, who produce results only through the work of others, do not personally produce anything. They don't design and build products and provide services, they don't teach students, they don't sell products and services, they don't discover and develop sources of energy, and they don't take care of patients, cook meals, and clean floors in hospitals. The only reason for the existence of such leaders is to eliminate or mitigate the constraints on real work and clear the way for higher levels of effectiveness and productivity.

If production is enhanced through improved relevance, higher quality or greater levels of output as a consequence of the actions of leaders, positive leverage is created. If such enhancement does not occur, negative leverage attaches to the presence and work of the leader. This circumstance leads us to reaffirm the belief described in our book *Beyond Reductionism* that there should be something like a Hippocratic Oath for leaders: "First, do no harm!"[1]

The consequences for leaders whose efforts fail to add value and improvement in the work of others should be the same as those for engineers who design bridges that collapse, doctors who make people sick, and teachers who cause students to hate learning. The hubris and sense of certainty associated with some leaders in high positions often brings about an illusion of control, yet many leaders simply do not know what goes on in their organizations at the level where the real work is done. The practice of "killing the messenger" while serving to protect the illusion, is an effective method for ensuring that people will withhold information from leaders and avoid telling them the truth.

When a leader's sometimes flawed assumptions and beliefs about reality go unchallenged, these assumptions and beliefs are in control of the organization to a far greater extent than what the leader says and does. In contrast to their fellow leaders who fail to succeed, effective leaders are more secure, less afraid of the truth, more comfortable with uncertainty, more humble and less inclined to believe that they have to be in complete control in order for results to be produced.

The fourth hypothesis from Chapter 1 states: *The essential task of leadership is to bring about and sustain an environment conducive to the growth of knowledge.* The growth of knowledge is an effective and unambiguous basis for leading organizations. It frames and enables the engagement of individuals and groups in the process of accessing and reconciling diverse and idiosyncratic perspectives for the purpose of achieving higher levels of relevance and performance. We will argue in this chapter that perhaps the greatest positive leverage a leader can produce is the object of this hypothesis—creating and sustaining a set of conditions hospitable to the truth. A tightly interconnected set of factors that either constrain or facilitate the growth of knowledge is proposed in this chapter. If and how leaders mitigate the barriers or the constraints to the growth of knowledge and how they support or fail to support the factors that facilitate the growth of knowledge are explored in the sections that follow.

Factors That Constrain the Growth of Knowledge

The factors that constrain the growth of knowledge are barriers that operate subtly and sometimes not so subtly to inhibit and restrict learning. The barriers that emerge as chief attractors of interest are 1) reductionism,

2) organizational politics, and 3) the aspects of culture that perpetuate an anti-learning status quo.

Reductionism

Reductionism is both a philosophical judgment about the nature of phenomena and a method for investigating such phenomena. It has a venerable reputation in science and is responsible for much of what we know about the natural world. In The limits of Reductionism in Medicine, Andrew Ahn and others affirm: "Since Descartes and the Renaissance, science has taken a distinct path in its analytical evaluation of the natural world. This approach can be described as one of 'divide and conquer,' and it is rooted in the assumption that complex problems are solvable by dividing them into smaller, simpler, and thus more tractable units. Because the processes are 'reduced' into more basic units, this approach has been termed 'reductionism' and has been the predominant paradigm of science over the past two centuries."[2]

The remarkable successes of science lead many scientists to take "reductionist" as descriptive of their method to be high praise. For them, it means that their focus is on the fundamental and essential and that everything irrelevant is methodically removed as "noise." To call science reductionist, however, may also be a criticism and can point to fundamental factors that scientists may overlook. It can also lead us to simple answers and an overly narrow focus that cause us to believe we understand when we don't. Questions often arise concerning what is fundamental and essential and what is noise and, therefore, irrelevant? Reductionism, as translated and adapted from natural science, has progressively become a factor in social science for the past one hundred years or so. It has come to be seen as either a blessing or a curse, especially in the study of organizations.

Edward O. Wilson, the respected biologist considered one of the world's greatest living scientists, is the author of the book *Consilience: The Unity of Knowledge*. Professor Wilson both celebrates reductionism and identifies its failings within the framework of his development of the idea of consilience. He defines consilience as the proposition that "Everything in our world is organized in terms of a small number of fundamental natural laws that comprise the principles underlying every branch of learning." Consilience seems to mean "grand universalism," a category of what has been called strong reductionism.

Stephen Rothman writes, "Grand universalism proposes that, at least in theory, we should be able to explain everything, all of the natural world, with a single, most fundamental understanding that is at once both completely general and totally comprehensive—an algorithm to which all other understanding can be reduced. Some physicists, most famously Albert Einstein, and mathematicians have worked hard to unify all the known physical forces of the universe into a grand united theory, or a theory of everything."[3]

The idea of universalism is taken a step further in the notion of a hierarchy of scientific disciplines from the most fundamental to the least fundamental in the order of mathematics, physics, chemistry, biology, and the social sciences. Consilience or grand universalism is exciting and intellectually appealing. It is reminiscent again of the classic novel, *Magister Ludi* by Hermann Hesse, set in the idealized context of Castalia. Resident scholars in Castalia become engaged in thought of the purest form as synthesis through which mathematics, philosophy, art, music, and science are appreciated simultaneously.

Returning to Wilson, he argues: "To dissect a phenomenon into its elements, in this case (the) cell into organelles and molecules is consilience by reduction. To reconstitute it, and especially to predict with knowledge gained by reduction concerning how nature assembled it in the first place, is consilience by synthesis. That is the two-step procedure by which natural scientists generally work: top-down across two or three levels of organization at a time by analysis, then bottom-up across the same levels by synthesis."[4] This two-step procedure is a marvelous conception and perhaps it is how physicists and biologists work in narrowly constituted settings. However, the second part of the procedure breaks down in the analysis of social systems and even in multidisciplinary natural science. Perhaps this problem (the second part of the procedure) will be solved some time in the future but for the present, we don't know how to solve it. Concerning even natural science, Wilson goes on to say, "The greatest obstacle to consilience by synthesis, the approach often loosely called holism, is the exponential increase in complexity encountered during the upward progress through levels of organization. I have already described how an entire cell cannot yet be predicted from a knowledge of its scrambled molecules and organelles alone. Let me now indicate how bad the problem really is. It is not even possible to predict the three-dimensional structure of a protein from a complete knowledge of its constituent atoms."[5] To return to the problem of reductionism, what do we fail to know about the whole of any reality if we cannot reconstruct that reality from the constituents about which we think we know?

The subject matter of this book is not the philosophy of science and we are not qualified to criticize the methods of the "hard" sciences. It has become commonplace, however, for the methods of natural science, especially reductionism, to be applied in a context beyond the study of physical or natural phenomena. Based on our experience, it is our belief that these methods, specifically reductionism, are more curse than blessing and generally ill suited to the demands of multidisciplinary science and, more to the point, to the social sciences, especially to the analysis and management of organizations. By definition, while organizations are social constructions representing multiple disciplines, functions, interests and beliefs, they are profoundly oriented to the whole, without which, organizations would have no meaning. The shortcomings of reductionism as applied to the analysis and leadership of organizations can be understood in how reductionism induces a failure to grasp the interdependent nature of organizational life and opens a path to the process of reification.

Reification is the process of regarding something abstract as a material or concrete thing. It is the apprehension of human phenomena in non-human terms. Social reality is complex, contradictory, paradoxical, and ambiguous. Organizations, as expressions of social reality, are abstractions and embrace this untidy reality. To treat this world as tangible, objective, and concrete is to reify it and to misperceive it. Reification lies at the heart of mechanistic views of organizations and objectification in the extreme. Through reification, human beings are capable of describing a reality that denies their own humanity.[6]

Reductionism conceals the whole of reality in many ways and in many circumstances. In a general sense, however, our view of reductionism as a constraint on the growth of knowledge in organizations comes into focus around the tendency to treat organizational reality as either strictly objective or purely subjective and to lose a sense of the whole of the relevant reality in the process. Rothman argues, "Reductionism is often equated with an objective description of reality. Accordingly, human perceptions that do not conform to a specific reductionist view may be seen as imaginary, or not objectively real. If one experiences something—a thought, a feeling, an understanding—that cannot be explained in reductionist (e.g., neurobiological) terms, then such experiences are illusory. Or, if they are real, it is nonetheless as if they were imagined because we cannot 'objectively' confirm them."[7] Conversely, a near exclusive orientation to subjective factors is reductionism as well in the sense that such an orientation would seek to reduce organizational reality to human subjectivity and fail to take account of the objective dimension of the organization's reality. To illustrate, consider an objectively centered engineering, finance, accounting, or economic view of an organization's reality in contrast to a more subjectively focused psychological, social psychological, anthropological, or sociological view. Such unipolar views are not uncommon and are indicative of reductionism as a potential barrier or constraint on learning and the growth of knowledge. In any form or context, reductionism can mask the true nature of reality and, therefore, renders attempts to know incomplete. Reductionism may move us to perceptions of certainty in the midst of ambiguous circumstances. It protects us from the perception of threat to the beliefs and views that make us secure and comfortable. Perhaps, reductionism is the ultimate collective defense mechanism; perhaps, further, its resilience is due to its potential to protect us from the anxiety associated with the complexity of modern life and, in the process, to essentially cure our existential angst.

Organizational Politics

Human rationality and capacity are bounded. Organizations as institutional forms, therefore, come together to deal with inherent human limitation through division of labor and structured relationships. The movement of structure in the direction of power relations and competition causes organizations to become essentially political in nature. The success of any organization depends on the performance of the whole. To the extent that any circumstance results in the actual or perceived success of any group of individuals or any organizational component while the organization as a whole fails to achieve its potential, competition and negative political dynamics exist. The constraint of politics on the growth of knowledge pertains to competition between the contending interests of groups and individuals for power, influence, and advantage in an organization. While some competition is inevitable in any collection of human beings, cooperation must prevail over competition if achieving the purpose of the organization depends on solving problems, learning, and the growth of knowledge. The willingness to engage with others as colleagues, to forgo personal gain, and to expend the required psychic energy to achieve common goals are essential characteristics of a spirit of cooperation. As argued earlier in this book, the *motivation* to know and to achieve is the only, if imperfect, remedy to unrestrained competition and the only consistent route to good will and cooperation.

The term "politics" designates as well as any other the total complex of relations among people in a society or an organization. On the surface at least, the term is neutral or indifferent. However, the general meaning of politics as a constraint on learning and the growth of knowledge is pejorative and implies organizational dysfunction. Politics suggests an environment of defensiveness where individuals protect vested interests, pursue hidden and private agendas, and engage in artful and possibly dishonest activities. Human nature and the behavior of leaders are the factors that put political dynamics in motion. Human beings often seek to protect and contribute to their own personal interests. These interests include career advancement, job security, and job related rewards, a sense of control and power over resources, and other people and the well-being of subgroups to which individuals belong and relate. Jared Diamond in his book *Collapse* refers to political actions by individuals as "rational bad behavior. ... Some people reason correctly that they can advance their own interests by behavior harmful to other people. Scientists term such behavior 'rational' precisely because it employs correct reasoning, even though it may be morally reprehensible. The perpetrators know that they will often get away with their bad behavior, especially if there is no law against it or if the law isn't effectively enforced. They feel safe because the perpetrators are typically concentrated (few in number) and highly motivated by the prospect of reaping big, certain and immediate profits."[8]

Without diminishing the contribution of individuals as individuals, it is rarely disputed that groups of individuals are the context for the solution of most problems and the execution of most functions in organizations. The relationship of politics to leadership is best understood through the realization that leaders tend to influence others within the context of groups. In what seems to be counterintuitive, however, many leaders continue to reward individual behavior, including their own, and not group behavior. When leaders fail to reinforce desired group and organization wide behavior in favor of the behavior of individuals, the stage is set for internal competition and organizational politics. According to the organizational theorist Edgar Schein, perhaps this circumstance endures as a result of traditional western conceptions of the individual as something potentially quite distinct from the group and something to be developed in its own right.[9]

It is assumed that leaders seek to influence the members of groups and organizations to bring about their commitment and voluntary involvement toward achievement of desired outcomes. The failure of leaders to focus on the whole of the organization and achieve effective group performance, which can be complex and difficult, causes leaders to seek ways to control the organization for the purpose of improving performance. As much as hierarchy and bureaucracy are out of favor and derided, the search for control seems to continue to lead to hierarchy and bureaucracy. Ironically, hierarchy and bureaucracy set up and perpetuate political dynamics, create an illusion of control, and act to constrain performance. Hierarchy brings about an orientation to narrow sub-goals and sub-optimization. Hierarchy consumes energy and time and plays a role in negative or diminishing returns to scale— that circumstance defined by lower levels of productivity and output driven by higher levels of resource and activity. Hierarchy puts up walls and segregates people; it slots them into predetermined ways of perceiving and being perceived. It fuels notions of turf, territoriality, and competition; it provokes defensiveness in response to perceived threat, all of which is generally described as "politics." As in the case of politics, some degree of hierarchy and bureaucracy is inevitable; reasonable hierarchy that serves the organization's purpose may even be desirable. The challenge for leaders is to minimize political factors and mitigate their negative and constraining effects on learning and the growth of knowledge, restraining the development of hierarchy and related bureaucracy to that which actively supports the achievement of purpose while providing space for individual initiative and creativity.

Culture

Culture may either constrain or facilitate the growth of knowledge. The dynamics and role of culture are fully explored in Chapter 9. Nevertheless, for the purposes of this chapter it is necessary to recall the meaning and potential leverage associated with the fourth hypothesis from Chapter 1: the essential task for leaders is to bring about and sustain a culture conducive to the growth of knowledge. In general, culture can be seen as a set of beliefs and assumptions that have become objective and taken for granted and the behavior that flows from such beliefs. The notion of culture as a constraint on the growth of knowledge refers to a culture that 1) perpetuates beliefs inconsistent with reality, 2) promotes narrow and incomplete understanding of key organizational circumstances, and 3) sustains self-serving and manipulative behavior by some people at the expense of others and the organization as a whole. When the beliefs about an organization and its environment are tacit and unexamined, the behavior of organizational members will be determined to a far greater extent by its culture than by what its leaders *say*. Leaders often espouse culturally and politically correct values. These values, however, may be inconsistent with the actual beliefs embedded in the organization's culture. What leaders *do* is what matters. To the extent that culture establishes and preserves a negative political environment and nudges individuals and groups to reductionist perspectives, there is a clear need for consistent and sustained leadership action. If leaders reward simplistic solutions to problems and behavior that puts individuals and groups at odds with each other, the culture will evolve in such a way that associated anti-learning beliefs and behaviors will become institutionalized and, ultimately, the norm.

Factors That Facilitate the Growth of Knowledge

We have seen how reductionism, organizational politics, and the aspects of culture that perpetuate the status quo are factors that constrain the growth of knowledge in organizations. Three important factors associated with establishing and sustaining the conditions required for the growth of knowledge are 1) perception of the proper relation among the objective and subjective dimensions of any reality, 2) clarity of purpose, and 3) the beneficial attributes of a progressive culture. In addition to the positive influence of these factors in their own right, they function directly to help overcome the barriers to the growth of knowledge.

Objective/Subjective Balance

Organizations exist for objective reasons and objective reality frames their existence. Organizations, however, are collections of human beings who have beliefs, needs, imaginations, biases, idiosyncrasies, and egos. Organizations, therefore, represent a reality that is both objective and subjective. The phrase objective/subjective balance does not suggest a simple and ongoing state of equality, but rather a state of adjustment and stability between apparently opposing or divergent influences or elements. Use of the term balance, in other words, refers to perception of the proper relation between the objective and subjective dimensions of reality in any circumstance. We have argued that treating any reality as either exclusively objective or subjective is reductionism and will obscure the meaning of the whole. Thinking about "wholes" in organizations embraces thought about various potential realities and their combinations, including 1) natural reality, i.e., the physical, chemical or biological processes associated with an organization's products, technology and environment; 2) material reality, e.g., physical assets, cost structures and earnings; 3) nonmaterial reality, as in its culture and its assumptions about the meaning of success and failure; and 4) conceptual reality as expressed in the ethical and socially emergent dimensions of the life of the organization. Material, nonmaterial and conceptual realities have objective dimensions. They are, however, constructed by human beings and by definition are subjective in character as well. Even natural reality has a subjective dimension, which is expressed in how individuals comprehend and make sense of natural or physical phenomena.

The pendulum in management emphasis and organizational change efforts appears to swing back and forth between objective and subjective focus. The excesses that define the extremes of swings in one direction seem to be the consequences of acting within the extremes of the other. We have seen organizations become so oriented to subjectivity through addressing the "soft" skills in management and teambuilding for the sake of congenial and conflict free relationships, that the objective reasons for the existence of managers and teams and the organization itself were obscured. At the other end of the pendulum's swing, we find organizations that become fully directed to influence objective performance. Such factors as productivity, cost reduction, and market dynamics completely override the need to motivate, reconcile competitive or contradictory beliefs, and develop the commitment, creativity, and spirit of people.

In his paper "The Epistemology of Strategic Consulting," James Phills describes how, ironically, an exclusive orientation to objective factors by both consultant and client often results in client organizations that fail to take objective advice. These organizations fail to adapt their strategies in response to objective changes in their markets and in the nature of their competition. Consultants conduct objective and formal economic and competitive analyses of critical strategic problems and opportunities, but two levels of subjectively driven inertia become obstacles to change. The first of these pertains to the failure to grasp the imperative for change in the first place and the second to failure to change even when the objective rationale for change is apparently appreciated. Phills argues, "In attempting to understand the roots of the primary and secondary forms of inertia, one culprit suggested by research on strategic change is the competitive beliefs (including assumptions and values) that guide strategic choice and action." These competitive beliefs, held by various members of an organization and reflecting a strong subjective influence, contend with each other for dominance. "Moreover, the process of influencing such beliefs in developing and implementing strategies is a task that has an important subjective/behavioral, as well as a technical/analytical component. Indeed, this task is often difficult for management consultants who are often quite sophisticated in using applied economic frameworks to diagnose competitive problems, but who still frequently encounter significant difficulty in using such diagnoses to facilitate strategic change in organizations."[10]

Purpose

It has become commonplace, yet no less valid, to suggest that a strong sense of purpose lies at the heart of all great achievements, including the growth of knowledge. Purpose is a straight forward concept and its meaning is no more complex than "an object or an end to be attained." However, as the construct around which the negative effects of politics, hierarchy, and bureaucracy can be mitigated and alignment and commitment can be developed among organizational members, a more specific and expansive definition is required. Our definition begins with the notion that purpose must relate to the whole of the organization and, at the same time, be comprehended and framed as the basis for action by all levels of the organization.

At any level, purpose must have an external focus, i.e., organizations must reach outside themselves to those they serve, their customers and clients (both internal and external), communities, markets, etc. While vision and mission are aspects of purpose and usually define "our reason to be" at a high level, they are not enough. Standing alone, expressions of vision and mission tend *not* to inform decision making, priority setting, and resource allocation. Fully articulated purpose at any organizational level must include a distillation of concrete, objective outcome goals underpinned by mission and vision. The achievement of such goals must be commonly understood in measurable or otherwise observable terms. Expressions of purpose at all levels must guide organizational members in doing their jobs, relating to other members, selecting tasks, and choosing courses of action with accountability to produce results tied to overall purpose. According to our understanding of purpose as a facilitating factor in the growth of knowledge, the following tests for purpose may be applied:

- Is purpose consistent with the higher order motives of the organization (usually expressed in vision and mission)?
- Does purpose have a pragmatic orientation, i.e., is it an expression of external *consequences* of effort as opposed to the effort itself?
- Given that resources are always limited, does purpose enable trade-off decisions to be made among competing alternatives?
- Is the achievement of purpose generally recognizable, i.e., is achievement measurable or at least unambiguous in terms of observable effects?[11]

Purpose and output are closely tied to the concept of leverage, which we have described as the central idea in our understanding of leadership. The output or the results of the work of any unit of an organization and the organization as a whole is only relevant to the extent that output relates to purpose. Output is not effort or activity; output is the result of effort, the consequence of activity. If a hospital's purpose is improvement of patient outcomes, output associated with number of procedures performed with no effect on patient outcomes is not relevant output. If the purpose of a design group is production of product designs that will enable the organization to compete effectively, output consists of completed designs that work correctly, that meet stated requirements, and that are ready to go to manufacturing. Anything else, while possibly useful in the design process, is not output.

As defined earlier in this chapter, leverage in relation to leaders pertains to actions that produce a multiplier effect on the work of others. By leverage, we mean creating the greatest "good" per unit of resource employed. Without a definition of "good," leverage makes no sense. In other words, without a clear sense of purpose and relevant output generally comprehended as that which is good, leverage is a meaningless concept. The collective motivation to know, to hold beliefs that are both justified and as close to true as possible, is provided by purpose. Such motivation, as asserted earlier in this chapter, is the only known route to cooperative behavior and the only neutralizer or nullifier of internal competition and politics.

Culture

As we have seen, culture may embody the constraints to the growth of knowledge and manifest them as hardened, crystallized ways of being. In the same way, culture may incorporate the facilitators of the growth of knowledge to foster and sustain positive, learning-oriented attitudes and behaviors. The attributes of a progressive culture that values critical thinking and dialogue include a collective motivation to learn and know, aligning beliefs with reality. Such a culture transcends political and reductionist dynamics and fosters a genuine openness to diverse ideas and ways of thinking. Leaders play an important role, arguably the most important role, in the creation, preservation, and change of the beliefs that drive collective behavior. To understand how to act consistently with this role, a leader must first understand the attributes of the relevant and existing culture. A leader's assessment of culture begins with observation of what decisions are made and what behavior is typical in specific circumstances and shifts to working in reverse to infer the beliefs that organizational members hold. It has been suggested by some organizational theorists that such inductive logic is inappropriate and that, instead, the assessment should rely on what members of organizations *say* are their beliefs.[12] In our experience, this is a profoundly unreliable approach to understanding culture with the inductive approach producing far greater accuracy in describing cultural dynamics. The essential insights leaders are required to bring to the process of mitigating negative cultural attributes and advancing new ones are 1) culture will not change unless the beliefs (espoused or not) that underpin behavior change, and 2) the primary embedding mechanisms for culture formation and perpetuation are what leaders pay attention to and either reward or sanction. If leaders maintain symmetry between what they say and what they do and if they recognize and promote the attributes of a progressive culture within which transparency, critical thinking, and collective learning occurs, the growth of knowledge will be enhanced and leaders will have enacted their essential task.

LEADERS AND THE GROWTH OF KNOWLEDGE

We have seen how certain factors constrain and others facilitate the growth of knowledge and how leaders may or may not act to diminish the constraints and engage the facilitators. We have seen how culture may be a barrier or a beneficial instrument in the growth of knowledge. The chief executive officer of a successful international airline expressed to us his belief that it is not so much the traits of a leader that matter as the conjunction of the traits of the leader and those of the organization and its culture. From our perspective, the functions of leadership and the influence of barriers and facilitators to the growth of knowledge come into focus around culture, around the central responsibility of leaders to align the institutional beliefs of an organization with reality. The implications of this central responsibility are examined within the framework of the questions: *What role do leaders play in not knowing and what role do leaders play in knowing more fully?*

What Role Do Leaders Play in Not Knowing?

Misconceptions of relevant reality hold sway. Individual members of organizations may misconceive reality as it pertains to any circumstance, but it is the duty of leaders to act so that such misconceptions are supplanted with accurate ones. Certain individuals may be predisposed to see any situation in material or financial terms; others may be inclined to see any natural or physical reality in nonmaterial or conceptual terms. How individuals seek to know may influence perceptions of reality. In other words, the tools of learning brought to bear on any reality shapes the perception of that reality. The failure to take account of the internal and external dimensions of relevant reality as well as the objective and subjective dimensions are common failings. The effects of misconceptions of reality are far reaching. Such effects may include the "solution looking for a problem" phenomenon as in expending scarce resources in attempting to solve the wrong problem or seeking to exploit phantom opportunities. Organizations can become very efficient at working within some context that has little or no bearing on reality. Misconceptions of reality are allowed to take hold and continue to exist when leaders fail to understand the range and differences of potential realities and when they fail to ask the right questions and encourage collective engagement in answering such questions.

Beliefs incongruent with reality are allowed to exist. When the character and dimensions of reality are understood, to what extent are the beliefs of the organization congruent with reality? It is paradoxical that relevant reality could, in general, be understood but incompatible beliefs could continue to induce behavior. The James Phills article, discussed earlier in this chapter, described this paradox as a form of inertia. As noted in Chapter 7, there is a degree of intransigence or resistance to change associated with the structure of our collective beliefs. Political dynamics can also influence beliefs even when organizational members know better. Leaders fail when they allow politics to hold what an organization believes about itself and its environment in its grip. Reductionism can reduce collective imagination and perceptions of the horizons where organizations and environments meet. The effects of such beliefs can be catastrophic; the organization could believe that real threats to its success and survival are non-existent and fail to act to counter such threats. Leaders fail when the inability to challenge incongruent beliefs is sustained. As a result of political dynamics, leaders may punish those who challenge existing beliefs or, equally damaging, they may fail to support and reward those who challenge the status quo. A culture that reflects existing conditions and reinforces existing beliefs will spawn behavior that reinforces such potentially limiting beliefs. Among the consequences of the inability to challenge incongruent beliefs is the failure to adapt to the changing internal and external reality.

The application of inappropriate or invalid approaches to believing/ knowing is undertaken and perpetuated. Individuals bring their dominant ways of knowing, their epistemic styles to organizations. Reductionism or political dynamics or culture or a combination of these factors may also shape collective epistemic styles. Such epistemic styles may or may not be valid for the reality in question and may be the source of false beliefs. A crucial role for leaders, therefore, is to inquire: Are we asking the right questions? Do our methods fit the questions? In other words, leaders provide the last opportunity to fit reality with approach to knowing should individuals and groups fail to do so. Regardless of the institutional and other forces underpinning any existing epistemic style, leaders must know that while an empirical approach to knowing is highly relevant for natural reality, it is not relevant at all to conceptual reality; that while coherentism is highly germane to knowing about conceptual reality, it is at best secondarily relevant to material reality; that while pragmatism is highly relevant to nonmaterial reality, it is inappropriate for any natural or physical reality; and that no approach to knowing that disregards subjectivity is valid for any constructed reality. The consequences of applying inappropriate or invalid approaches to knowing are false beliefs, wrong answers to questions and flawed solutions to problems; succinctly, the consequences are the failure to know.

An organization with which we had some connection reflected a convergence of the factors identified above in response to the question: what role do leaders play in *not* knowing? The organization in question, a functional unit of a multi-national, technology-driven company, had been formed to provide an interface between the research and application arms of the company. This unit had been recently established and staffed to provide a technology transfer function and the leader of the unit had arranged for a series of interventions led by an outside party designed to develop the new organization. At first, the reality surrounding this organization seemed clear enough, encompassing the roles and functions of the research organization and its principal internal client (the application organization) and the details and structure of the technology transfer unit itself. In seeking to frame the existence of the new organization and develop it, the leader's initial motives and instincts were insightful and appropriate, yet they added complexity to perceptions of the organization's reality. She intended for her organization to develop a description of its role and operating mode, incorporating significant added value to the process of moving new technology into practice. Her view was that the role and operation of the organization should in some way produce value that exceeded the sum of the individual components of product and technical expertise. The added value would be associated with influencing the research agenda on the front end and packaging and delivering multi-disciplinary approaches to applications of technology on the back end.

The knowledge to be developed at this stage in the life of this new organization included answering such questions as: How can we determine the technical capability growth initiatives that will provide the greatest leverage for the users of technology? How can we support the delivery of the right people with the right skills and the right technology to the right projects at the right time? What is the most effective balance between incremental improvements in technology and pursuing breakthroughs? Is there a "whole greater than the sum of its parts" associated with multidisciplinary approaches to capability growth?

Through the early work of the organization, it became clear that there were two distinct and divergent conceptions of the role and function of the organization operating among the members. The first conception held that the purpose, outcome goals, role, and function of the organization should be defined in relation to the business goals of the larger organization. The second held that it was not possible to make such a direct connection with business goals, that the work of the new organization held intrinsic value, and that attempts to quantify it would diminish it. In short, the first view conceived the new unit as a service organization and the second conceived it as a potential driver of the overall business. Attributions of the advocates of each conception with respect to the other were classic and significant. The second group of advocates saw the first as simplistic and obsessed with being able to count things and the first camp saw the second as motivated to avoid accountability for doing anything useful and favoring some nebulous and unsubstantial "good."

The problems for the organization were 1) its need to come to grips with its relevant reality or set of realities; 2) to become aligned around a common understanding of reality, role, and function; and 3) to answer the central questions facing the organization. The first failing of the leader and the organizational members pertained to undervaluing the subjective dimension of the organization's reality, viewing the differences between the two conceptions as purely objective and failing to reconcile the underlying dynamics as a consequence. Since defensiveness and political dynamics continued to operate, the objective differences between the two camps and the incongruent underlying beliefs were not addressed and the role and function of the organization did not become clear, much less shared by all the members of the organization. The members of the unit seemed to become stuck in a pattern of collective if competitive navel contemplation and the internal discourse became unaccountably obscure. Two significantly opposed approaches to knowing were being brought to bear in the process of seeking to answer the central questions and coming to know what the organization needed to know. The camp oriented to business goals reflected a *pragmatist* epistemic style while the advocates of the second conception reflected a *rationalist* or perhaps a *coherentist* epistemic style. The categories of reality in question for this organization ranged from *natural* (related to science and technology), to *material* (financial implications) to *nonmaterial* (cultural factors) to *conceptual* (the anticipated gestalt). While the pragmatist style had a broader and probably more relevant reach than the rationalist style, neither was well suited to this organization's full and comprehensive reality (the full scope of categories of reality embodied in the state and context of the organization).

While the leader of this organization had good intentions and a good initial conception of how to proceed, she did not lead the group to a resolution of the influential subjective dynamics operating in the group, allowing reductionist perceptions to come to the surface and endure. Clarity of purpose did not emerge as expressed in an incomplete understanding of role and function. The group was not led to a reconciling or bridging approach to knowing, such as *contextualism* or *hermeneutic phenomenology*, as a route to moving perceptions of reality to a common understanding and answering the relevant questions. Our contact with the organization was lost. Whether the group ever achieved its potential is not within our ken. At the time of our association, however, the group had not been led to learn what it needed to know and struggled through a lack of a common perception of purpose, role, function, and reality.

What Role Do Leaders Play in Knowing More Fully?

The collective ability to identify and define the implications of knowing is enhanced. The motivation to transcend differences and political dynamics and reach beyond simplistic and incomplete conceptions of reality, the motivation to *know* in contrast to merely believe, is provided by a clear and objective purpose. Effective leaders work to provide clarity of purpose and to ensure that such purpose is widely understood. There is probably no other way to provide such motivation. When the members of an organization are led to develop purpose through a *collective* process, purpose is more likely to become a *collective* purpose that resonates with individuals as well as the group. When purpose is clear and shared, the implications of knowing and acting within a framework of truth and justification are important. The essential effect of the ability to produce a clear purpose and define the implications of knowing is a group of people who *want* to know; embedding this desire to know as a cultural attribute in how wanting to know becomes a way of life.

The ability of groups to accurately identify and define the reality in question is improved. Identifying and defining the specific reality or the whole of a set of relevant realities associated with a given circumstance are significant knowledge producing activities. Comprehension of reality provides the base against which beliefs about reality can be assessed and points to the epistemic style(s) or approach(es) to knowing that will most likely yield the greatest knowledge. Understanding the reality connected with any circumstance, i.e., problem, opportunity, or any other situation, is related to defining the circumstance and ascertaining that the perceived circumstance is the relevant one. Another way to think about defining the relevant reality is asking the right questions as opposed to seeking to produce the right answers. Since an accurate conception of reality is a necessary first step in developing purpose, it is imperative for any group to be led to understanding the relevant reality if the members of the group are unable or disinclined to do so on their own.

Leaders can bring certain tools to bear on the task of defining the relevant reality. Systems thinking is such a tool and differs from traditional forms of analysis. Systems thinking focuses on how the phenomenon or circumstance being studied interacts with the other constituents of the system. Douglas and Wykowski maintain, "A system is a set of interconnected elements. Systems thinking is a way of thinking about the interdependence of elements potentially leading to an enhanced perception of the whole. Systems thinking is a logical framework encompassing descriptive images and clear language for comprehending and communicating the dynamics of organizational life. It acknowledges that the interaction of factors in organizational circumstances can be dynamically complex and that linear and reductionist approaches are often inadequate."[13] Systems thinking is a tool that is an expression of important aspects of *coherentism* and *hermeneutic phenomenology*, both of which are epistemic styles especially applicable to knowing about complex, multidimensional organizational realities.

Groups are better able to identify and define the approaches to knowing being brought to bear on the reality in question. Without the intervention of a leader, the tendency will be for either a collective epistemic style, evolved over time and perhaps consistent with the culture, or the approach to knowing most favored by the dominant personality in the group to be applied to knowing about the relevant reality. Awareness of how the individual members of a group seek to know is necessary in order to assess whether or not such epistemic styles are valid, given the nature of the reality in question. A dialogue-supporting culture, the motivation to know, and the actions of leaders will help bring about openness and transparency to enable the engagement by group members at this level. As described in Chapter 6, it follows that one's dominant approach to knowing informs the structure and shapes the content of what one believes. Since beliefs may have to be challenged and epistemic styles may have to be given up in favor of more relevant ones, leaders need to know about these dynamics in order to execute the next step.

The ability to identify and develop consensus around the valid and/or reconciling approaches to knowing is improved. The assumptions at this stage are that the problem is understood and the right questions are being asked. The operative question is now: what method(s) fits the questions? This is analogous to asking, what approach to knowing is most relevant to knowing about this reality? The obvious point here is to apply the most relevant approach to knowing in order to know all we can about this reality, to align our beliefs with reality, to produce the right answers, to solve the problem, to understand as fully as possible, and to take the most efficacious action.

Since this book has philosophical underpinnings regarding reality and knowledge, it's appropriate to recall the comments of Daniel Robinson, an Oxford University philosopher, as we approach the end of the chapter on leaders.[14] In an interview, Professor Robinson was asked: what can philosophy tell us about how to make difficult choices and determine the right course of action? His qualified response was 1) be more deliberate *(in comprehending the nature of reality, the validity of beliefs, and how to know about the reality in question)*, 2) trust passions less, 3) trust reason more, and 4) trust limits most *(knowledge is rarely absolute, most of what we know is contingent and subject to reinterpretation). (Parenthetical comments are the authors'.)*

Happily, there is another chapter to the Marco Polo story from Chapter 7. The general manager of the business function responsible for the Marco Polo project assumed temporary leadership of it and took action that resulted in an ultimately successful endeavor. The essential constraints to learning resulting in a limited and flawed view of reality were fully engaged when the general manager took action to counteract this reductionism and set of negative political dynamics. Given the scope of the GM's usual responsibilities, we were engaged to help her recover Marco Polo as a viable project. She defined her needs as 1) to get as close to the truth as possible as soon as possible regarding the essential dynamics of this team, 2) to be able to define the options for proceeding with a high degree of confidence, 3) to be able to determine the best set of options among the possible array of options, and 4) to be able to reconfigure and reorient the team to enable successful execution of the chosen approach or set of options. A cornerstone of our practice as consultants is an orientation to understanding the objective and subjective dimensions connected with any reality involving human beings through qualitative research. We conducted extensive interviews and interpreted a comprehensive personality and leadership style instrument with each team member. Subjective issues were identified and assessed with each person and the entire group, which also addressed the objective purpose of the team in a workshop setting.

The team was presented with a working hypothesis pertaining to the reality of Marco Polo and was led to a refinement and an understanding of it by most members of the team. The reality would be described as a combination of material and nonmaterial reality categories. The essential perceptions regarding expectations for the work of the team and the internal dynamics associated with the project and the team framed the "reconceptualization" of the project, underpinned by its purpose. This work positioned the GM and the group to be able to challenge the beliefs of some team members and the determination that some beliefs were clearly incongruent with reality, as it had come to be understood. Notable among these was the belief that the company-wide globalization mandate gave the project the ability to make demands on the primary client organization and impose its own preferred courses of action. The political dynamics in the group were due primarily to the actions of one member whose beliefs did not change, even given a fresh look at the project's reality and purpose. It was theorized that a *foundationalist* epistemic style provided a dogmatic structure to these beliefs and that the member was unlikely to change. Action was taken by the GM to reassign this person to eliminate this source of internal competition and politics.

As described in Chapter 7, the epistemic styles or approaches to knowing in this group were varied. We postulated that they ranged from an extreme *empiricism* to *rationalism* to *foundationalism*, none of which was suited to knowing about the complex reality facing the group. Understanding the problem and the dynamics in the group was undertaken using a *hermeneutic phenomenology* approach. *Pragmatism*, as a bridging epistemic style, was determined to be the approach to guide the work of the team, to solve problems, and to take action. While not everyone was completely comfortable, the members of the team came to understand how pragmatism could reconcile ways of thinking and knowing, given the character of the reality in question. A combination of actions by the GM and the work of the group resulted in the recovery of the project. Marco Polo was reframed, reconstituted, and repositioned. The team members became aligned around the new conception of the team's reality and its purpose. The downside of subjectivity was mitigated and the group learned how to use the strengths of its individual members to its advantage.

REFERENCES

1. Douglas, Neil and Terry Wykowski. 1999. *Beyond Reductionism: Gateways for Learning and Change.* Boca Raton: St. Lucie Press.
2. Ahn, Andrew C., Muneesh Tewari, Chi-Sang Poon. 2006. The Limits of Reductionism in Medicine: Could Systems Biology Offer an Alternative? *PloS Medicine* 403:335–338. http://medicine.plosjournals.org.

3. Rothman, Stephen. 2002. *Lessons from the Living Cell: The Limits of Reductionism.* New York: McGraw-Hill.

4. Wilson, Edward O. 1998. *Consilience: The Unity of Knowledge.* New York: Alfred A. Knopf, Inc.

5. Wilson, Edward O. 1998. *Consilience: The Unity of Knowledge.* New York: Alfred A. Knopf, Inc.

6. Douglas, Neil and Terry Wykowski. 1999. *Beyond Reductionism: Gateways for Learning and Change.* Boca Raton: St. Lucie Press.

7. Rothman, Stephen. 2002. *Lessons from the Living Cell: The Limits of Reductionism.* New York: McGraw-Hill.

8. Diamond, Jared. 2005. *Collapse: How Societies Choose to Fail or Succeed.* New York: Viking Press.

9. Schein, Edgar H. 1992. *Organizational Culture and Leadership* 2nd ed. San Francisco: Jossey-Bass Publishers.

10. Phills, Jr., James A. 1996. The Epistemology of Strategic Consulting: Generic Analytical Activities and Organizational Learning. In *Organizational Learning and Competitive Advantage,* ed. Bertrand Moingeon, Amy Edmondson, 202 – 223. London: Sage Publications.

11. Douglas, Neil and Terry Wykowski. 1999. *Beyond Reductionism: Gateways for Learning and Change. Boca Raton:* St. Lucie Press.

12. Schein, Edgar H. 1992. *Organizational Culture and Leadership* 2nd ed. San Francisco: Jossey-Bass Publishers.

13. Douglas, Neil and Terry Wykowski. 1999. *Beyond Reductionism: Gateways for Learning and Change.* Boca Raton: St. Lucie Press.

14. Robinson, Daniel. 2007. All Things Considered, September 30. Washington: National Public Radio.

9

Culture

ANTICIPATORY SUMMARY

The collective beliefs of an organization as embodied in its culture largely determine its patterns of behavior. Collective beliefs which are true and reflect knowledge produce relevant products and services, a proper balance among such factors as growth, earnings, sustainability, and risk and lead to successful adaptation and survival. On the other hand, false collective beliefs produce invalid assessments of reality, inappropriate action, products and services out of phase with markets, and lead to failure to adapt and decline.

An adaptive culture is defined by the ability to continually align collective beliefs with reality and, therefore, to know. The characteristics of an adaptive culture include: the collective motivation to *know*; an orientation to the idea that belief and even knowledge are always contingent; a tolerance for ambiguity and challenge; and a highly developed sense of collaboration. This concluding chapter addresses the special and deeply influential role of culture in the growth of knowledge.

The Meaning and Dimensions of Culture

It has been clear from the beginning that a primary focus of this book is on knowledge and the growth of knowledge as a cultural attribute, as a way of working and participating in organizational life in contrast to the narrower conception of knowledge as an asset. Culture and the concept of interacting subcultures in an organizational context are defined in this segment of Chapter 9, and the proposition that culture exists on two planes or in two dimensions is identified and explored.

The Dynamics of Culture

The essential dynamics of culture are defined as a circular process: people create culture; culture becomes its own reality; culture shapes people. The paradox of culture is that, while culture begins in the minds of individual human beings, it evolves, becomes objective and exists apart from people, and then completes the circle becoming subjective to people as they internalize its hardened attributes. This segment of Chapter 9 explores the dynamics of the formation and perpetuation of culture, including the co-active dimensions of belief and behavior.

Culture and the Growth of Knowledge

The beliefs and actions of individuals, groups and leaders converge in culture to support or restrain the growth of knowledge. Culture itself may create the illusion of knowledge. What an organization believes about itself and its environment may or may not be justified and true. These assertions frame the answers proposed in this segment to the questions: How does culture constrain the growth of knowledge? How does culture facilitate the growth of knowledge?

Culture Change versus a Culture of Change

The subject matter in this final segment of Chapter 9 is creating and sustaining an adaptive culture in contrast to the conventional model of culture change as episodic and linear. In a significant way, this entire book has been about an alternative view of culture change. Our alternative view is connected with building a culture animated by the growth of knowledge, suggesting that an adaptive culture is not reflected in the state of lurching from one static set of cultural attributes to another, but rather in sustaining a culture defined by the ability to continually align collective beliefs with reality.

CULTURE

What an organization believes about itself and its environment, as embodied in its culture, largely determines its hardened and ingrained patterns of behavior. The phrase "what an organization believes" is shorthand for what the members of an organization are led to believe by the culture and, reciprocally, what the culture absorbs and objectifies from the beliefs of the members. Our beliefs assert: "This is the way the world is." What culture imposes and members believe, however, may or may not be true; culture may create the illusion of knowledge. To the extent that non-conformity exists between an organization's beliefs and reality, the organization is crippled by embedded and crystallized delusion. On the other hand, the fruits for an organization of knowing about itself and its environment are successful adaptation, survival, effectiveness and growth.

A primary focus of this book, from the preface to the current chapter, is knowledge and the growth of knowledge as a cultural attribute, as a way of working and being in contrast to the narrower conception of knowledge as an asset. The field of knowledge management (KM) pertains to managing the intellectual assets of an organization such as its strategic technology and process know-how. KM is generally technology-based and embodies organizational processes that seek a mutually reinforcing combination of the data and information processing capacity of technologies and the creative capacity of human beings. Our conception of knowledge within the context of this book is distinctly *not* knowledge management. A culture, however, that supports the growth of knowledge would set the stage for not only successful stewardship and management of an organization's knowledge-related assets but for the growth of such assets as well.

This concluding chapter addresses the special and deeply influential role of culture in the growth of knowledge. The influence of culture is enormous and silent unless there is a deliberate effort to understand the nature and consequences of the culture in question. The process of aligning belief with reality is an intentional process that results in the transition from belief to knowledge. Such transitions as they relate, for example, to an organization's human resources, operating and financial performance, strategy and marketing plans represent occurrences of organizational learning. When the transition is from *institutional belief* to *institutional knowledge*, culture change has occurred with the potential to transform the life of the organization. The term *institutional* is used as a modifier to suggest the institutional dynamics associated with both belief and knowledge when one of these or both are represented in culture. Institutional dynamics exist when either belief or knowledge becomes objective and when either collective state of mind (believing or knowing) takes on a life of its own and is resistant to change.

In large measure, institutional beliefs are responsible for behavior in a systematic and near-deterministic way. Institutional dynamics associated with mere beliefs may formalize and legitimize inappropriate or ineffective behavior and cause such actions to be taken for granted and unquestioned. When institutional beliefs are justified and true in an absolute or in a relative and probable sense, however, mere belief becomes knowledge and behavior will tend to be effective and suited to the circumstances or the reality in question. The transition of belief to knowledge within a context of culture is a special occurrence of learning and comes with the potential of producing a high degree of leverage in enhancing the capacity of an organization to achieve its potential. A word of caution is indicated, however, based on the fact that institutionalization, by definition and in connection with either belief or knowledge, produces collective states of mind resistant to challenge and change. What counts as knowledge at some moment in time may not *be* knowledge in the future. For example, an assessment of an organization's competitive environment may have been valid, i.e., consistent with reality, at some point in the past but profoundly inaccurate in the present. There is a requirement, therefore, to sustain a collective awareness of knowledge as contingent and subject to change. The ability to build and sustain institutional self-awareness in order to learn and adapt is an indispensable aspect of culture for organizations seeking long-term success.

THE MEANING AND DIMENSIONS OF CULTURE

The social anthropologist Clyde Kluckhohn wrote, "By 'culture,' anthropology means the total life way of a people, the social legacy the individual acquires from his group. Or culture can be regarded as that part of the environment that is the creation of man."[1] The culture of an organization or any group has been defined by Edgar Schein, one of the founders of the field of organizational psychology, as "A pattern of shared basic assumptions that the group learned as it solved its problems of external adaptation and internal integration, that has worked well enough to be considered valid and, therefore, to be taught (consciously or not) to new members as the correct way to perceive, think and feel (and act) in relation to those problems."[2] (Parenthetical comments are the author's.) According to the anthropologist Edward Hall, culture refers to customs, i.e., practices and behaviors but also to "ways of organizing life, of thinking and of conceiving the underlying assumptions about social life and man himself. ...Cultures are historically created designs for living, explicit and implicit, rational, irrational and non-rational, which exist at any given time as potential guides for the conduct of man. Another important aspect of culture is language, which includes the way events are categorized and symbolized."[4]

These definitions of culture and our understanding of it point to the proposition that culture exists on two planes or in two dimensions—behavior and the information that sets behavior in motion. Behavior is the aspect of culture that we see. Behavior is what we do and is represented in the symbolic and physical manifestations of what we believe or know. The difference between classical behavior-focused conceptions of culture and our understanding of it is the focus placed on the information expressed as beliefs or knowledge. As we will explore later in this chapter, under-standing culture begins with careful observation of what people do, but the aim is to be able to reliably infer what people believe. "Think of cul-ture as a pool of information, mainly stored in the brains of a population of people. This information gets transmitted from one brain to another by various social learning processes," Boyd and Richerson wrote in their book *The Origin and Evolution of Cultures* where they complete their char-acterization of culture as: "...information capable of affecting individuals' behavior that they acquire from other members of their species (group) by teaching, imitation, and other forms of social transmission."[5] To be clear, the term "information" refers to ideas, attitudes, assumptions and values, which are held and expressed as beliefs and knowledge.

There is a clear distinction between what leaders often describe and assert as their organization's "core values" and the information, i.e., the beliefs and assumptions that actually shape what the organization does. Schein's analysis of culture proposes a direct and linear relationship between *actual* assumptions or beliefs, the values or beliefs members of organizations *say* they hold, and behavior. In our experience, espoused values do *not* directly affect behavior. If there is a relationship between espoused values and basic beliefs, and often there is not, it is certainly not because what is actual is what is expressed or because saying it makes it actual and true. In his 1990 book *Overcoming Organizational Defenses*, Chris Argyris expresses this distinction in terms of espoused theories and theories-in-use. Espoused theories are those values or beliefs that orga-nizations talk about and, perhaps even believe about themselves at some level, while theories-in-use refers to the actual assumptions or beliefs embedded in the culture that determine behavior.[6] Argyris finds incongruence between these theories to be widespread, a circumstance borne out in our own experience. Culture is often not in conformity with what the members of organizations say they believe and value and, seeking to understand any given culture, contrary to Schein's assertions, is most productively pursued by observing what people do, not what they say. A large service organization with whom we worked in the American west proclaimed in posters and laminated pocket cards that their culture was open and honest. In individual and group settings, however, members of the organization reported that "open and honest is a two-edged sword." They meant that one may be open and honest, but one would also likely lose their head in the process. The actual belief, although the espoused value expressed something different, was that contradictory or challenging opinions should not be expressed.

Culture among the various units of an organization is rarely uniform. In differentiated organizations, i.e., those with numerous functions and occupational and professional groupings, multiple stocks of belief are typically operating and interacting in unpredictable and often unintended ways. As a result of training and professional socialization, members of such groupings as engineering, manufacturing, sales, research and development, administration, basic science, applied science, marketing, and so on operate out of defining sets of assumptions and beliefs about how the world works and what's important. As individuals with a common orientation come together in units within an organization, other sets of assumptions can be expected to emerge reflecting the context of the units within the organization. While an overall organization-wide culture will exist, the existence of subcultures will influence the overall culture and cause uneven comprehension of its attributes.

Our work with an academic medical center illustrates how subcultures can mask and contradict the nature of the culture the overall organization is seeking to evolve. The leaders of this organization saw its future success and impact linked to interdisciplinary research and clinical practice and sought to move the organization in this direction. A great deal of effort was expended in promoting the idea of interdisciplinary work and shifting organizational and support structures consistent with this idea. The subcultures associated with the basic science and clinical disciplines, however, did not change. The attributes of culture connected with science in this organization were internally contradictory and difficult to define. The highest levels of the organization espoused a culture attuned to interdisciplinary effort. The members of administrative and support functions seemed to actually believe the organization was oriented to the integration of disciplines. The actual assumptions and beliefs at the level where the basic and clinical science was done, however, were that value is associated with discipline-specific effort, not work of an interdisciplinary nature. The embedded conceptions of reward and recognition based on focused work in narrow, discipline-based settings remained in place and the movement toward a true interdisciplinary focus languished.

THE DYNAMICS OF CULTURE

The essential dynamics of culture are defined as a circular process: people create culture; culture becomes its own reality; culture shapes people. The paradox of culture is that, while culture begins in the minds of individual human beings, it evolves, becomes objective over time and exists apart from people and then completes the circle, becoming subjective to people as they internalize its hardened attributes. Culture becomes like the paint on the walls, rarely noticed but always present. People come and go but cultures endure. Culture emerges in a natural and unconscious way in any ongoing setting or circumstance involving multiple human beings. That culture predictably comes into existence and is recognizable in its effects is an interesting human phenomenon. It is even more interesting to consider how culture takes on a life of its own and is highly resistant to change, persevering over generations of allegedly self-determining individuals.

The Formation of Culture

In *The Social Construction of Reality*, Berger and Luckman argue that human beings lack the necessary biological means to provide stability and a degree of consistency in their behavior. Human existence, thrown back on its biological resources by itself, would be chaotic. Human beings have highly unspecialized and undirected desires and instincts. Humans, therefore, are motivated and able to apply their biological resources to a wide and constantly variable and varying range of activities. Human existence, however, takes place in a context of relative order, direction, and stability. The question then arises: from what does the stability of human existence derive? At least part of the answer is that the "world-openness" intrinsic to man's unique biological make-up is always preempted by social order, which leads to the question, in what manner does social order itself arise?

The most general answer to this question is that social order is a human creation, produced in the course of ongoing externalization. In other words, human beings produce and institutionalize the social order as they relate and adapt to their environment. The social order, the constructed character of human society, as an instance of objective reality defines culture for our purposes. Institutionalization, as the essential process in the formation of the social order or culture, has been introduced within the context of constructed reality to refer to the dynamics of objectification and the structure of beliefs, knowledge, and behavior.[7]

The twin forces of habitualization and legitimation were introduced in Chapter 3 as the drivers of institutionalization. Habitualization precedes institutionalization and refers to any actions that are repeated frequently and can be reproduced at any time with an economy of effort. Berger and Luckman write, "This frees the individual from the burden of 'all those decisions' providing a psychological relief that has its basis in man's undirected instinctual structure. Habitualization provides the direction and the specialization of activity that is lacking in man's biological equipment, thus relieving the accumulation of tensions that result from undirected drives. And by providing a stable background in which human activity may proceed with a minimum of decision making most of the time, it frees energy for such decisions as may be necessary on certain occasions. In other words, the background of habitualized activity opens up a foreground for deliberation and innovation."[8]

Sometimes, attitudes and basic beliefs in the form of dogma shape behavior in the initial instance and become habitualized; sometimes awareness of what has habitually worked in the past and belief in the efficacy of such actions informs behavior. In either case, coupled with the results of legitimation, the information dimension of culture comes into being and takes shape. The function of legitimation is to make objectively available and subjectively plausible the beliefs and behaviors that have become objective through habitualization on the way to institutionalization. Legitimation implies justification and legal or otherwise authoritative status. "Legitimation justifies the institutional order by giving a normative dignity to its practical imperatives. It is important to understand that legitimation has a cognitive as well as a normative element. In other words, legitimation is not just a matter of 'values.' It always implies 'knowledge' as well. Legitimation not only tells the individual why he should perform one action and not another; it also tells him why things *are* what they are. In other words, 'knowledge' (or belief taken as knowledge) precedes 'values' in the legitimation of institutions (or culture)."[9] (Parenthetical comments are the authors'.)

The Perpetuation of Culture

The mere fact of the existence of culture does not explain its enduring power to influence behavior even when the beliefs that animate behavior and behavior itself are out of phase with reality. Culture's essential mechanisms of control seem to be 1) latency and 2) how the attributes of culture become subjective to members of the culture.

Culture operates as latent in the sense of lying hidden and generally out of collective and individual consciousness. Since organization members are typically unaware of the nature of relevant culture, it often fails to rise to the level of notice. Rom Harre observes in *Social Being* that any social entity or institution exists not just as its observable, daily manifestations but also as the beliefs, habits of mind, prejudices, knowledge, and expectations of its constituent members. We can see that an institution is not so much ideal, conforming to some standard of utility or soundness, as latent, lying out of sight and perhaps reflecting eccentricity. Because of the large degree of latency within any culture, it is reproduced anew each day from the stored beliefs, knowledge, and skills of its members.[10]

As individuals, through exposure and socialization, internalize the hardened attitudes, perspectives, and beliefs represented in culture, these mental states become subjective, altering the subjective natures of these individuals. Any attempt to change the beliefs that have become subjective to individuals threatens the certainty and comfort these beliefs represent and tends to trigger defense of them, thereby locking them more firmly in place.

Latency and the process of cultural attributes becoming subjective to individuals are represented in the information dimension of culture. This dimension, encompassing beliefs, assumptions, attitudes, and even knowledge and its potential to endure and resist change, is well understood from various perspectives. Regarding the information dimension of culture, each of these perspectives represents a perpetuating and legitimizing circle and no fundamental question or elemental challenge should be allowed to cross its threshold without a high degree of stress and pain. Ludwick Fleck introduced the terms the "thought collective" and the "thought style" in the 1930s. "The individual, within the collective is never or hardly ever conscious of the prevailing thought style which almost always exerts an absolutely compulsive force upon his thinking, and with which it is not possible to be at variance."[11] As a philosopher of science, Thomas Kuhn described his insights regarding the nature of scientific progress and introduced the term "paradigm." For Kuhn, paradigm represents the institutionalized assumptions or beliefs that relate to "normal science" within any discipline at any point in time. "The scientific community is largely bound by the presuppositions it holds, such premises in turn providing the rules discerning the perceptual limits of problems and solutions."[12] The physicist David Bohm was interested in fostering dialogue across paradigms and among individuals whose thinking is circumscribed by different sets of assumptions and beliefs. He used the term "tacit infrastructure" to name these sets of interlocking components of institutional beliefs.[13]

In a contributing chapter to the book *Rethinking Organization*, Frank Blackler described a theory proposed by Roberto Unger to underpin a more integrative approach to organizational and social change. Writing from a political science perspective, Unger's key theoretical concept is the notion of "formative context." Through this, he focuses on the arrangements and beliefs that people take for granted and on the ways in which they identify and pursue their interests. Such beliefs are pervasive in their effects for they give coherence and continuity to the roles that people enact in everyday life. Normally unrecognized by those who are affected by them, formative contexts are an accepted set of pragmatic, institutional, and imaginative assumptions and beliefs that guide the ways in which interests are defined and problems are approached.[14] The "institution-in-the-mind" is the term fashioned by Shapiro and Carr to express their psychologically based perspective on the information dimension of culture. Their insights are especially attuned to how shared or collective interpretations of organizational life become subjective in the minds of organization members. The organization is composed of the diverse fantasies and projections of its members. Everyone who is aware of an organization whether as a member or an observer has a mental image of how it works. Though these diverse ideas are not often consciously negotiated or agreed upon among the participants, they exist. In this sense, all institutions exist in the mind and it is in interaction with these in-the-mind entities that we live. Of course, all organizations also consist of certain real factors, such as people, profits, buildings, resources, and products. But the meaning of these factors derives from the context established by the institution-in-the-mind.[15]

Basic assumptions, tacit infrastructure, thought style, paradigm, institution-in-the-mind, formative context—all of these refer to the information dimension of culture or institutional belief as seen through different lenses and understood in different frameworks. This, as we have come to understand culture, is the essence of it and the principal reason for its ability to endure.[16]

Relevance of the Naturalistic Perspective

Although we surveyed naturalized epistemology in Chapter 4, other than acknowledging the relevance of evolutionary epistemology in knowing about and shaping nonmaterial reality, naturalism has not been pursued in this book. In its most expansive sense, naturalized epistemology reduces forming beliefs and ultimately knowing to cognitive science and to the chemical, neuronal, and synaptic bases of brain function. As noted earlier, the prospect of naturalistic explanations of how and what we know are tantalizing and neurobiology may be able to explain how we know someday. It cannot do so today, however, and almost no one describes how he or she knows and relates to differences in approaches to knowing in naturalistic terms.

In general, we have adopted what has been called the "naturalistic fallacy," which is taken to mean that we cannot derive "ought" from "is" and that explaining behavior as "natural" does not render intellectually, ethically, and morally suspect behavior as acceptable. The naturalistic fallacy asserts that, while human beings are animals, human behavior cannot be reduced to natural explanations. According to VanWieren, "This is because human beings have a choice to behave differently; they have consciousness, intentionality, agency, and are cultural-social animals, not instinctual animals."[17] Regarding culture, it is also true that we have developed the ideas that culture is a constructed reality and that the relevant ways to know about culture take account of human subjectivity, concepts which seem to be at odds with naturalism.

Evolutionary epistemology belongs to the category of naturalized epistemology. However, our analysis of the character, genesis, and perpetuation of cultural reality places the analogical version of evolutionary epistemology as compatible with conceptions of culture as constructed reality. As a naturalistic theory of knowledge, evolutionary epistemology sets forth an important if analogical connection between the growth of knowledge and biological evolution through natural selection. Within the context of evolutionary epistemology, the rise of culture is understood as a process of belief and/or knowledge development. Robert Boyd and Peter Richerson are well known across a wide range of disciplines for their work on evolution and culture. Developing the idea of social learning as the driver and substance of culture, they argue that culture completely changes the way that human evolution works. "The capital fact is that human-style social learning creates a novel evolutionary trade-off. Social learning allows human populations to accumulate reservoirs of adaptive information over many generations, leading to the cumulative cultural evolution of highly adaptive behaviors and technology. ...Because this process is much faster than genetic evolution, it allows human populations to evolve adaptations to local environments— kayaks in the Arctic and blowguns in the Amazon"—examples of masterful adaptations in a changing and diverse world.[18]

Along with the work of Sir Karl Popper, the work of Donald Campbell is key to our understanding of evolutionary epistemology. According to Campbell, a variation-and-selective-retention process is fundamental to all genuine increases in knowledge and to all increases of fit of culture to environment. "In such a process" Campbell writes, "there are three essentials: (a) Mechanisms for introducing variation; (b) Consistent selection processes; and (c) Mechanisms for preserving and/or propagating the selected variations."[19] Evolutionary epistemology is descriptive. It aims to explain how culture is created, sustained, and changed. Approaches to knowing about culture pertain to knowing about the attributes of an existing culture as well as knowing about the dynamics of cultural influence and how culture can be changed. Our understanding of culture is consistent with evolutionary notions of culture, especially the analogical form. As we argued in Chapter 5, the analogical form of evolutionary epistemology, coupled with, for example, hermeneutic phenomenology, pragmatism, coherentism, or contextualism seems to be relevant to nonmaterial reality and culture in particular and will be explored later in this chapter under the heading Culture Change.

CULTURE AND THE GROWTH OF KNOWLEDGE

In Chapters 6 and 7, we explored how individuals acting alone and in concert with others in groups influence the growth of knowledge in organizations. In Chapter 8, we saw how leaders have an uncommon effect on the growth of knowledge through the influence of leverage, in either a positive or negative sense. The beliefs and actions of individuals, groups, and leaders converge in culture to support or restrain the growth of knowledge. These foundational arguments from Chapter 1 pertain to culture and the growth of knowledge: *Human action is set in motion by belief. Institutionalized beliefs are embodied in organizational culture. Action is valid and has value when the belief that drives it is aligned with reality. The growth of knowledge in organizations is largely the result of learning to align belief with reality.* These arguments frame the answers proposed below to the questions: *How does culture constrain the growth of knowledge? How does culture facilitate the growth of knowledge?*

How Does Culture Constrain the Growth of Knowledge?

Culture can predispose us to fail to recognize and understand the relevant reality. We have argued that multiple realities have a bearing on life in organizations and that how these realities are conceived and how knowledge about them is sought have practical implications. We described a systematic "ontology" or classification of these realities in Chapter 3 encompassing natural, material, nonmaterial, and conceptual realities. These realities were also described as multi-dimensional. There are objective and subjective dimensions to each of these realities, varying in degree and nature. The constructed realities (material, nonmaterial, and conceptual) have internal dimensions, relating to the organization itself, and external dimensions pertaining to the organization's environment. Institutional beliefs about reality, the collective beliefs which have become embedded in culture, will predispose the shaping of organizational members' assumptions about the nature of any reality. Such predispositions could cause a conceptual reality to be misperceived as material, a physical reality to be interpreted as nonmaterial, or a subjective aspect of reality to be ignored or discounted. The failure to grasp the character of reality associated with any circumstance cripples the ability to form true beliefs about such reality. As described in the next paragraph, institutionalized epistemic styles or approaches to knowing can play an important role in failing to recognize the relevant reality.

Culture can harden and embed invalid or inappropriate approaches to knowing. When dominant epistemic styles take hold and endure over time, like beliefs and behaviors, they become institutionalized and embedded in culture. There is a tendency to put to use such styles or approaches to knowing regardless of their validity in general or their applicability to the specific reality about which knowledge is sought. This state of being is likely to lead to the production of false beliefs. Approaches to knowing based on notions of certainty and deduction are of dubious value in organizational life, irrespective of the nature of the reality in question. Foundationalism and rationalism are examples of such approaches and will tend to strengthen existing beliefs and constrain the growth of knowledge. Culturally sanctioned conceptions of "how to know" (institutionalized approaches to forming beliefs and knowing) can lead members to believe that the reality best suited to the "enshrined" approach to knowing is always the relevant reality, whether or not it is. In this manner, culture may predispose members to perceive *any* reality in a uniform way. One is reminded again of Maslow's axiom, "If you only have a hammer, you treat everything like a nail." For example, when empiricism is the essential belief-forming tool and is an intrinsic feature of an organization's collective and institutionalized cognitive and epistemic style, all reality appears to be natural or physical in character. While empiricism is appropriate for natural reality, its application to constructed realities is a constraint on the growth of knowledge, leading to false beliefs, wrong answers, and flawed solutions to problems. Although pragmatism as an attribute of culture is potentially suited to knowing about constructed reality, its application to natural reality is analogous to applying Maslow's hammer to a screw.

Culture perpetuates our false beliefs and inhibits our ability to challenge them. Given that a relevant reality exists and our collective and institutional beliefs are out of alignment with this reality, how is this incongruence sustained? In other words, why do the features and peculiarities of a constraining culture persist? The proposition that beliefs are comprised of two parts—the actual *content* of belief and the *structure* regarding content—was described in the Figure 6.1. Whether the *content* of our beliefs is true or false, the institutional and possibly structural character of these beliefs will serve to perpetuate them. The instruments of perpetuation are twofold and were described earlier in this chapter. First, beliefs embedded in culture tend to be latent, operating out of the consciousness of members of organizations. If we are unaware of the influence and even the existence of such beliefs, they continue to assert their authority. Second, when we internalize the objective and hardened beliefs associated with culture, these beliefs become our own and subjective to us; any threat to them is a personal threat. When beliefs have both become a part of culture and their *structure* points to standards associated with determinism, reductionism or dogmatism, such beliefs will function to perpetuate the status quo or fail to take account of the whole of reality or both. Determinism in this sense refers to the belief that a preordained future is unavoidable; reductionism refers to the belief that the whole can be comprehended by simply reducing phenomena to constituents; dogmatism refers to the absolute belief in some set of "given" principles.

Our experience in a high technology products and services company, briefly described in Chapter 1, illustrates how culture can constrain the growth of knowledge. At the time of our initial involvement, the company was about 15 years old having been founded by an engineer who, along with his co-founder, continued to be involved in the company as non-executive chairman and vice chairman. The company had been successful in a niche market and held a dominant position in a high profile segment of that market. A new chief executive officer was recruited at about this time and the founder and former CEO formally stepped aside to the role of non-executive chairman. The assumptions about the business held by the former CEO and most of his long-term associates, based on the past and their strong beliefs, were that the company was well positioned for the future. Linear projections were provided for the new CEO, which suggested that the proper course for the future was to do the same—only more of it. The new CEO, having known the company and the founders for a number of years, accepted their highly optimistic assessment of the company's prospects with little question.

However, as the new leader assumed his post and became engaged in the operation of the company, the assumptions that were so clear in the chairman's mind, beliefs that seemed to be driving behavior in the organization, looked less and less like reality. At the level of observed behavior, the organization was profoundly inward looking. Many members of the organization seemed smug, self satisfied, and antagonistic to criticism of any sort. Customers, while loyal and continuing to value the company's products, viewed the organization as generally arrogant and uninterested in their opinions. At the level of performance, while the company was profitable, all the important indicators pertaining to future performance were headed in the wrong direction. Product margins were falling, the level of earnings was declining, strong new competitors were emerging, and market share was being lost in the segment where it had been dominant. These factors, to the extent they were recognized at all, were attributed to the sales organization, which was seen as unmotivated and unskilled. The attachment of blame for bad news to the sales department notwithstanding, the new CEO concluded fairly quickly that the past did not necessarily represent the most effective way forward and began the process of thinking about and introducing change.

The change process was difficult to initiate and even more difficult to bring to the point of possessing a degree of momentum. The culture of the organization as represented by its deeply held beliefs viewed customers as incompetent and unable to make proper decisions. Further, the company's products were seen as superior even though their designs were dated and had not been advanced to match the capabilities of competitors. The changes the new CEO sought to introduce were related to becoming market- and customer-oriented and undertaking aggressive programs of product enhancement and development. While these initiatives were clearly needed, many members of the organization resisted them, both overtly and subtly, from the chairman down. Initiatives of this sort were dramatically at odds with the organization's culture. Although the assumptions pertaining to the company's products and competition had been accurate in the past (the company had in fact been a pioneer in its field), the culture as expressed by its beliefs was clearly out of phase with current reality.

Some members of the organization fully and energetically embraced change and some short-term success was achieved; the consequences of the efforts of these people belied their small number. Strong new product marketing and customer relations programs were instituted along with the achievement of significant change in the nature and quality of the company's core products. Market success accompanied these programs and, based on observable changes in market performance, the chairman found it difficult to argue against ongoing and more significant change. The CEO was eventually allowed to lead an extensive reshaping of the company from its capital and ownership structure to its core technology and organizational framework. New areas of opportunity were identified, business planning was accomplished, new investment capital was acquired, and new leaders were recruited. It could be argued that everything in the company changed—everything, that is, except the essence and effects of its culture.

It seemed at the time that the company had become oriented for long-term success. But the process of change had taken a great deal of time and truly fundamental change had only just then become possible. As defined by its old self, the company and its products were late in their life cycles. The pressures were intense, therefore, to move quickly within the context of the company's reformulated existence and generate anticipated, higher levels of performance. The CEO had burned important bridges, especially with respect to the chairman, and had left himself exposed with other key board members. When performance was slow to materialize, the old assumptions and beliefs crept back out of the shadows having never really gone away. In the presence of this opportunity, the CEO was ousted and the market and product plans were altered and ultimately abandoned except in rhetorical terms. When the stresses became acute, the old cultural imperatives re-emerged, creating organizational confusion and resulting in the resignation of key leaders. The company survived for a period of time, but it eventually lost financial viability and failed. While other companies acquired certain assets, the company ceased to exist as a corporate entity and the equity of shareholders became worthless.

This story is a complex and multifaceted one. The CEO and others made mistakes but, with the benefit of hindsight, this organization's demise was due to its culture. Irrespective of the efforts of many people, the real change that was enacted and the actions of individuals who truly understood the character of the organization's reality, the culture, the basic beliefs and driving assumptions from the past held sway and drove the company out of existence.[20] The decision makers in this company failed to grasp the relevant reality. They put aside challenges to their conceptions of reality and failed to extricate themselves from hardened, culturally sustained patterns of thinking and believing.

How Does Culture Facilitate the Growth of Knowledge?

We have seen how culture can be a constraint on the growth of knowledge through 1) embedded predispositions about the character of reality, 2) hardened and entrenched ways of knowing, and 3) a collective cognitive style reflecting some combination of determinism, reductionism, and dogmatism. In interviews connected with our projects and as part of research for this book, some variation of the following question was asked: What are the hallmarks of an organizational culture that would provide an optimal environment for achieving an organization's potential? Representative answers to this question include:

- A clear sense of purpose and direction coupled with the ability to adapt and change
- A culture that fosters the skills of leaders to coach and lead employees through periods of change—a learning culture that comprehends

what works and what doesn't, adapting and incorporating changes quickly—a culture that acknowledges that business results are important but how results are achieved is also important, not leaving a trail of bodies in the wake of success

- The culture should inspire the idea of leaving the world better than we found it, including leaving the organization better than we found it.
- The culture should reward and foster doing the right things the right way the first time; it should support finding and sustaining the proper balance among key variables such as growth, earnings, cost, sustainability, and risk.
- The culture should produce enough tension to be challenging and able to unlock creativity, where new ideas are welcomed. It should not be so competitive, however, that some ideas are destroyed in order for others to win; the culture should support winning teams and not winning individuals.

These views are consistent with our own. In summary, the primary attributes of a culture that functions to facilitate the growth of knowledge are clarity of direction and an orientation to hypothesis (recognizing that knowledge is contingent), probability (acknowledging that truth is rarely absolute), and the logic of induction. Such a culture will influence us to seek to understand the character and dimensions of reality and to challenge our beliefs—to *know*, as opposed to merely believe.

Culture can enhance the ability to identify and define the implications of knowing. A culture unambiguously oriented to objective purpose can provide the stimulus to seek to know. Our definition of purpose as developed in Chapter 8 argued that purpose must relate to the whole of the organization and, at the same time, be comprehended and framed as the basis for action by all levels of the organization. Purpose must have an external focus and represent a distillation of concrete, objective outcome goals, underpinned by mission and vision. Such goals must be commonly understood in measurable or otherwise observable terms. This aspect of how culture can facilitate the growth of knowledge pertains to the collective desire to know. It pertains to wanting to know and creating the motivation for the members of organizations to overcome all the reasons why we don't know, individually and collectively, and to engage in the difficult work of coming to know more fully.

Culture can foster collective awareness of the factors associated with the growth of knowledge. Is the reality in question natural, material, nonmaterial, conceptual, or a combination? Is it internal, external, or a conjunction? What are the dimensions of the objective and subjective components of the relevant reality? What are our individual and collective beliefs about the relevant reality? How are we seeking to know about this reality? To what extent are our beliefs congruent with reality? To what extent are our approaches to knowing matched with the character of reality? The ability of culture to support the asking of these questions and, more importantly, to understand what the questions and answers mean and imply enables this necessary step in setting the stage for the growth of knowledge.

Culture can compel members of organizations to gain consensus around valid and/or reconciling approaches to knowing. We have argued that a culture that facilitates successful adaptation and the ongoing transition of belief to knowledge nurtures approaches to knowing based on certain or all of the concepts of hypothesis, probability, and induction. Depending on the character of the reality in question, approaches to knowing described in Chapters 4 and 5 such as empiricism, pragmatism, hermeneutic phenomenology, coherentism, and contextualism satisfy this requirement. The validity of epistemic style is often simply a matter of mapping the character of the reality in question with the most relevant ways of knowing about such a reality. When knowledge is sought about a circumstance reflecting multiple realities, when there is doubt or disagreement about the character of the reality in question or when multiple epistemic styles being brought to bear on the circumstance produce contradictory results, certain approaches to knowing may be able to bridge or reconcile divergent epistemic styles. These bridging or reconciling approaches include hermeneutic phenomenology and contextualism and pragmatism when the circumstance reflects one or more constructed realities.

The most positive organizational culture we've experienced in recent years was that of a global business unit within a very large, multi-faceted manufacturing company. We had the privilege to work on several projects for this business unit, ranging from 1) focus brought to bear on geographically based business units to 2) the integration of a new manufacturing facility to 3) work with the overall leadership team. Our perception of the culture is based on our own direct contact with the organization as well as with conversations with former unit members who had moved on to other assignments within the company. The culture in this organization transcended individuals in specific roles. New people came into the organization; others assumed different roles and others left the unit all together. It general, the business unit was regarded as a healthy environment. People liked working there and when they were promoted and took other assignments worried whether they would find a similarly stimulating and supportive environment. There was mutual respect in the unit and people actually seemed to like each other. They tended to see and affirm each other's strengths and to utilize them. We observed an absence of cliques and situations of one subgroup plotting against another. There was a marked sense of collaboration and the entire unit operated from the belief that we all succeed or none of us do. This unit was far from just a group of people that got along together well. Leadership in the unit was strong; it was focused on business results and was highly regarded within the corporation for performing well. The culture facilitated the growth of knowledge and enabled the unit to successfully adapt in a dynamic and highly competitive market.

Clarity of direction continued to evolve during our association with the business unit. The context of this evolution was the Business Framework, a construct that sought to answer such questions as: Why do we exist? What are our objectives? How can we win and continue winning? What are our work focus areas? The Business Framework moved steadily in the direction of articulating desired outcomes, giving substance to a well-defined sense of purpose, able to be translated or "cascaded" throughout the organization. The group was highly motivated to understand and align its beliefs and assumptions with reality. As a part of our work in each project, we interviewed members of the organization and developed an analysis of perceptions and an interpretation of the various dimensions of the organization's reality. This work was based on inductive logic and a phenomenological approach to knowing. It was validated by the members of the organization and used to address subjective issues within a framework of what was objectively important to the group. What was proposed and presented as useful perspectives regarding controversial issues were framed and understood as hypotheses and open to challenge and the input of a range of voices. Members of the organization seemed to have a tolerance for ambiguity, enabling them to think in terms of probabilities and not certainties and to enable the organization to push itself into new situations and out of its comfort zone. Although the products and processes associated with this business unit were technical in nature with underpinnings based in science, most issues pertained to marketing, competition, economics, culture, and ethics. Given this circumstance and the fact that various ways of knowing were represented in the various groups, pragmatism became the de facto epistemic style in the group regarding these issues, bridging the diverse ways of knowing.

The objective consequences of the positive and knowledge-enhancing culture of this organization were notable. It became and sustained a position as one of the most profitable product business units in the wider corporation. In seeking to understand its competitive reality, it engaged in "war gaming" in its various geographical subunits. Team members played the role of competitors in simulated competitive situations to assess competitive behavior, assets, and capabilities. In one of its commodity-like product lines, it introduced innovative product stewardship ideas such as supplier-managed inventory to increase its market share. In the process of moving into a global competitive and customer environment, it actively sought the perspectives of American, Asian, and European leaders to design a successful global approach for the business. The organization's business was cyclical. In the midst of a down cycle and at the bottom of its trough, it evaluated all aspects of its business operations and made incremental changes in manufacturing, supply chains, and fixed and variable cost structures. When the cycle turned up, the level of business and profitability escalated beyond normal expectations. In the midst of an up cycle, plans were made for the next down cycle to shift output to a product line less affected by cyclical dynamics to ease the financial stress associated with the next downturn. One of the geographical units had undergone dislocations through a reorganization brought about by the divestiture of some assets. This unit was able to adapt and to prosper. Throughout a particularly challenging episode, the leadership of the business unit was able to grasp the reality of the situation, make appropriate changes, and turn a potentially damaging set of factors into a positive circumstance.

CULTURE CHANGE VERSUS A CULTURE OF CHANGE (CREATING AND SUSTAINING AN ADAPTIVE CULTURE)

Adaptation is an increment of knowledge. As noted earlier, the variation-selection-retention model of evolution by natural selection has come to be seen by some social scientists as a metaphor for the development of culture as a process of knowledge growth. Others, with a stronger orientation to naturalistic explanations, see the model of natural selection as literally how knowledge grows and how cultures form and evolve.

Within the context of cultural evolution, variation refers to the belief and related behavior options available at any moment in time. Analogically, this variation comes from the idea of mutation in biology. For purposes of illustration, we could speak of a collection of organizational belief/behavior pairs that form a set or a subset of variations such as: 1) people are expendable/exploit them, 2) people matter/respect and support them, 3) internal competition is good/pit people against each other, 4) collaboration is good/reward cooperation, 5) efficiency is most important/focus on cost, 6) effectiveness is most important/focus on strategy and competitiveness, 7) balance matters most/question and reconcile extremes, and 8) adjustment to changing conditions is most important/hold beliefs and assumptions lightly. Karl Weick observed, "In general, it is assumed that 'the more numerous and the greater the heterogeneity of variations, the richer the opportunity for an advantageous innovation."[21] Advantageous innovation refers to the potential for the growth of knowledge and successful adaptation.

The process of selection pertains to selection of specific beliefs and behaviors among the available variations. Boyd and Richenson wrote, "Selection acting on culture is an ultimate cause of human behavior just like natural selection acting on genes."[22] Karl Weick describes Campbell's insights regarding selective retention processes as reflective of both selective *systems* and selective *criteria*. Selective systems have been observed to bear upon: 1) selective survival based on relative fitness for efficient collective action, 2) selective diffusion or borrowing of the behaviors of prosperous groups by groups that are less prosperous, 3) selective imitation of the actions of certain individuals to yield the psychological processes of individual conformity, 4) selective promotion or elevation of individuals to leadership roles who choose variations that appear to be more adaptive, and 5) rational selection based on planning and anticipation. While what has been described as *criteria* and *systems* seem to overlap to some extent, the identification of selective retention criteria include: 1) accept that which brings pleasure and reject that which brings pain, 2) accept novel variations and reject conventional ones, 3) accept the rational, reject the irrational, 4) accept variations that bring quick responses and reject those bringing slow responses, and 5) accept and retain the variations decision makers attend to, enact, and monitor and reject those for which decision makers are inattentive.[23]

With the selection of variations, a retention-propagation system is required to hold on to and sustain selected variations. In *The Origin and*

Evolution of Cultures, Boyd and Richerson describe how human groups have beliefs, norms, and values and how the cultural transmission of these traits can cause them to be retained and propagated for long periods of time. "The norms and values that predominate in a group plausibly affect the probability that the group is successful, whether it survives, and whether it expands."[24] The formation and perpetuation dynamics of culture favor that which works. It appears to be reasonable, therefore, to assume that when selected and retained beliefs and associated behaviors have become habitualized, legitimated, and institutionalized and culture has become objective, such beliefs are (or at least were) congruent with reality. We know, however, that this is not always the case. Even when original conditions remain the same, i.e., when reality is unchanged, cultures are not always consistent with reality. An advantage of culture is that individuals don't always have to invest the energy in forming beliefs and deciding how to behave. The trouble (and an important reason for cultural/reality inconsistency) is that an enthusiasm for easy adoptions of traditions or imitation can lead to perpetuating the maladaptions that sometimes arise.

Within the extended life of a successful organization, the capacities that give rise to culture and shape its content tend to be adaptive on average. However, the behavior observed in any particular circumstance at any particular time may reflect evolved maladaptions.[25] Even granting the truth of beliefs within the context of original conditions, circumstances and environments are subject to change and when reality changes, some basic beliefs are no longer valid. When reality overwhelms belief in highly developed cultures, this is exactly the moment when more options in the form of variations (of belief and behavior) are required. Campbell, however, describes how the dynamics of culture act to put the brakes on change, writing, "Too high a mutation (variation) rate jeopardizes the preservation of already achieved adaptations (cultural attributes). There arise in evolutionary systems, therefore, mechanisms for curbing the variation rate. The more elaborate the achieved adaptation, the more likely are mutations to be deleterious (threatening to culture), and therefore the stronger the inhibitions on mutation. For this reason we may expect to find great strength in the preservation and propagation systems, which will lead to a perpetuation of once-adaptive traits long after environmental shifts have removed their adaptedness."[26]

Given the profound influence of culture to determine behavior and the fact that culture can *be* wrong and can *go* wrong, there is a need to consciously and intentionally change culture. Of course, cultures evolve on their own but the rate of natural change may be wholly inconsistent with rates of change in their environments or relevant realities. Cultures are resistant to change but conscious change is possible. As we argued in Chapter 8, knowing about the character of relevant reality and the attributes of existing culture are necessary first steps in intentional culture change. The source of illumination in deciphering existing culture is what the members of organizations *do*, not what they *say*. Rather than seeking to establish what members of organizations say they believe, attention must be brought to bear on the decisions that are made and the patterns of behavior that are typical in specific circumstances and work in reverse to infer the beliefs that members hold. The essential idea then is to co-opt the natural processes of evolutionary change, i.e., to introduce variation of potential beliefs and behaviors, to examine selection systems and criteria within the context of the reality in question, and to seek to retain and perpetuate new beliefs and behaviors. Two principles apply in evolving and sustaining a different culture: 1) culture will not change unless the beliefs (espoused or not) that underpin behavior change and 2) the primary embedding mechanism for culture formation and perpetuation are what leaders pay attention to and either reward or sanction.

These thoughts represent a departure from what we could call conventional or traditional conceptions of culture change as articulated by Kurt Lewin in the 1940s and subsequently by Schein and others. According to Schein, conventional ideas are expressed as a sequence of "unfreezing," "cognitive restructuring" (changing), and "refreezing." "If any part of the core structure (culture) is to change in more than minor incremental ways, the system must first experience enough disequilibrium to force a coping process that goes beyond just reinforcing the assumptions that are already in place. The creation of such a disequilibrium Lewin called unfreezing." Cognitive restructuring introduces variation and selection. Once an organization has been unfrozen, the change process proceeds through cognitive redefinition of some of the core concepts in the assumption set. Refreezing is analogous to the dynamics of retention. "The final step in any given change process is refreezing, which refers to the necessity for the new behavior and set of cognitions to be reinforced."[27] The conventional model of culture change is episodic and linear and based on an organization's stage of existence, i.e., early growth, midlife and maturity and decline. Our interest is in an *alternative* view of culture change, one that is not episodic and doesn't take account of an organization's stage of existence, which is virtually impossible to know except in retrospect and tends to predispose thinking and limit potential.

In a significant way, this entire book has been about an alternative view of culture change and this final topic—Culture change versus a culture of change—is a fitting conclusion. The essential question in culture change is: change to what, acknowledging that "what" is a moving target? We believe the answer we have proposed is universal, non-episodic and non-linear. The answer and the focus in this book are on the growth of knowledge as a cultural attribute, as *a way of working and being*. In other words, the alternative view is connected with building a culture animated by the growth of knowledge, suggesting that an adaptive culture is not reflected in the state of lurching from one static set of cultural attributes to another, but rather in sustaining a culture defined by the ability to continually align collective beliefs with reality. Some will argue that periodic states of equilibrium, when beliefs are not open to challenge, is required for high levels of organizational performance. Our view is that the desired equilibrium is one where testing collective beliefs against reality is institutionalized, making implicit an inherent richness of potential variations of beliefs and behaviors. The growth of knowledge in organizations is seen as the essential benefit of learning. Since the key active idea is growth, knowledge is not seen as absolute or static and the emphasis is on a *continuum of transitions* along the *continuum from belief to knowledge*.

REFERENCES

1. Kluckhohn, Clyde. 1949. *Mirror for Man*. New York: McGraw-Hill Book Company.
2. Schein, E. H. 1992. *Organizational Culture and Leadership*, 3rd ed. San Francisco: Jossey-Bass.
3. Hall, E. T. 1959. *The Silent Language*. New York: Anchor Books/Doubleday.
4. Argyle, Michael. 1989. *The Social Psychology of Work*, 2nd ed. London: Penguin Books.
5. Boyd, Robert, and Peter J. Richerson. 2005. *The Origin and Evolution of Cultures*. New York: Oxford University Press.
6. Argyris Chris. 1990. *Overcoming Organizational Defenses: Facilitating Organizational Learning*. Boston: Allyn and Bacon.
7. Berger, Peter L. and Thomas Luckman. 1967. *The Social Construction of Reality: A Treatise in the Sociology of Knowledge*. New York: Anchor Books, a Division of Random House.

8. Berger, Peter L. and Thomas Luckman. 1967. *The Social Construction of Reality: A Treatise in the Sociology of Knowledge.* New York: Anchor Books, a Division of Random House.

9. Berger, Peter L. and Thomas Luckman. 1967. *The Social Construction of Reality: A Treatise in the Sociology of Knowledge.* New York: Anchor Books, a Division of Random House.

10. Harre, Rom. 1979. *Social Being: A Theory for Social Psychology.* Oxford: Basil Blackwell.

11. Fleck, Ludwig. 1935. *The Genesis and Development of a Scientific Fact,* 1979 Trans. Chicago: University of Chicago Press.

12. Kuhn, Thomas S. 1970. *The Structure of Scientific Revolutions,* 2nd ed. Chicago: University of Chicago Press.

13. Bohm, David and F. D. Peat. 1987. *Science, Order and Creativity.* New York: Phantom Books.

14. Blackler, Frank. 1992. Formative Contexts and Activity Systems: Postmodern Approaches to the Management of Change. In *Rethinking Organization: New Directions in Organizational Theory and Analysis,* ed. Michael Reed, Michael Hughes, 273–294. London: Sage Publications.

15. Shapiro, Edward R. and A. Wesley Carr. 1991. *Lost in Familiar Places: Creating New Connections Between the Individual and Society.* New Haven: Yale University Press.

16. Douglas, Neil and Terry Wykowski. 1999. *Beyond Reductionism: Gateways for Learning and Change.* Boca Raton: St. Lucie Press.

17. VanWieren, Jon. 2007. Decisions, Decisions, Decisions…Intentionality, the Growth of Knowledge and Cultural Evolution: Establishing Evolutionary Reasoning in the Social Sciences. For the International Consortium for the Advancement of Academic Publication. http://theoryandscience.icaap.org.

18. Boyd, Robert, and Peter J. Richerson. 2005. *The Origin and Evolution of Cultures.* New York: Oxford University Press.

19. Campbell, Donald T. 1987. Evolutionary Epistemology. In *Evolutionary Epistemology, Rationality, and the Sociology of Knowledge,* ed. Gerard Radnitzky, W.W. Bartley, III, 47–89. Chicago: Open Court.

20. Douglas, Neil and Terry Wykowski. 1999. *Beyond Reductionism: Gateways for Learning and Change.* Boca Raton: St. Lucie Press.

21. Weick, Karl E. 1979. *The Social Psychology of Organizing,* 2nd ed. New York: McGraw-Hill.

22. Boyd, Robert and Peter J. Richerson. 2005. *The Origin and Evolution of Cultures.* New York: Oxford University Press.

23. Weick, Karl E. 1979. *The Social Psychology of Organizing,* 2nd ed. New York: McGraw-Hill.

24. Boyd, Robert, and Peter J. Richerson. 2005. *The Origin and Evolution of Cultures.* New York: Oxford University Press.

25. Boyd, Robert, and Peter J. Richerson. 2005. *The Origin and Evolution of Cultures.* New York: Oxford University Press.

26. Campbell, Donald T. 1965. Ethnocentric and Other Altruistic Motives. In *Nebraska Symposium on Motivation,* ed. D. Levine, 306–307. Lincoln: University of Nebraska Press.

27. Schein, E. H. 1992. *Organizational Culture and Leadership,* 2nd ed. San Francisco: Jossey-Bass.

Postscript

Will Durant begins his twelve volume *Story of Civilization* with this definition: "Civilization is social order promoting cultural creation. Four elements constitute it: economic provision, political organization, moral traditions, and the pursuit of knowledge and the arts. It begins where chaos and insecurity end. For when fear is overcome, curiosity and constructiveness are free, and man passes by natural impulse toward the understanding and embellishment of life."[1] "Understanding and embellishment of life" expresses the knowledge and the art that flows from the freedom and support to be curious and creative. Analogously, the social order represented in successful organizations is constituted by four similar and essential elements: material and economic support, people and a defined set of relationships, a clear purpose, and the quest for knowledge.

The management of modern organizations is concerned with an array of topics including the purposeful development and deployment of people and other resources, operational and financial control, strategy, the application of technology, marketing, external relations, etc. At the core of the practice of management and the composite set of relevant topics, however, are the four essential elements. In other words, at the base of everything we think about and do as managers are these elements: providing purpose or a reason to exist, acquiring the material means to pursue the organization's purpose, securing and organizing human resources, and learning with the consequential knowledge to properly relate and adapt to the organization's environment and internal circumstances.

In spite of what appears to be a highly developed vocation of management, too many consciously managed organizations do not achieve their potential. To be sure, there are examples of successful organizations. Sometimes success seems to be due to the actions of managers; sometimes success seems to come about in spite of management intervention. Irrespective of the exceptions, the fact that many organizations do not achieve their potential seems to point to a failure of the practice of management. The consequences of this failure are many and varied: opportunities for creativity and innovation are lost, solutions to problems are not found and enacted, cures for diseases are not discovered and developed, economic gains are not realized, jobs are not created, human potential is wasted, and improvements in quality of life are not produced. The following observations pertain to disappointing organizational circumstances in the United States as the writing of this book comes to a conclusion.

> The healthcare industry is comprised of large and small organizations including health service providers, insurance companies, drug and medical equipment manufacturers, and government. The industry is approaching twenty percent of Gross Domestic Product. While healthcare is significantly more expensive in the United States than in any other developed country, many millions of people do not have routine access to health services and healthcare outcomes are no better and, in some cases, worse than in other parts of the world. The American automobile industry, once the envy of the world, has simply failed to innovate and adapt. It has lost market share, jobs have migrated to other parts of the world, and it has been rescued from oblivion by the federal government. Many of the organizations that inhabit the banking and financial services sector in the United States, and in the rest of the developed world as well, have been profoundly mismanaged to the extent of bringing entire national and regional economies to the edge of financial depression. It could be argued that this financial crisis is more accurately a matter of malevolence or simple greed but, at its heart, this is a failure to *know* and to lead appropriately.

We plainly are not as good at managing organizations as we tend to think we are. Some will argue that these times call for leaders and not managers and that the problem is that we need to rediscover the inexplicable and latent qualities of visionary and charismatic leadership. But how is leadership defined? In a practical sense, what does it mean *to lead* versus *to manage*? In our opinion, the perception of a dichotomy between management and leadership is a false one and engaging in the semantics of leadership versus management muddles the topic and moves nothing forward. Why are we not simply focused on intelligence, knowledge, perspective, judgment, and competence, whether we call it management or leadership?

Although organizations are complex and dynamic social entities with both objective and subjective traits, the practice of management increasingly sees them as black boxes with inputs and processes to be manipulated to yield hypothetically optimal outputs. In terms of what matters to managers, we routinely witness the victory of whatever can be quantified over everything that can't. Successful organizations mature and persist over decades yet, due in part to the influence of financial markets and the acquiescence of managers, such managers of businesses tend to focus on the short term. In the quest to be "savvy" and businesslike, even managers of nonprofit organizations such as educational and healthcare organizations seek to emulate business, look past their deepest purpose and set of real stakeholders, and adopt the methods of purely shareholder-focused commercial enterprises. Organizations are composed of many functions and working parts. Even though it is blatantly obvious that organizations succeed or fail as whole and integrated entities, managers often reduce their line of sight and their efforts to a narrow subset of concerns.

We believe the practice of management needs to be philosophically reoriented. In other words, we believe that how organizations are conceived and how they are established, sustained, directed and controlled needs to be reoriented based on a more fundamental understanding of social, individual, and economic reality. We are not alone in this belief. For example, Gary Hamel, the celebrated author of *The Future of Management* and other best selling management books, has argued that among the list of challenges associated with management in the twenty-first century, the first is "restructuring the philosophical foundations of management." Hamel was ranked by the *Wall Street Journal* as the world's most influential business thinker. *Fortune* magazine has called the London Business School professor the world's leading expert on business strategy.

The themes and subject matter of this book are learning, the growth of knowledge, and change or the capacity to adapt. The practice of management is clearly about more than this set of themes. Nevertheless, as we have argued, learning and the growth of knowledge are among the elements that form the core of what we call management. If there is a general need to reshape the philosophical foundations of management, there is a specific need to philosophically reorient organizational learning and the growth of knowledge. This book has sought to connect, in a substantive and concrete way, learning and change in organizations with the philosophical subject matter of knowledge, belief, truth, justification, and reality. The actual aim of the book, therefore, to the appreciation of some and the consternation of others, has been to occupy a space at the boundary of management and philosophy, at least with respect to learning, the growth of knowledge and related factors. Four hypotheses have been identified and developed within the context of this boundary. Briefly restated, these include: 1) Optimal ways of knowing are reality-specific, 2) the growth of knowledge is influenced by the personal and subjective attributes of the individuals engaged in the process of coming to know, 3) within the work of groups, specific approaches to knowing can transcend and help to bridge or reconcile diverse approaches to knowing and contradictory perceptions of reality, and 4) the essential task of leadership is to bring about and sustain a culture conducive to the growth of knowledge, reflecting an increasing fit of culture to the environment.

The table in Figure P.1 defines the boundary between certain management issues or problems and specific aspects of philosophy and summarizes the book's essential hypothesis-related arguments at this boundary. The pair of essential yet simple ideas in this book were identified in the beginning as 1) the uncontroversial premise that our beliefs or assumptions largely determine the decisions we make and the actions we take, and 2) the novel central argument that *how* we form the beliefs we hold significantly influences *what* we believe and whether our beliefs are likely to be true and, therefore, representative of knowledge. The relative truth of our beliefs determines their alignment with reality. Since what we do is determined by what we believe, our actions tend to be valid and beneficial depending on the knowledge content or degree of truth represented by our beliefs. How we form our beliefs is equivalent to our epistemic style or our approach to knowing. We have seen that there are two essential points related to the central argument: 1) There is a need to match ways of knowing with relevant reality, and 2) approaches to knowing embedded in culture must be those that support an orientation to hypothesis, probability, and the logic of induction, avoiding those that fuel dogmatism, determinism, and reductionism.

Believing and knowing are both mental states; the difference is what matters. It is common to be encouraged to challenge our beliefs to strive for reason, clarity, and knowledge. It is less common but more effectual and consequential, as we have argued throughout this book, to understand and challenge our belief-forming processes. This is how we become more aware of what we truly believe and how we assess the veracity of our beliefs.

Management	Boundary	Philosophy
Organizational Learning		
What is the object of learning?	Multiple realities have a bearing on life in organizations. Taking account of the character of the reality in question is developed as an important step in the process of seeking to know.	Theory of Reality (Ontology)
What is the meaning of learning?	Learning is equated with the growth of knowledge. The concept of knowledge is deconstructed and defined in a practical and operative way.	Theory of Knowledge (Epistemology)
What are the dynamics of learning?	Optimal ways of knowing are reality-specific. In other words, specific approaches to knowing are relevant to specific realities.	Ontology/ Epistemology
	Certain theories or approaches to knowing are able to bridge or reconcile divergent approaches to knowing.	Epistemology
Individuals and Groups		
Diversity	How we form beliefs (seek to know) is a fundamental and influential aspect of diversity. Individuals and groups tend to have a dominant approach to knowing.	Epistemology
Structure, content and influences of belief	Belief formation is comprised of two parts, structure and content. The structure of what we believe shapes and sustains the content of our beliefs as informed by perception, memory, attribution and emotion.	Epistemology and Cognition
The potential of individuals	Consciousness or awareness of psychological processes (largely governed by developmental factors) is a crucial cognitive condition in the individual seeking to think critically - to know, to form true beliefs.	Genetic Epistemology
Leadership and Culture		
Culture change	In analogical form and in terms of the increasing fit of culture to the environment, the variation-and-selective-retention process associated with biological evolution informs how culture is created, sustained and changed.	Evolutionary Epistemology Sociology of Knowledge
Sustaining an adaptive culture	Effective leaders bring about and sustain a culture oriented to hypothesis rather than belief. Such leaders identify and manage processes to reconcile divergent epistemic styles and perspectives within the context of an accurate conception of relevant reality.	Epistemology/ Ontology
Organizational integration and performance	The growth of knowledge is explored as a function of an integrated view of individuals, groups and leaders and as an attribute of culture. Organizational successes and failures are described as the consequences of either knowing or believing falsely.	

FIGURE P.1

Summary of themes and arguments at the boundary of management and philosophy.

REFERENCE

1. Durant, Will. 1935. *The Story of Civilization*: 1. New York: MJF Books.

Index